1988

1988

# DESIGNING
# TO SELL

Vilma Barr and
Charles E. Broudy, AIA

# DESIGNING TO SELL

A Complete Guide to Retail
Store Planning and Design

McGraw-Hill Book Company
New York   St. Louis   San Francisco   Auckland   Bogotá
Hamburg   Johannesburg   London   Madrid   Mexico
Montreal   New Delhi   Panama   Paris   São Paulo
Singapore   Sydney   Tokyo   Toronto

**Library of Congress Cataloging in Publication Data**

Barr, Vilma.
   Designing to sell.

   Bibliography: p.
   Includes index.
   1. Stores, Retail—Planning.   2. Stores, Retail—Design and
construction.   I. Broudy, Charles E.
II. Title.
HF5429.B318  1985         725'.21         85-8823
ISBN 0-07-003838-4

        2 3 4 5 6 7 8 9 0     HAL/HAL     8 9 8 7 6

ISBN 0-07-003838-4

The editors for this book were Joan Zseleczky and Georgia
Kornbluth, the designer was Elliot Epstein, and the production
supervisor was Sally Fleiss. It was set in Bodoni Book by University
Graphics, Inc.

Printed and bound by Halliday Lithograph.

*Frontispiece:* Interior of Ann Taylor shop, Newbury Street, Boston.
Design by Charles E. Broudy & Associates. (Photograph by Paul
Warchol.)

This book is dedicated to:

*My daughter Lesley and my son Glenn*

VILMA BARR

*My wife Judy, my sons Josh and Matt, and my mother Anna Broudy*

CHARLES E. BROUDY

# Contents

# Preface

Throughout the research and writing of *Designing to Sell*, the authors tested the contents against the needs of a dual reader model: the designer and the merchant. Designers have to understand the business of merchandising and view each design solution as both an answer to a space design problem and a direct contribution to the client's profitability. For merchants, becoming familiar with the design process and the basic technical aspects of architecture and interior space planning will help in the assessment of ideas for their own store or stores.

Included here are over 200 photos, illustrations, and tables to enhance the text and show the principles of retail store planning and design in actual use around the country. To make the book a practical and useful reference, three basic objectives were established:

## 1. *Filling an education gap*

The training of architects and designers does not generally include the fundamentals of marketing and economics. Unless these professionals earn M.B.A.s or obtain similar business experience, they have limited comprehension of the laws of supply and demand, as well as the factors that drive domestic and international trade.

On the other hand, a business education will rarely contain such a course as "Design Decision Making for Managers: A Basic Introduction for Nondesigners." Retail marketers (and those in other areas of business) frequently make decisions to spend considerable sums on the physical plant without a rudimentary knowledge of esthetics, design trade-offs, and life-cycle costing.

## 2. *Going beyond the obvious*

In the narrowest sense, the end result of a retail store design could be defined as an assemblage of goods housed in or on display equipment, within an enclosure constructed to keep the wind and rain out, and heat or cooling in. But what more? What else does the customer want or hope to get out of the exchange of legal tender for merchandise?

The authors had hoped to include published data on the effect of the retail store environment on the buying patterns and actions of the customer. Our research failed to produce a single relevant, quotable document. The field of environmental psychology has not yet attempted to quantify the dynamics of store, customer, and merchandise.

Readers, therefore, are asked to accept our premises that, first, the environment created for retail selling becomes a medium of communication between the seller and the buyer, and second, a store's environment helps to shape and augment the shopping experience. "More than a place to shop, a great shopping experience" was the headline of an ad to attract tenants to St. Paul's new Galtier Plaza. "Visit the Chalet . . . where shopping becomes a truly delightful experience," said the announcer of a radio spot aimed at Chicago's upscale food shoppers.

## 3. *Setting quality standards for retail store design*

The subtitle of this book is *A Complete Guide to Retail Store Planning and Design*. We have attempted to treat the subject matter as completely as possible within the confines of one book. Many of the chapters could well have been expanded into separate volumes, but this concise yet comprehensive treatment in a single book seemed better suited to the task at hand.

The comments and suggested procedures in the text, together with the high-quality and relevant illustrations, present an overview of the field. We have stressed careful analysis, thoughtful design, and realistic budgeting. These factors, when combined with the right proportion of flair and style, can produce exciting, creative public spaces. We hope our book will encourage merchants and designers to create retail stores that will be commercially viable and visually dynamic.

*Vilma Barr*
*Charles E. Broudy*

# Acknowledgments

The authors would like to express their appreciation to Ernest R. Burden, AIA, for encouraging us to take our book idea to McGraw-Hill; to Joan Zseleczky, editor for architecture, construction, and civil engineering books for McGraw-Hill Book Company, for her enthusiastic support and guidance throughout the creative and production processes; and to Professor Mercia Grassi of Drexel University for suggesting the Drexel-sponsored seminars that preceded this book.

We are grateful to Leonard R. Korobkin, PE, of Gamze, Korobkin, Caloger, Inc., Engineers, Chicago, for supplying the "Retail Store Illumination" section of Chapter 8, "Lighting," as well as all of Chapter 9, "Systems and Energy."

The authors wish to thank the contributors for sharing their experiences and observations:

- Edward A. Brennan, president and chief operating officer, Sears, Roebuck & Co.

- W. Scott Ditch, vice president and director, corporate public affairs, The Rouse Company

- Donald Fisher, founder and chief executive officer, The Gap Stores

- James B. Klutznick, senior vice president, Urban Investment and Development Co.

- M. Leanne Lachman, president, Real Estate Research Corporation

- Anthony W. Miles, vice president, The Boston Consulting Group

- Geraldine Stutz, president, Henri Bendel

- Robert J. Witt, chairman and chief executive officer, Boyd's

We would also like to thank the following:
Joan Papadopoulos, formerly creative services director of Real Estate Research Corporation, for supplying a number of photos used in the book; H. G. A. Hall, for generous coordination assistance; Joyce Mega and Cynthia Corrello, for transcribing tapes, typing drafts, and generally helping me to organize the manuscript; and Arthur P. Contas, an advisor and friend.

*Vilma Barr*
Chicago

Architects Charles King, Jr., and Edward Einhouse, associates of Charles E. Broudy & Associates; Sandie Pope, our office manager, for handling myriad typing and clerical tasks; Brian Rushton, museum shop consultant; Max Raab, an early and supportive client; and Richard Liebeskind, a long-standing client.

*Charles E. Broudy, AIA*
Philadelphia
December 1984

# DESIGNING
# TO SELL

# Designing for Retail

When the retail business moves, it moves fast. And its physical environment must move with it.

Function, selling strategies, display, and visual elements all have to work together to move merchandise. The true mark of ingenuity in retail store design is how successfully the designer contributes to *stock turns*, that is, moving the merchandise, the reason the merchant is in business.

Trends in retail store planning and design tend to have a quicker turnaround than do the more evolutionary swings that characterize banks, offices, and health care and educational facilities. Most retail managers are willing to evaluate innovative store design ideas and solid new concepts. If merchants have a hunch a store design will work, they do it. Then they watch the sales-per-square-foot figures to see how right they were.

Retail sales in 1983 amounted to $1170 billion, compared with $1080 billion the year before. Retailing is an industry based on rapid adjustment to such factors as consumer spending patterns and sociological swings. Change and flexibility are built into the business.

What makes retail design different from other forms of architectural and interior design?

• The store itself is an active selling tool, a promotional device to attract people to shop.

• The store's ambience adds to a product's image of worth and value to the buyer.

A retail store is a dynamic organism with many interlocking systems. In addition to the furnishings (or

**Santa Monica Place, Santa Monica, California. People play out their hopes and aspirations in the "theater" of the retail store. The designer supplies the backdrop, lighting, and forms to create the mood that leads to profitable selling for the merchant and satisfying buying for the customer.**

*Architects:* Frank O. Gehry & Associates, and Gruen Associates. *Courtesy:* The Rouse Company.

"hardware"), an important aspect of designing for retail is the "psychological software." Creating a retail store is comparable to designing a stage set. Shopping is an experience in which people act out their innermost hopes, dreams, aspirations, and desires. A shopping excursion is a personal minidrama for the customer. The merchant is the playwright. The designer supplies the background with furnishings, lighting, spatial relationships, and form to create the mood for buying.

# Today's retailing territory

"You've Got to Know the Territory!" sang the turn-of-the-century traveling salesman in the classic musical comedy, *The Music Man*. Today's retailing territory for designers combines a grasp of the psychology of selling, a feeling for the excitement of the marketplace, and a working knowledge of merchandising distribution channels. The design and sig-

nature look of a retail store reflect the owner's merchandising philosophy, so it is essential that the planner-designer have a sharp perspective on top management's thinking.

Just because a retailer opens a store, erects a sign, and sells good products, there is no guarantee that sufficient customers will come in to return a profit on operations. Merchants know they run the risk of missing a large part of the market if they do not integrate other ingredients—how the items are merchan-

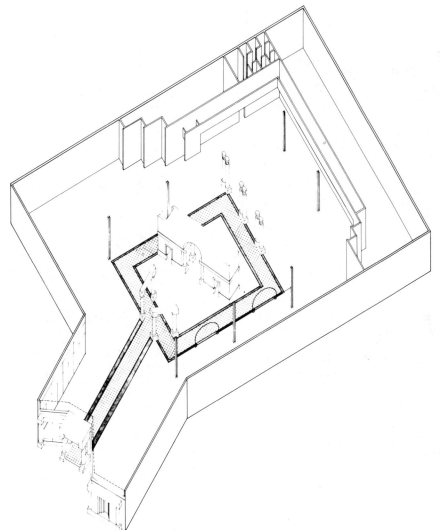

**(Far left)** Creating a retail store is like designing a stage set that reflects the owner's merchandising philosophy and signature look. For the Julius Lewis store in the Hickory Hills Mall, Memphis, postmodern is the design idiom for the 19,200-square-foot store in which all casework, shelving, display, dressing rooms, lighting, etc., are movable. Architectural fragments—a triumphal arch, neon arches, double columns—lead to implied entrances of departments.

*Design:* Walk Jones & Francis Mah, Inc. *Photo:* Nick Wheeler.

**(Left)** Isometric of the Julius Lewis store, Memphis, Tennessee. Primary circulation is a fixed path of travertine marble, used in conjunction with hardwood and oriental carpets. Movable dressing rooms can be bunched together to form walls; rods can be hung on one side and shelves on the other.

*Architect:* Walk Jones & Francis Mah, Inc. *Store design and fixture layout:* Barnova & Vasi.

dised, how they are presented, what kind of "zing" or aura is created. The Limited women's apparel chain has zing; Tiffany's and Harrod's have an aura; Bloomingdale's and Macy's combine both zing and an aura.

The retailing arena attracts hard-driving business people with a flair for showmanship, a gambling instinct, and spatial awareness. Every inch of space their store occupies is critical to profit. The retail yardstick is sales per square foot,

the measure of merchandising productivity. The space must work, and work hard, for the owner.

Decisions by merchants to build or remodel are not made on whim. The decision-making process in a neighborhood shop is certainly far less complex than in a multistore, multicity chain, but the marketing reasoning is the same. The designer has to know where the merchant-client is coming from, economically and emotionally, and where she or he wants to go.

To whom is the merchant appealing? Every retailing organization segments the market. Merchandisers of staple goods, such as food stores, appeal to broad segments of the population. Big-ticket and high-style retailers—furniture, jewelry, apparel—are targeted to thinner slices of the market.

Merchants are in constant communication with their customers, analyzing, redefining, and reprofiling the motives and patterns that govern buying decisions. When demand

Water Tower Place, interior

Water Tower Place

GUM

GUM, interior

slackens, the retailer adjusts the supply.

The market-sensitive, facilities-conscious merchant wants the most attractive and functional store that returns the greatest volume for the least amount of money. If the client retailer tells you to create a design that vacuums customers into the store and magnetizes them to the displays and racks inside, then that is the basis of the design program. Follow it, and do not lose sight of it. Allocate the budget and develop the design theme around it.

Remember that a successful retail store thrusts out, so shoppers see what the merchant wants them to see, with the best light, the best color, the best background and ambience.

# Retail time line

Retailing has undergone vast changes over the course of time, as has the construction industry itself. Retailing's genesis was in the bazaars of the mideast, in the Cas-

The concept of the urban mall had its beginnings in the last century. A prime contemporary example is Water Tower Place on Chicago's Magnificent Mile shopping area, north Michigan Avenue. The eight-level shopping mall, part of the 74-story multiuse Water Tower Place (white building), contains Lord & Taylor and Marshall Field & Co. branches and 100 specialty stores. In Moscow, the GUM department store on Red Square faces the Kremlin. Its interior design forecasts today's enclosed vertical urban malls.

WATER TOWER PLACE   *Architects:* Loebl, Schlossman & Hackl and Murphy/Jahn Associates. *Consulting Architect:* Warren Platner Associates. *Courtesy:* Urban Investment and Development Company.
GUM   *Photos:* Charles E. Broudy.

In traditional marketplaces, individual purveyors first directly exercised the laws of supply and demand in a group selling situation. The concept has been expanded into the urban "festival malls" that came on the scene in the United States beginning in the mid-1970s. Part of New York City's port area on the East River near the Brooklyn Bridge opened in 1983 as the South Street Seaport. Buildings up to 200 years old have been integrated with new structures for shopping and dining.
*Design:* Benjamin Thompson & Associates. *Courtesy:* The Rouse Company.

bah and the Medina. Peddlers with camels and mules also carried goods to customers in caravans across the deserts.

In the Middle Ages, the stalls and carts moved into western Europe. Some of the purveyors were all-day, every-day tradespeople. Others came into town on market days bringing goods with them for a day for two, returning to their own farms or cottages between trips. Medieval retailing would probably be charged with restraint of trade today. While fairs and bazaars still flourished, guild-

controlled shops entered the picture. The guilds set the prices and quality standards and the hours of business. Sellers were required to carry goods that did not compete with guild artisan-produced merchandise.

"Market days" for food as well as durable goods continue today in all parts of the world, from Mexico to New England, from Scandinavia to the Gulf Coast. As convenient and accessible as today's mass-merchandising outlets are, these traditional markets maintain the fun and personal interaction with "trading," and some of our modern merchandising success stories such as Boston's Faneuil Hall Marketplace, San Francisco's Ghirardelli Square, and Baltimore's Harborplace borrow the best of both worlds.

The Industrial Revolution signaled the end of dependence on cottage industries and a close-by supply of agricultural products. Mechanization of production and transportation propelled the growth of cities and accelerated the maker-to-user cycle.

Mass merchandising had its beginning in the United States in New York in 1826 with the founding of the Lord & Taylor and A. T. Stewart department stores. Thirty years later, Elijah Otis installed the first steam-driven elevators in the Stewart and E. G. Haughton stores. In 1863 a new Stewart store utilized cast-iron front construction developed by James Bogardus. This construction enabled the prefabrication of structural parts that characterized the early multistory warehouse-style structures that continued into the next century.

A number of our present giant retailing institutions were founded in this era. R. H. Macy & Co. started its New York City operation in 1858. Kansas City's Emery-Bird-Thayer began in 1863, and Strawbridge & Clothier opened in Philadelphia in 1868. In this same period, John Wanamaker's "Grand Depot" in Philadelphia was attracting customers to a single-story converted freight warehouse. Wanamaker, who did much to reverse the "caveat emptor" (let the buyer beware) method of selling, later relocated into one of the country's most elegant retail palaces.

In 1872, the first mail-order house, Montgomery Ward & Co., was established. F. W. Woolworth & Co., was founded in 1879. Sears, Roebuck & Co., which now extends

Carson Pirie Scott & Co.

John Wanamaker

Retailing classics and classical inspiration. Louis Sullivan's curved entrance to Carson Pirie Scott & Co. dominates the corner of State and Madison Streets, Chicago. The colonnaded Chestnut Street entrance to John Wanamaker, Philadelphia. The store's elegant main court with "The Eagle," a favorite meeting place for shoppers. Daily concerts on the Great Organ in the court are a Philadelphia tradition. In Tucson, the 1983 enclosed Foothills Mall has courtyards and arcades that form an interior streetscape.

CARSON PIRIE SCOTT & CO. *Photo:* Carson Pirie Scott & Co. Audio/Visual Department. JOHN WANAMAKER *Photos:* Vilma Barr. FOOTHILLS MALL *Design:* RTKL Associates, Inc. *Photo:* Joe Aker.

into the insurance, investment, banking, and real estate fields, began in 1886.

With the opening of Marshall Field & Company and Carson Pirie Scott & Co. in Chicago in the 1890s on State Street, the department store as an architectural and mercantile showplace reached its pinnacle. Their objectives were service, customer comfort, a high degree of flexibility of operation, and a broad selection of merchandise in separate sections of the store. They became multilevel commercial landmarks and joined their neighboring skyscraper office blocks to weave a vigorous urban fabric.

Louis Sullivan's masterful Carson Pirie Scott & Co. building suppressed the vertical columns in order to stress the horizontality of the structural bays. At the same time, Sullivan masked any sense of support by the elaborate coiling thickets of iron ribbons at the ground level. In contrast, the upper floors assumed a kind of horizontal velocity, Sullivan's statement of the pace of the busy State Street thoroughfare.

By the 1930s, the traditional ways of doing business were pushing up costs for the country's major department store enterprises. Building operation, displays, advertising,

John Wanamaker, interior

Foothills Mall, interior

extensive credit operations, and free delivery—all part of the retailing price structure—spawned a new kind of competition. Chains, like J. C. Penney, founded in 1924, stressed price and convenience, rather than selection, and aimed at the working-class market. Central buying organizations and management, including real estate and construction, applied the economies of multiples to all parts of the organization.

"Outlet" stores that sold "distressed" merchandise appeared, and these stores were the precursors of the post-World War II discount explosion. From semiluxury merchandise to staples, the outlet store and later the discounter cut the then-average 40 percent markup, and offered the customer lower prices. They stressed reduced overhead as part of the bargain mood and environment. While some discounters still maintain their "plain pipe racks" visual identity, other operations now resemble the traditional retailer in appearance and make their profit on buying power, more dense displays of merchandise, tighter selection, and targeted-market promotional efforts.

**The materials used in a store must relate to the targeted customer and to the merchandise on the selling floor. At the Roots clothing store in Morristown, New Jersey, merchandise presentation is subtle and classic to appeal to an upper-income suburban customer. Accent lighting, wood paneling and flooring, and oriental rugs give warmth and depth to the displays and stock areas.**

*Design:* Charles E. Broudy & Associates. *Photo:* Lawrence S. Williams, Inc.

Changes and innovations in packaging have done much to influence the way displays are set up, departments are arranged, and traffic patterns are planned. Blister polypacks put the supermarkets into the non-food business to stay, dispensing a plethora of goods from cat toys to razor blades. Freestanding display modules boost sales for designer jeans and light bulbs alike.

# What makes retail run?

The materials used in a store's design have to "talk" to the targeted customer. If the store does not look current or timely or if it does not express the look the merchant feels customers will respond to, it should be remodeled. The store must look physically right to complement the merchandise being displayed and sold. Any mismatch between store location, store design, the merchandise, and its presentation can pull down a store's profits and may eventually foretell its demise. Before top management embarks on a building or renovation program, they must have a clear idea of why and how much money they are spending and match this with the store's mission.

Retail decision makers closely watch the changing demographics of communities and neighborhoods in their trading area. At any time, they must be able to describe in detail who their customers are and what level of service will be presented to them.

Many retail stores must be super-flexible because of swings in the economy or changes in presentation policy. A merchant can project needs and then change the plan entirely 6 months later, a fact sometimes misunderstood by designers.

Management determines the store's building and remodeling budget as a return on investment. If the merchant budgets $20 to $30 per square foot for remodeling, the cost justification must answer the question: How many gross margin dollars generated in income will be needed to pay off the project?

A remodeling project starts with a planned sales increase projection. The space may be redesigned so that it is 20 percent more efficient, thus requiring fewer salespeople. Many stores now are reducing the size of their larger units due to the increased cost of displaying and storing merchandise. A new layout can call attention to the ease of shopping and convenience by coordinating presentations on the sales floor.

# A share of the retail store design market

The better understanding that planners and designers have of retailing, the more valuable they are to merchants. (Also see Appendix, "Developing A Retail Store Practice.")

There are more opportunities than ever to design for retail. From the big multioffice architectural-engineering-interiors firms to the individual practitioner's office, designers can find both the quality and the quantity they seek for this kind of work:

- Specialty stores are everywhere, from enclosed urban malls to suburban strip centers to hotels.

- Discounters tend to have multiunit chains operating in shopping centers, strip centers, and in neighborhoods.

- Retail shops are an important part of many new and remodeled office

In the shop of the Boston Museum of Fine Arts recent addition, custom-designed display towers showcase a variety of items. The towers complement the architectural space and add to the products' image of worth and value to the customer.

*Design:* Shop by Charles E. Broudy & Associates; addition by I. M. Pei & Partners. *Photo:* Charles E. Broudy.

structures, giving life and vitality to ground and lower levels.

- Shops in museums and libraries have become profit makers for many institutions and offer interesting design challenges.

- Community restoration and rehabilitation (rehab), from Society Hill, Philadelphia, to Soho in New York, to Chicago's Printer's Row, stimulate new retail opportunities.

- Foreign-owned companies are opening outlets around the country, from bread specialty shops to specialty clothing stores.

## Getting to the bottom line

Whether a neighborhood food store or a glossy suburban specialty branch, two basic tenets apply:

- Get the confidence of the client early in the project. Let the ideas flow to the client. Loosen up. Keep exploring and do not be afraid to break new ground if it will help the client achieve expressed goals. Clients are more responsive to creative designs.

- Explore the maximum possibilities. Do not accept the first design you put down on paper. Under deadline and time pressures, you may be tempted to defend a safe, easy solution. The final design may be simple in execution, but the beauty and attraction will reflect the insight and thoughtful planning that went into it.

There are no standard solutions in retail store design. Showcasing the merchandise in a lively, stylish, and imaginative setting is the primary pervading element. The designer's product is the most appealing atmosphere possible from which to move goods. That spells bottom-line success for the merchant and the designer.

## Bibliography

Gosling, David, and Barry Maitland: *Design and Planning of Retail Systems*, Whitney Library of Design, New York, 1976, pp. 2–17.

"Retail Sales Up 0.1% in December, 9.1% in '83," *The New York Times*, January 14, 1983, p. 21.

Scully, Vincent: *American Architecture and Urbanism*, Praeger, New York, 1969, p. 110.

# 2

# Store Design from the Exterior

**Question:** At what point should the designer begin to plan the store exterior?

**Answer:** Start to plan the exterior when the merchandising program is defined for the store interior. Design with unity. There cannot be incongruities between the exterior and the interior. Both must project the same message to the same market.

The purpose of the exterior is to *sell*, through use of materials, lighting, signage, and windows. This is true for stores facing the street, the highway, or the enclosed mall's promenade.

Merchants expect their storefront to help them achieve an edge over the competition. The number of merchandise vendors is limited, and with neighboring stores carrying the same or similar goods, the design of the exterior and windows presells customers before they walk in.

Commissions for interior store design work will outnumber those for the exterior by 5 or 6 to 1. A merchant may feel it important to do a full or partial interior remodeling every 4 or 5 years to look current. The outside can look perfectly fine for a dozen years or more if the design is not dated. Other than a design for a trendy store or chain, it is more prudent to adopt an approach that is simple and classic while at the same time distinctive and creative.

## A "silent salesperson"

Unless you are told otherwise by your client, the main objective of the storefront is to *vacuum or funnel shoppers into the store*. This is true for stores in just about any price range. The owner is paying a premium for frontage on a busy street, highway, or mall because that is where the pedestrian and vehicular traffic is. Traffic means action, and profit.

Directing traffic into the store with an appealing storefront is the designer's job—to translate the available length and width between the party walls into a sales-stimulating, long-lived dimensional advertisement.

The elements of store exterior planning and design are:

- Site selection, location, and access
- Size, shape, and parking
- Environmental considerations
- Materials for storefronts
- Windows
- Awnings and canopies
- Portals and doorways
- Vestibules and entryways
- Signage
- Lighting

## Site selection, location, and access

Entire volumes have been written on the theories of store location and site selection. Space in this book allows only for an overview of the topic. The designer can become more familiar with the many economic and demographic considerations of retail store and shopping center site decision by independent readings. The following organizations are excellent sources of literature:

- Urban Land Institute, 1090 Vermont Avenue, Washington, DC 20036 (202-289-8500)
- National Retail Merchants Association, 100 West 31st Street, New York, NY 10001 (212-244-8780)
- International Council of Shopping Centers, 655 Fifth Avenue, New York, NY 10022 (212-421-8181)
- Real Estate Research Corp., 72 West Adams Street, Chicago, IL 60603 (312-346-5885)

It is not unusual for the merchant to ask the store designer to look at and evaluate a site under consideration, from the standpoint of its physical potential. Very often, this evaluation represents a "presentation" by which the merchant can judge the designer's awareness of the retail scene. Designers only occasionally become involved with the siting of a bank, school, or office building. Merchants, with their predilection for instinctive action, want to know what the designer thinks, pro or con, about one or another site before making up their minds.

If the designer is asked to visit a site and respond with a "go" or "no-go" judgment, the designer should ask for copies of all available relevant demographics and market studies and obtain current zoning ordinances. The merchant is looking for a physical fit—the site in relation to the merchandising objectives. The designer's report—written, illustrated, or verbal—can take the place of the usual, formal, prepared "presentation." What the merchant wants to know is: If you were the owner of my store, would you locate here?

What do the raw demographic figures say?

If the area has a high percentage of residents age 68 and over, remember that they do not like to walk too far. Distances over 150 yards from car to the entry of a shopping center could pose a problem.

Younger shoppers (under 21) spend less than the average.

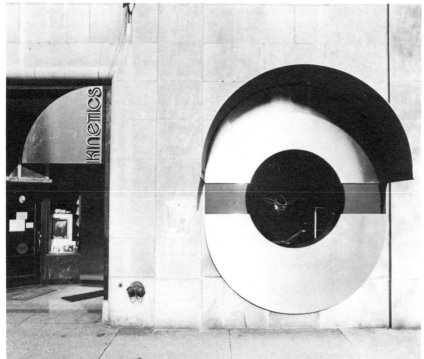

The main objective of the storefront is to attract shoppers into the store. It is the designer's job to translate the space between party walls into a sales-supportive, three-dimensional advertisement. For the Kinetics Gallery in Philadelphia, the original limestone facade was punctuated with a hooded, framed circular show window. The awning over the entry door turned the gallery name on end. Remodeled retail space in the Playboy Building (originally the Palmolive Building) adheres to the strong vertical lines of the structure. The classic lines complement the tenants: Mark Shale, a quality clothier, and Bally shoes.

KINETICS GALLERY    *Design:* Charles E. Broudy & Associates. *Photo:* Charles E. Broudy.
PLAYBOY BUILDING    *Photo:* Laura L. Mueller. *Courtesy:* Real Estate Research Corporation.

**Kinetics Gallery**

**Playboy Building**

In the 25 to 45 age group, earning $20,000 to $40,000 per year is the middle market.

People in the traditional professions tend to spend more than the average.

Will the merchandise being offered "fit" with the trading area's strongest income group? Low-end products (not discounted better goods) will not fit into a high-rent district. A pricey fashion store will not do well where low- to middle-income consumers form the base for the trading area. These may sound like time-honored truisms, but mistakes are made, and some of the country's most sophisticated retailers make them. Small independents and chains have less chance to recover from a bad decision than do bigger multistore operations.

What can sway a merchant to take a risk on a site? Sometimes the answer is "industry gifts," enticements offered by the landlord to sign up a tenant. These are usually in the form of allowances for construction, ranging from 10 to 100 percent. At the upper end of the gift scale, the deal becomes virtually a turnkey operation: The landlord does all the construction, and the lessor moves in. If the landlord increases the allowance to make a second-rate location more appealing or to fill up a slow-renting mall or center, the merchant is taking his chances by signing a lease.

Here are some basic categories to help the designer profile the client's store:

· *Destination store:* Shoppers will travel to the location of a particular store to shop for a certain item or items. A major department store is a destination store.

· *Destination area:* This term usually refers to clustering of a certain related group of stores, like jewel-er's row or antiques row, rather than one particular store.

· *Traffic generator:* Actively promoted shopping malls or downtown areas draw traffic, on foot or by car. Municipal agencies often maintain statistics on the number of people or cars passing a certain point.

· *Neighborhood center:* These centers draw from approximately a 1.5-mile radius and can be a traditional street-front shopping area or a strip center. A number of strip centers over 10 years old are being remodeled to concentrate on a particular type of merchandise such as apparel.

· *Community center:* These centers draw from a 3- to 5-mile radius. Stores provide convenience goods and services and some lines of shopping goods. Centers should be located for access from major thoroughfares.

· *Convenience center:* The customer is a "buyer" making a purchase and getting out. A high-density center means high turnover, and the axiom to follow is to provide more parking rather than less. When a convenience center gets the reputation of always having filled parking spaces, people will begin to avoid it.

· *Regional center:* These centers draw from up to a 20-mile radius, to a downtown area or a major shopping center with one or more anchor "destination" stores. They should be easily reached from well-marked expressway interchanges.

## Size, shape, and parking

A regularly shaped space makes for a more efficient layout. Frontage along a street or highway is very important. A triangular-shaped parcel with 10 feet along a highway and thousands of feet behind it does not offer a good presence even if the demographics appear favorable. Good presence consists of:

· Good vehicle access
· Good approach
· Good entrance
· Good appearance
· Good lighting
· Good signage

Provide as much parking as possible, on grade or in multilevel structures. Municipal zoning codes establish the minimum requirement. While no designer wants to stand accused of blighting the landscape with acres of parking lots, the fact remains that America moves on wheels, and those wheels represent traffic to the retailer. Trees, plantings, and berms can attractively relieve the flat expanse of a parking lot. The ratio of square feet of building to square feet of parking is subject to the size of the shop or shopping center and the local zoning codes. Remember to provide for handicapped parking.

## Environmental considerations

Regional enclosed malls of 350,000 square feet and over (gross leasable area, or GLA), not including anchor department stores, often are designed with two or more levels. Site costs are reduced, as are walking distances. Connecting multilevel parking is appropriate here, to

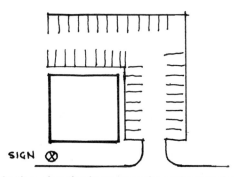

When selecting a location in an open site, make sure the slope of ground is not too extreme. Highway access to parking lot and sign tower or building sign is important.

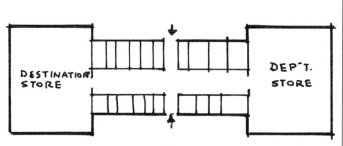

When selecting a shop location in an enclosed mall, choose a site near a department store or destination store. Be as close to the entrance as possible; be where the traffic is.

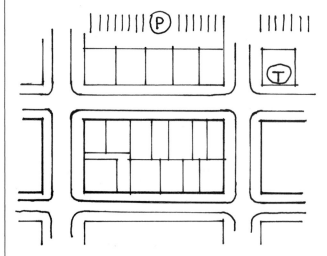

Major factors: *T* Public transportation; *P* Parking. Economic level of adjacent stores.

**Advice for Siting of Stores**

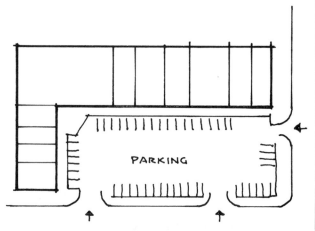

Parking access and visibility of signage are primary conditions of a strip center. A canopy is also a consideration.

reduce openair parking and as a convenience.

Environmental considerations include: topography, drainage, subsoil conditions, zoning, utilities, and environmental impact statements.

A qualified civil engineering or landscape architectural firm can be retained by the store planner to define requirements and handle technical aspects of planning and construction. The store designer and

the consultants should work as a team so that the esthetic objectives as well as the legal requirements are met.

· Try to keep earth moving to a minimum. A steeply sloping site can be adapted for retail site use, but the costs for contouring should be well understood before proceeding.

· Control of storm water runoff, through sedimentation and reten-

tion ponds, is part of the site program.

· Utilities should be in place close to the site. Responsibility for extending the sewer and waterlines to the site should be dealt with early in the site evaluation by the owner and the municipality.

· Some communities require extensive buffering between residential and commercial zoning categories.

The type and amount of space between the store or shopping center and neighboring homes should be identified and costs projected to meet these stipulations.

Approvals from agencies and public advisory groups are required for both new construction and remodeling. To meet various laws and statutes, the owner may have to file an extensively documented environmental impact statement dealing with water and air quality, traffic estimates, analysis of future water and power needs, construction timetable, and other items. Concerns of plan commissions, arts councils, and historical committees must be met with presentations and/or written documentation.

Even if the project is on a fast-track schedule, the same approvals have to be obtained. Designers should develop a realistic schedule so the merchant is clear about the approval process from the beginning of the project. Skipping an approval step or missing a deadline may mean job-delaying backtracking for the store designer. If the merchant wants to open in time to take advantage of the end-of-the-year holiday buying period or other seasonal events, the designer should consider this fact as a given constant throughout each phase. Other than an unforeseen act of God, merchants do not have much patience with excuses for not meeting an opening date.

**Beachwood Place, Cleveland, provides 2300 parking spaces for 455,000 square feet of space (116 stores and eating places).**
*Design:* RTKL Associates, Inc. *Courtesy:* The Rouse Company.

Combining materials for street-front and mall shops: Little Daisy in Palo Alto, California uses wood and bronze mirror-frame windows for an exterior storefront. Ann Taylor on Oak Street, Chicago, Illinois, in an adaptive reuse of a townhouse, utilizes oak doors, bronzed aluminum frame, clear glass, and projecting awning.

*Designs:* Charles E. Broudy & Associates. *Photos:* Charles E. Broudy.

Little Daisy

Ann Taylor

# Materials for storefronts

Cost, appearance, and availability are the three basic guidelines for material selection. Almost any material can be used if the designer has the freedom and the budget. How the materials will be handled depends on the designer's creativity and ability to interpret and communicate the merchandising message. Constraints include restrictions imposed by ordinances or by the mall or shopping center owner's standards (Table 1). Stainless steel, for example, might be unacceptable in Georgetown Park, in Washington, D.C., a shopping complex with a strong Victorian ambience. Other considerations are:

· *Regional weather:* Natural stucco is fine for California and the southwest and southern states, but it will not give long service in the frost belt.

· *Neighborhood compatibility:* Unless the designer and the merchant agree that the shock effect will be good for business, anything (modern, colonial, shiny, brightly colored) should be avoided if it does not complement the area's existing structures.

· *Time, cost:* Shipping Pennsylvania stone to Louisiana, or Ohio brick to Oregon, needs sufficient lead time and funds.

· *Maintenance:* Wood is handsome and distinctive but usually needs regular maintenance. Some metals are elegant but require polishing to keep their luster.

## Table 1  Materials for Storefronts

| Material | Considerations | Best uses |
|---|---|---|
| Wood | Gives warm, soft look. Natural finish will be destroyed by elements; needs constant maintenance. Some woods, such as oak, need multiple coats of shellac or varnish. Others, such as cedar shingles and redwood, weather naturally and require little upkeep. | Versatile; can be used to advantage in all design settings, contemporary as well as period. |
| **Metals** | | |
| Bronze, brass | Handsome. Expensive. Needs maintenance to keep brightness and sheen. | Appropriate for quality appearance, jewelry, and fine-apparel stores. |
| Aluminum | Coated (duranodic) comes in many colors and finishes, both satin and polished. Lightweight. Pliable. | Popular because of contemporary look and low maintenance. |
| Stainless steel | Low-maintenance. Expensive. Long-lasting. Malleable. | Very good for urban installations. Cool and sleek effect. |
| Baked or porcelain enamel steel | Available in bright colors. Long-lasting. | Good application if sharp contrasts are required. |
| **Masonry** | | |
| Natural stone, brick, marble, granite | Selection will usually be regional because of availability and transportation costs. Fairly high cost, even with veneers. Very low maintenance. | These materials work well in environments where they pick up the theme of materials set by surrounding structures. Convey solidity, timelessness. |
| Stucco | Can be worked into interesting shapes. Variety of textures available. Can go over concrete block. Manufactured with insulation backing or lightweight metal or wood framing. Not recommended for cold climates. | Excellent for exteriors and interiors of stores in warm-weather climates. Pliability is major asset. |
| **Glass** | | |
| Glass block | Combines solid facade with translucence. | Can be teamed with other materials in contemporary design plan. |
| Transparent glass | Emphasizes interior store activity. May be security problem. Ultraviolet rays could damage merchandise. | Best material for permitting views of merchandise and store interior. |
| Opaque glass | Available in colors. Carrara (black) glass can be dramatic when installed as a facade. | Good for deco, modern, or contemporary designs. |
| Transluscent glass | Used for clerestory windows where light but not transparency is needed. | Effective if back-lit. Presents a warm glow in evening hours. |
| Mirrors | Reflectance gives dimensional quality. Lightweight. Can be framed with metal for street fronts or malls. | Can be used in urban or natural settings but should reflect a dramatic or visually appealing view. |
| **Plastics** | | |
| Acrylics (clear and opaque); laminates | Very adaptable. Good for canopies. Sometimes permitted for storefronts in malls. | Work well for signage and canopies. For larger installations, get manufacturer's estimated life of product for your region. |

# Windows

A store's display window talks directly to the potential customer about the goods inside.[1] Like a poster outside of a theater or movie house, it gives a small preview of the attractions inside.

As noted earlier in this chapter, the purpose of the store's exterior and the windows is to sell—certain categories of goods to certain customer segments. High-priced jewelry is often shown in small cube windows, precisely illuminated and artfully arranged (limited market, restrained display). Electronic equipment from calculators to stereos is closely packed in fluorescent-lit closed-back windows (broad appeal, large display).

Most display windows belong to one of two types: closed back, mak-

ing its own environment, and open back, where the store itself forms the backdrop for the window display. A cross between the two utilizes partial shutters or hanging banners behind the windows to partition the space between storefront display and selling floor. Apparel merchants differ in their closed- versus open-back preference. Some prefer the additional interior hanging or shelf space that a closed-back window provides. Others believe the sight of the merchandise selection inside is a strong draw, well worth sacrificing a few linear feet of interior display space.

If the store has a visual merchandiser or display director, his or her ideas and merchandise presentation techniques should be incorporated into the window design. Often lighting will determine the shape and design of the store's window and front. Lighting can be exposed, hidden, or theatrical, or any combination of the three. The window should be dimensioned so that the installed lighting does not hit the top of a

mannequin's head or a display object. Leave "aiming distance" from the light source to the displayed object.

Portable platforms allow display directors the flexibility to mount settings at floor level or in tiers. Space allotted to the window should be sufficiently deep to accept effectively lit platforms.

Often enclosed mall stores will have no windows at all. Here, retail establishments open onto a controlled environment. Gondolas and other display units are just a few

**Most display windows have either an open back, allowing shoppers to view the activity and selection inside the store, or a closed back, where the partition between window and store interior can be utilized for shelf or hanging space inside the store. Mary Walter, an Evanston, Illinois, women's clothing store in an office building lobby, has a closed-back, angled shop window.**

*Design:* Raymond J. Green & Associates Architects Inc. *Photo:* Howard N. Kaplan.

---

[1] Other discussions of windows can be found in Chapter 7, "Colors, Materials, and Finishes" and Chapter 8, "Lighting."

feet inside the store. Tenants in vertical high-priced urban malls like Chicago's Water Tower Place maintain a traditional doors-and-windows approach; shops in midprice malls like The Bourse in Philadelphia and most suburban malls are a mixture of traditional and open front. More storefronts in malls featuring popular priced merchandise are open to make patrons feel welcome and to encourage their entering.

The store designer can help the merchant set up visual standards for displaying merchandise in windows. Through a series of sketches, the designer can suggest groupings or positioning of items with appropriate lighting and possibly props. Here, designers can use their imagination and show how to hang items, floor mount them, or suspend them.

# Awnings and canopies

Awnings and canopies offer protection from the rain and snow to customers, and to window-displayed merchandise from the sun. They can carry the store's name, thereby becoming a sign. Or they can do both at the same time.

Many materials can be fabricated into awnings and canopies of different shapes. In addition to traditional canvas, other materials such as glass, wood, metal, and plastic can be made into bubble or arch shapes as well as the standard 45-degree angled extension from the outside wall.

In some urban areas, canopies extend to the curb line from the entry doorway to give a very elegant impression as well as overhead protection to customers leaving their cars and taxis. At the Old Orchard Shopping Center near Chicago, hard

Plaza del Lago

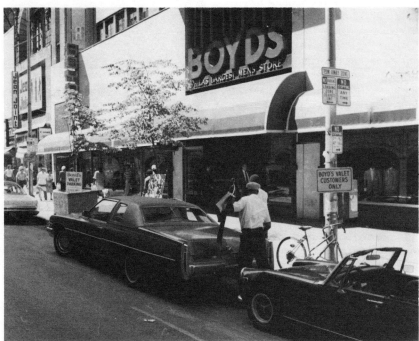
Boyd's

The designer can select from a variety of materials and shapes for overhead coverings above windows and doors. Boldly striped fabric awnings are a graphic eye-catcher at the Plaza del Lago center, Wilmette, Illinois. Similarity in material and shape lends unity to the storefront of Boyd's men's store in Philadelphia which occupies four separate adjoining buildings.

PLAZA DEL LAGO   *Photo:* Joan Papadopoulos. *Courtesy:* Real Estate Research Corporation.
BOYD'S   *Design:* Charles E. Broudy & Associates. *Photo:* Vilma Barr.

canopies overhead are part of the walkway system that connects clusters of stores.

Awnings can lend a unifying effect to rehabbed stores. In an existing street-front setting, a merchant may take over an adjacent store or stores for expansion purposes. If the merchant does not want to go through the expense at that time of putting in new storefronts, awnings can give a semblance of visual unity. At Boyd's, an upper-price men's store in downtown Philadelphia, four separate dissimilar storefronts in older buildings were tied together by the awning design. The store spent over $1 million on interior renovation but did not want to go to the expense of new fronts because the buildings were slated for demolition, a fact known to the owners when the modernization program began.

Many enclosed malls will allow canvas awnings or canopies because they do not consider the fabric a permanent material. Check the tenant's criteria or get special permission from the landlord if you are considering this type of storefront element. Inquire also whether retractable hardware has to be included as part of design.

# Doorways and entry portals

Doorways make a very personal statement to the user. With one motion, the customer is removed from the boundless expanse of the outside to the controlled commercial environment of the retail store. Doorways welcome people in. They can also keep them out. And they are a cause for security concern.

Theoretically, doors are not needed for enclosed mall stores. Some merchants opt for doors if they want more of a streetscape

**Stanford University Shopping Center**

**Gallery at Market East**

**Hillside Shopping Center**

**Safeway Stores**

look. Doors can also deter entry by potential nuisance makers such as youngsters with drippy ice cream cones. Often, stores with the typical side-hinged swinging doors will keep them open during business hours. The exception is the retailer (like an expensive jewelry or fur store) who wants to maintain an exclusive aura to discourage certain market segments from entering.

Here are the most common types of doors currently used for retail stores:

· *Swinging:* Side-hinged glass doors can be framed with many different materials. Clear tempered glass with no frame is another option.

Entrances and entrance-surrounding structures can be fanciful, human-scale, oversize, or high tech, among other themes.

At Stanford University Shopping Center in Palo Alto, California, playful arched canopies and arcades are an interesting counterpoint to colorful paving blocks. A series of steps and landings leading from heavily trafficked Market Street in Philadelphia prepares the visitor for the open spaces and controlled shopping environment at the Gallery at Market East. A complete remodeling of the 500,000-square-foot Hillside Shopping Center near Chicago created a new identifiable main entry for the mall which is located below grade of the nearby expressway. Safeway Stores, Inc., opened four prototype stores in 1982 that are really minimalls without walls separating the various types of merchandise. At the 61,000-square-foot Arlington, Texas, store, exposed structural framework, a glass storefront, and an inner skylight create an open atmosphere.

STANFORD UNIVERSITY SHOPPING CENTER    *Photo:* Charles E. Broudy
GALLERY AT MARKET EAST    *Design:* Bower & Fradley. *Courtesy:* The Rouse Company.
HILLSIDE SHOPPING CENTER    *Design:* Chicago Design Group, Ltd. *Photo:* Stephen Libbin.
SAFEWAY STORES    *Courtesy:* Safeway stores.

• *Side sliding:* These doors were the most popular for enclosed mall stores 10 to 20 years ago. Usually framed in aluminum or other metal material, they are pushed open and stacked in side pockets. Open metal mesh is now a popular material for doors which can be pulled from above as well as from the side. Tambour sliding doors, which have clear or opaque inserts adhered to a flexible backing, are on the market, and they offer increased security over the open mesh kind. Automatic or manual operation can be specified for most sliding doors.

• *Accordian fold:* An adaptation of the side slide door, these can be fabricated of open mesh or solid panels which give the impression of a wooden door.

• *Revolving doors:* These doors have good air-lock properties to keep out cold air and dust, but they are not considered fire exits, so a manually operated door beside the revolving door is usually required for egress in emergencies, as well as for use by the handicapped.

• *Custom doors:* Ornate wood and metal doors, gates, and antique doors can be converted to commercial use by replacing glass and other elements by careful repair work. Hardware should be reinforced to meet current security standards. Custom doors can effectively project a feeling of style and quality for any type of store. Sleek contemporary doors in a suitable metal or other material can make this same type of statement.

• *Heated entrances:* In the early 1970s, some stores experimented with open entries defined only by heat registers at top and bottom. A flagrant waster of energy, most heated entries have been replaced with solid partitions.

• *Automatic openers:* Foot-activated treadles are in use primarily in supermarkets and large drugstores.

Security at doorways is a major consideration (see Chapter 11, "Security"). Most large department stores with multiple entrances now have either guards or electronic surveillance units to monitor traffic. Small- and medium-sized stores should have one front entrance. If there are side or back doors for receiving or to meet fire exit requirements, alarms should be installed.

# Vestibules

Vestibules are primarily for stores located in bad weather climates and for outdoor-facing stores only (never for enclosed mall stores). They are windproof, weatherproof, coldproof enclosures that save energy. Vestibule flooring should collect dirt and snow before they are carried to carpet, tile, or wood floors inside.

Many products are on the market to provide a nonslip surface undamageable by water, grit, and sand. These range from natural flagstone and slate to nonslip aggregate, terrazzo, and tile; rubber flooring and mats; and carpets. A two-level product provides slotted metal with carpet slat inserts that scrapes foot bottoms. Grit and moisture are deposited on a tray underneath.

In malls, where vestibules are not needed, the recess between the mall walkway and the inside of the store itself should be of the same material. Mall maintenance crews use mechanical scrubbers to clean floor surfaces, and if the store's entry material is not compatible, it can be ruined by large scrubbing and buffing machines.

Heat is sometimes introduced in vestibules. For a small store, a 3-foot 6-inch square space will probably get enough spillover heat from the store proper to keep it comfortable for the short amount of time customers are inside it. For larger stores and department stores with deep enclosed recesses, separate provisions should be made for air handling.

In hilly cities like San Francisco or Seattle, or older cities where rehab is popular, a common problem is how to relate the interior floor height to the lower sidewalk level. Many older buildings that were once townhouses have steps within the vestibule. If the client wants to eliminate steps by installing a ramp, allow 1 inch of height for every foot of ramp length (a 6-foot-long ramp will eliminate a 6-inch-high step). If the depth of the store allows for doors at both ends of the ramp to form a vestibule, it can be worked into the layout. For steps, the store owner should check insurance liability coverage and install one of the heavy-duty flooring products previously described.

# Signage

Signage is another area where the designer can do just about anything that is in good taste and legal.[2] The design objective is to have the sign work as a unit with the exterior style and materials, windows, and lighting.

As previously mentioned, approvals needed for the exterior plan may come from the zoning board, art

---

[2]Also see Chapter 13, "Signage and Graphics."

**Mary Walter**

Information that can be carried by a storefront sign includes the firm's logo symbol, logotype, or advertising tag line. At Mary Walter career clothing store in an Evanston, Illinois, office building, the store name is placed high on the glass entrance so it can be read at a distance. The framed neon sign above the entrance from an enclosed mall is part of the high-style design at Julius Lewis, Memphis, Tennessee.

MARY WALTER   *Design:* Raymond J. Green & Associates Architects Inc. *Photo:* Howard N. Kaplan.
JULIUS LEWIS   *Design:* Walk Jones & Francis Mah, Inc. *Photo:* Nick Wheeler.

**Julius Lewis**

Today's Man, Chestnut Street, Philadelphia.

Today's Man, a discount men's wear retailer selling medium- to higher-priced clothing, occupies a 8600-square-foot, two-level space on the Chestnut Street Mall in downtown Philadelphia. Completed in 1980, it is the company's first unit in the central business district.

1. Found to be structurally sound, the building has a classically detailed limestone facade. Charles E. Broudy & Associates, architects and store planners, removed the former recessed front while retaining the decorative elements. Infill materials are stainless steel and glass.

2 and 3. The previous tenant of the c. 1930 building was also a men's store. Deeply recessed windows were 40 feet wide and 40 feet deep to support the now-outmoded theory that shoppers should see as many styles as could be packed into a window display. The new window is flush with the fronts of taller neighboring buildings and incorporates the entrance door directly off the sidewalk. The open-back window allows shoppers a view of the store interior.

4. Street lighting casts sufficient illumination on the Today's Man sign so that no additional lighting is required, an expense-saving feature.

5. Mannequins mounted at the second-floor level are lit from fixtures in window.

6. The ceiling steps down from a height of 18 feet in the front of the store to 12 feet in the rear. The proscenium effect helps to draw shoppers to the rear.

7. Concealed lighting focuses interest on merchandise shown in the window.

*Design:* Charles E. Broudy & Associates. *Photo:* Peter Olson.

**(Left)** Roots, Morristown, New Jersey, is a men's, women's, and children's classic clothing store which exemplifies adaptive reuse of a 20-year-old, freestanding building, with an approximately 5000-square-foot addition. The total selling space is 11,000 square feet on two levels.

1. The brick addition complements the existing structure.

2. The three-dimensional sign is not illuminated, but lit from grade; and it is easy to spot by auto traffic.

3. The closed-back display windows are frameless, a contemporary technique that blends well with the traditional environment.

4 and 5. Transparent windows are a transition between the new addition with contemporary glazing and the older building whose windows are not suitable for eye-level merchandise viewing.

*Design:* Charles E. Broudy & Associates. *Photo:* Lawrence S. Williams, Inc.

**(Below)** Front of Hahn Shoes, Beachwood Plaza, Cleveland, Ohio, a mall store handling women's shoes, echoes shapes and forms used inside:

1. The stylized design expresses basic forms in an unconventional manner and was meant to attract attention in the closed center.

2. The see-through portion allows the viewer to look into the shop and to see merchandise on pedestals or tabletops.

*Design:* Charles E. Broudy & Associates. *Photo:* Charles E. Broudy.

**Representative facades for Ann Taylor
stores, 1964–1984**

*Design:* Charles E. Broudy & Associates.

**Freestanding new building with skylight monitor for New
Canaan, Connecticut, branch (1964).**

**Alteration of three-story art deco building in New York on
57th Street off Fifth Avenue utilized stainless steel trim and
detailing against black (1979).**

For interior malls throughout the country, store facade combined oak and canvas with glass bay windows (mid-1970s on).

Adaptive reuse of 2½-story building on Chicago's Oak Street combines bronze, aluminum, and glass (1978).

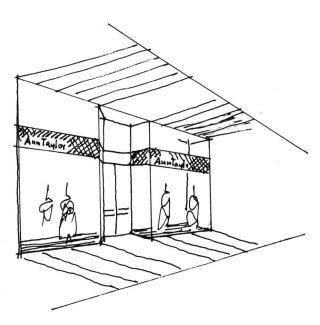

Because of the mild climatic conditions, black aluminum and glass were used for the Bal Harbour, Florida, unit (1980).

Rehab of former furrier's store on Boston's Newbury Street (1984).

commission, residents' groups, and shopping center management. Before designing or specifying a sign, the designer should check on:

- *Size:* This figure should include the total number of square feet permitted.

- *Hanging restrictions:* Some malls do not permit rigid signs or banners to be hung at a right angle to the store front.

- *Illumination:* Lighting should be contained within the sign or supplied from another source. If blinking lights are part of the design, make sure they are not violating a local ordinance.

Illuminated signs are more important for suburban and highway stores than for downtown stores, where street lighting often provides sufficient light for passers-by to read store signs.

For stores fronting on a highway, the merchant may want a freestanding sign that is readable by traffic moving at 50 miles per hour. In addition to signage attached to the building itself, the designer may become involved with a supplementary, freestanding, pylon-mounted sign. The challenge here is to handle this assignment with a well-disciplined approach. Garish examples abound as living examples of what not to do.

# Lighting the store exterior

Lighting the areas around a store or shopping center can have substantial influence on the establishment's image.[3] Specifically, proper lighting of parking lots, stores, and shopping center entrances can help satisfy six important needs:

- Safety

- Security

- Attraction

- Identification

- Beautification

- Unification

Good outdoor lighting design will help meet these objectives by using a variety of techniques—building floodlighting, area lighting, walkway lighting, landscape lighting, roadway lighting, and sign lighting. Proper design is comprehensive, encompassing all the lighting as part of an esthetically pleasing total plan.

High-intensity discharge (HID) systems are both energy-efficient and design-effective. Their high light output relative to wattage input combined with compact size assures this.

Regardless of the source chosen for area lighting, a valid rule of thumb should guide light-pole spacing: Do not place light poles more than 4 times their height apart from one another. Wider spacing will create glare and dark areas between poles. For both motorists' and pedestrians' safety and comfort, avoid unnecessary glare.

---

[3]Also see Chapter 8, "Lighting."

# Bibliography

*Lighting Application Bulletin—Stores:* General Electric Company, Nela Park, Cleveland, 1984, pp. 15–16.

*Retail Location Analysis Manual:* Prepared for the Ford Foundation by Real Estate Research Corporation, Chicago, 1967, pp. 7–12.

Telchin, Charles S., and Seymour Helfant: *Plan Your Store for Maximum Sales and Profit,* National Retail Merchants Association, New York, 1969, pp. 8–13, 49–68.

# 3

# How to Develop a Typical Program

**W**hy a program is needed

A program is a useful and necessary tool to define the needs of the client, the constraints around which the design will be developed, and the budgetary breakdowns to make the design feasible.

It can be as simple as a 1-page checklist or as complex as a multipage document of questions and answers, depending on the scope of the project. The program gives the designer and the client a basis for reference throughout the design process. Changes requested or required can be checked against the agreed-upon program to make sure that they coincide with the project's objectives.

The theory behind writing a program for a retail store design is not unlike program development for other types of building projects: offices, schools, recreation facilities, warehouses, or technical facilities. It is the designer's job to ask the proper questions that will provide the data base for the design. *Gather the client's merchandising thoughts, for these will form the program backbone.* The programming exercise will put into focus the broadbrush approach to the main problem and many of the details as well.

Your client—and you—should know why you did what you did to create the design. The program is the verbal blueprint that both of you can use as a reference and a guide. Designers are blessed with the ability to conceptualize and think graphically. Many of your clients do not have this God-given talent, but they do communicate with words. So the program presents a common ground of give and take.

Establish a data-gathering format that is comfortable for you. Some designers prefer typed $8\frac{1}{2}$- by 11-inch sheets; others set up horizontal spread sheets. Some prefer to obtain the answers during client meetings; others submit the program questions to the client to complete and then fill in specific points together.

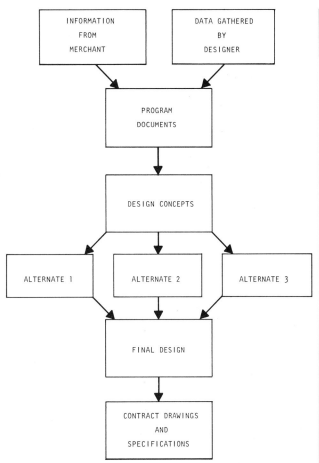

Programming and design process for a retail store. Developing alternatives is important.

**B**asic program questions

A. Overall considerations

   1. Exterior environment:

      a. What is the nature of the surrounding neighborhood? Define the adjacent commercial area: shopping center or block; strip or freestanding stores.

 b. How will existing colors, textures, architectural styles, and graphics affect your store's design?
Is traffic primarily vehicular or pedestrian?

2. Characteristics of the merchandise

 a. What will be sold in the store?

  (1) Clothing: men's, women's, children's

  (2) Accessories: belts, scarves, hats, hosiery, jewelry

  (3) Shoes

  (4) Home furnishings: furniture, carpeting, lamps and lighting, wall decor

 b. What will be the range of styles?

  (1) Basic, classic

  (2) Trendy, promotional

  (3) Seasonal

  (4) Impulse, or big ticket

  (5) Full markup or discount

 c. Merchandise breakdowns.

  (1) Percent each will account for total sales

  (2) Sales per square foot for each category

  (3) Stock turns per year

3. Who are the store's customers?

 a. Age

 b. Geographical distribution

 c. Income level

 d. Size range

B. Characteristics of the store

1. Type of service:

 a. Full service

 b. Self-service

 c. Combination

2. Plan of space:

 a. Linear

 b. Open

 c. Enclosed

 d. Random

 e. U-shape

3. Siting considerations:

 a. Proximity of merchandise to front, perimeter, or rear of store

 b. Location of cashier to merchandise

 c. How merchandise will be viewed by customers

C. Merchandising

1. Quantity:

 a. Number of styles, colors, numbers

2. Seasonal:

 a. Weather

 b. Holidays

 c. Calendar considerations (back-to-school, cruisewear, etc.)

3. Item pricing:

 a. Hang tags

 b. Stickers

4. Sign considerations:

 a. Type needed for floor and counter use

 b. Use of name brands as an important attraction

D. Merchandising specifics
(Define how much flexibility is needed to display and stock the merchandise.)

1. Wall displays, accessible by sales personnel

2. Wall displays, above 80 inches

3. Island displays

4. Secure displays, under glass

5. Manufacturers' displays

E. Stock

  1. Concealed in floor displays

  2. Stored in drawers or behind doors

  3. Stockroom and backup areas

  4. Remote storage

# Program shorthand: Six basic planning diagrams

A. Interior traffic flow characteristics
Traffic flow is based on the psychology of customers' movements inside a shop and the paths they take to the various departments. Most common patterns are: relationship to entrance and exits; front to back; side to side; and diagonal.

B. Merchandise siting
Customers respond to placement or location of products within a shop. Merchants have observed that shoppers gravitate toward staple items, and retailers place these in the rear. This placement draws people through the rest of the store, exposing them to merchandise and displays as they move through the space.

C. Visual display
High-impact displays should be cost-efficient and designed to draw in-store traffic to special sections of the sales floor. Freestanding, ceiling, floor, and wall elements can achieve this.

D. Security
Visual surveillance of the sales floor from a central point is an important part of the store owner's theft-deterring efforts. When tall displays or partitions are needed, allow for mirrors, cameras, or additional personnel.

E. Lighting
Rising energy costs have led retailers and designers alike to seek illumination solutions that are *value-engineered*—most efficient to operate over the life of the fixture—and most flattering to the merchandise. Store planners and lighting specialists have developed ingenious and attractive lighting plans, most frequently using the following types of lamps alone or in combination:

  1. Fluorescent

  2. Incandescent

  3. HID (high-intensity discharge)

  4. Low voltage

F. Storage, receiving, back-of-the-house requirements
The designer should understand fully how merchandise is brought into the department and how much will be in view of the customer and how much will be back-up, out of the customer's sight. In traditional, full-service shoe departments, nearly all the stock is concealed.

G. Other considerations

  1. Electronic requirements

    a. Computerized records and stock-keeping equipment

    b. Cash registers

    c. Charge account equipment

  2. Specialized local code requirements

    a. Sprinkler systems

    b. Fireproof materials

    c. Watts per square foot or other energy usage limitations

  3. Time frame

    a. Opening date

    b. Building code approvals

    c. Advance ordering of equipment and supplies

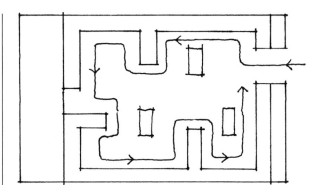

Traffic flow. The psychology of people movement and paths to various departments in the shop.

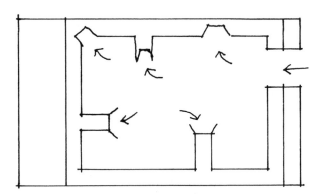

Visual display. High-impact displays or eye-catching design features are important, as they lead patrons to special sections of a store. Ceiling, floor and wall, or freestanding elements can help in achieving this goal.

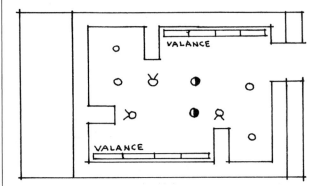

Lighting.   ▭ *Fluorescent:* Efficient, general illumination.
          ○ *Incandescent:* Warmer feeling, sophisticated.
          ◑ *HID:* Harsher, but more efficient incandescent.
          ♉ *Low voltage:* High-impact display lighting.

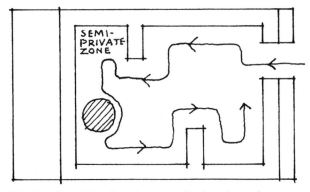

Merchandise siting. People respond to locations of products in the shop and gravitate toward staple items. Many merchants place staples in the rear, drawing shoppers through the store.

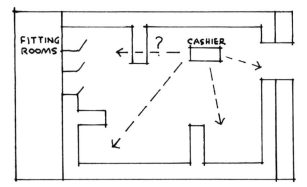

Security. The view of the customer is important. Theft in some shops is more prevalent because of visual blockage.

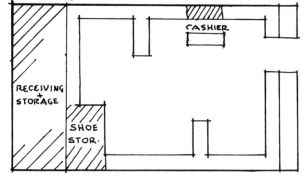

Storage, receiving, back of house. Storage is required at the rear of the facility for various products (i.e., shoes) as a backup to display merchandise.

**Program shorthand: the basic fundamentals of planning for retail stores**

# Creating and guiding the scheme

It was mentioned in an earlier chapter that designing retail stores is not unlike creating theatrical settings. Stage designers create fantasy; the audience accepts illusion.

Customer's imaginations are going at full tilt when they are shopping. They imagine how they will look in a new item of clothing, how a new cosmetic will make them more appealing, how a new chair will look in their living room.

Remember that:

- There are no absolutes in retailing. "Pie-in-the-sky" solutions *are* possible.

- In store planning, the designer can gamble with presenting unusual, imaginative ideas. Take advantage of the opportunity to exercise new design ideas.

Taste, timing and razor-sharp judgment produce successful retail stores.

You have gathered data to help you formulate the physical plan, and you are now at the drawing board, ready to design. *Create multiple alternative drawings, each well founded in concept.* Each alternative should address the fundamentals, the subjects of the program's questions.

Present three to five schematic alternatives to the client, and ask for reactions. Here is a guide to what to expect next:

- The client will challenge you to defend your design. You will be asked to explain your theory and concepts on the various ideas, touching on all the program areas.

- As you explain your schemes, adjust your position and understanding of the problem, and the client will do the same. This is an exercise in mental attitude, not a contest of wills or superegos.

- Practice "active listening" by restating the client's comments. Use phrases like "What I think I heard you say was . . . " and "Let me summarize what you said about. . . . "

## Establishing Project Communication

Communication with the client is a vital linking force throughout the entire planning and design process.

In dealing with large retail organizations, the designer listens to, digests, and sifts ideas and opinions from merchandising, financial, display, advertising, and operations people before establishing priorities for the design program. If the designer is receiving conflicting messages, these must be clarified before the actual design work can proceed.

Charles E. Broudy & Associates used a sketchbook questionnaire as part of the program for the design of a chain of men's apparel stores. Interviews with management had produced many ideas and concepts, but no clear direction was emerging. The medium used was a mini-comic book of multiple-choice responses to free-form association sketches. By tabulating the answers from several dozen executives, we were able to say to top management, "This is what the majority feels will work." The executives responded to the loose-line sketches and light-veined question-and-answer format, and we received the benefit of their insights and creative thinking to help the client establish a name and theme for the chain.

Take full advantage of graphic presentation techniques that clearly convey your design intentions. Your client may be as visually oriented as you are. Renderings highlighted by color help sell your ideas from the outset.

- Clients want to feel that they are getting valuable business judgment from you, as well as a design. Make sure that they feel they have taken part in a give-and-take situation, and know that you are doing your best for them.

- Before winding up the first design review, make sure that you feel that the subject has been stretched to its limits, *and that together you and your client can attain the ultimate quality solution.* Building accord and goodwill early in the design decision-making process makes the designer's job easier down the line.

At the initial and subsequent design reviews, learn to "think on your feet." Bend, mold, and modify your designs while the client is there. Certainly, some ideas will need quiet and solitary concentration to work out. But have the confidence to offer solutions on the spot and know that they are viable and can work. As a professional merchant and manager, your client faces situations like this every day—a new merchandise offer, a chance to get in on a manufacturer-sponsored promotion, or a new ad campaign. "OK, let's do it," she or he will often say to these opportunities. Your designs are opportunities for the retailer to make more profit. Emulate his or her style in this respect. It can work to your advantage if you will give it a chance.

Now you are ready to go back to the drawing board to refine one or two of the original schematic alternatives. You should have a sense that the answer is at hand, that you have received accurate client input to develop the final preliminary.

At the meeting to review the refined schemes, you may want to summarize the decisions made at the first meeting. Minimize the mental roadblocks or adjustments that will stall you from reaching a final scheme. Keep up the client's belief in your expertise throughout the process.

# 4

# Interior Considerations

The merchandise and the people who buy and sell it are the most important factors in organizing a retail design plan.

• *Bringing in the business is the high-road to success in retail store design:* And business means turnover. The more times a merchant can turn over the inventory in a year, the higher the return on the merchandise investment. A store can make $1000 on a watch, $3000 on a piece of furniture, or 50 cents on a T-shirt. The more times this gross margin figure is repeated, the higher the gross profit. Big-ticket items turn over less quickly than lower-price impulse goods. One successful women's apparel discount chain turns its inventory 12 times a year, an enviable record.

• *Each piece of merchandise should be approached as a modular component to be displayed:* Otherwise, the process becomes an exercise in creating shelves and rods. Retail store designers must visualize the space with its most important element, the merchandise, in place. If not, they are running the risk of inviting the most sacrilegious of all store design critiques: "The store looked great before we put the merchandise in it!"

• *Design for people:* The retail store designer creates the same environments for two vastly different user groups: the customer and the employee. To succeed, the designer has to make the space work for both at the same time.

## Get into the retail mood

The merchant-designer team gives the store its visual personality. Before a line is drawn, they have to project themselves inside that store and act as the consumer. An honest answer to "What would make me interested in buying *here?*" provides the program's backbone. Many subtle, unseen elements, like the senses of smell and hearing, play important roles in the overall theme development.

The merchant-designer team gives the retail store its visual personality. At Boyd's, a quality multilevel men's apparel store in downtown Philadelphia, a million-dollar rehab provides an elegant contemporary backdrop for merchandise and people. The transparent elevator was treated as an attention-catching sculptural element and as a source of vertical transportation. The skylight acts as a design focal point and also allows patrons to view colors and fabrics in a natural light.

*Design:* Charles E. Broudy & Associates. *Photos:* Robert Harris, Berry & Homer Photographics.

Analyze what makes you go into a store. How do you feel when you approach it? When you are inside? Elegant? Thrifty? Inspired? Where would you rather buy a new soap dish? Bloomingdale's? The neighborhood c. 1930 hardware store? K Mart?

Does the store say, "Stay out unless you want to spend a lot of money" or "I offer full service" or "I'm tasteful and conservative, solid and stable."

Consider a retail store as a functional setting. The store setting must function smoothly to support all participants: the buyers, the seller, and the merchandise. Unlike office design, which is suited to live workers, whose job-related movements are relatively low, and to furnishings which support data and word-related tasks, retail store design has its own dynamic foundation.

Many stores today in the same block, in the same shopping center, carry the same or similar merchandise. How a store projects its image is often what gives it the competitive edge. Combined with advertising and other media promotional techniques, a unique or different visual image will help identify the store *with* the goods, and attract customers. The designer creates excitement in the space through lighting, traffic flow, materials, and the rhythm of the displays.

Memorable retail interiors are like musical compositions, offering artfully conceived changes of pace and pleasant surprises.

Not everyone who walks through a store entrance has a specific purchase in mind. Star-quality retail design is awarded to interiors that help make lookers into buyers. Certainly other forces are involved—price, pleasant salespeople, eye-stopping displays, helpful signage—that lead to the interaction between the product and the consumer that leads to a sale. But the store itself is the major investment to back up the merchandise.

## Shaping the retail environment

Retail stores come in all sizes and shapes.

A merchant needs a location in a particular market to sell jeans and pants. A space that is 12 feet wide by 75 feet long becomes available at a good rental. In less than 3 months the designer has to turn this bowling alley interior into a busy specialty store. Where does the designer start?

This was an actual project for Charles E. Broudy & Associates, and we had to answer the basic question: How do we best move the merchandise? Inventory and selection were primary, and fast turnover was needed. There was not room in the store for more than one theme, and this had to be functional. The solution was a series of revolving bins that resembled Ferris wheels which "dispensed" the merchandise. The entire vehicle was called a "Pantwheel." It was manufactured to our design and specifications, and a patent application was filed.

These fixtures were operated by the customer and fit the mood of the merchandise. They also helped draw

Store design, merchandise presentation, display, price, and helpful signage and salespeople lead to product-consumer interaction that turns into sales. At the Bon Marche in Tacoma, Washington, installation of high-output fluorescent lamps that approximate home incandescent lighting has enhanced color rendition and reduced returns.

*Courtesy:* General Telephone & Electronics Corp.

Mary Walter

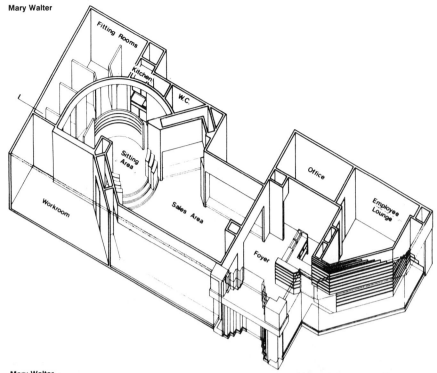

Mary Walter

Three creative solutions fulfill merchandising requirements for clothing, accessories, and eyewear. Mary Walter, an Evanston, Illinois, career women's clothing and accessories store, is shown here in an axonometric drawing and a photograph of the interior. To accommodate after-hours seminars, a free-floor area large enough to seat 30 people and hold a stage was designed into the selling area plus the waiting area used by people accompanying the store's customers. On the first floor of the remodeled Lytton's, a men's and women's specialty store on Chicago's State Street, traffic patterns are based on a 45-degree angle, to avoid an uninteresting straight-line path. Eyeglass "windows" at Wall & Ochs store in Philadelphia echo the actual merchandise and draw shoppers to look inside.

MARY WALTER  *Design:* Raymond J. Green & Associates Architects, Inc. *Photo:* Howard N. Kaplan.
LYTTON'S AND WALL & OCHS  *Design:* Charles E. Broudy & Associates. *Photo:* Charles E. Broudy.

Lytton's

Wall & Ochs

Ann Taylor, 5th Avenue and 57th Street

customers into the store's rear selling areas.

Impossible spaces are often the most exciting. A creative designer would rather work in a tough space like a narrow store, a triangle, or a space that wraps around a corner, than a square with four matching corners and a flat ceiling. Difficult spaces invite designers to expand their design horizons.

A good jumping-off point for a retail design is to pick a theme. It could be the movable merchandise wheel, like the jeans store, or a pure geometric shape. We used a circular pattern effectively for an eyeglass store and a shoe store, and we used semicircular elements for an art gallery.

Or the theme can be representative of the products sold. In abstract or realistic form, supergraphics can symbolize the items on display. Photographs can establish an end-user relationship with the product.

In dealing with a store-planning project, the designer has to treat areas like ceilings and walls above the typical sight line. These planes can be utilized to hang merchandise or displays so every inch of space works to support merchandise presentation.

Remember cubic footage, and take advantage of it.

For Newman's Toys, a small toy store in Philadelphia with a $5000 construction budget, we integrated the original pressed-tin ceiling into the decorative theme. With bands of color against a white ground, the set-

Ann Taylor, 3d Avenue

Two Ann Taylor women's apparel stores in New York City. The soft, sculptural, geometric forms of plush-covered seating in the shoe department of the store at 5th Avenue and 57th Street are accented by overhead lighting. The seating contrasts with the angular, reflective metal display units. In the 3d Avenue store, a dropped-ceiling unit provides illumination and makes a focal point of the raised sales platform.

ANN TAYLOR, 5TH AVENUE AND 57TH STREET   *Design:* Charles E. Broudy & Associates. *Photo:* Norman McGrath. ANN TAYLOR, 3D AVENUE   *Design:* Charles E. Broudy & Associates. *Photo:* Paul Warchol.

ting was bright, fanciful, and inexpensive.

From high ceilings, beams or baffles can be dropped to highlight a display island or define a traffic pattern, and subliminally create a space.

There are sufficient opportunities in most store design commissions for the architect and the interiors specialist to exercise their creativity to fit the client's requirements and the mood of the merchandise. On the other hand, not every display gon-

dola need be a separate problem calling for a customized solution. A number of manufacturers have stock lines of very acceptable fixtures, so take the time to seek them out.

If a thorough search fails to turn up display cases or fixtures that relate to the merchandise and the design theme, create a special design. When Charles E. Broudy & Associates did the shop for the Philadelphia Museum of Art, we wanted to display the extensive stock of art books so that the fronts rather than

the spines were on view. For art postcards, a system of stock control integrated into the display was necessary to handle expanded inventory. We created new display units for both books and cards and have subsequently utilized them in other museum shops. The fixtures are meeting the needs of the store owners and the patrons equally well.

Use quality materials when they enhance the merchandise, but do not put expensive materials in places where they do not mean anything to

**Fewer salespeople and higher operating costs emphasize the importance of flexibility in layout, as shown in this vignette in the linens section of the Cloverleaf Mall branch of Thalhimers Department Store in Richmond, Virginia.**

*Courtesy:* General Telephone & Electronics Corporation.

the customer or the items for sale. We invested in custom stainless steel for railings and perimeter store displays for the remodeled Ann Taylor women's apparel store at Fifth Avenue and 57th Street in New York City. The gleaming art deco–style bands complement the stock and displays and lead the shopper up the exposed stairway in the three-level open atrium. It has a functional as well as a design rationalization.

Flexibility and adaptability comprise the creative core of successful retail plans. Display stands, racks, counters, gondolas, lighting, and everything else that is not critical to the structural support of the building will probably be moved. The original balance that was so carefully achieved may only be hinted at 6 months after the store opens. Little in retailing is inviolate, but a sensible traffic plan and a unifying theme

that holds the space together should supply sufficient stability to uphold the design's integrity.

# Major forces in today's retailing business

## Self-service

Years ago, a retail clerk would tell a customer, "Well, Mr. Jones, I have some things I'm going to show you today. I remember what you liked the last time you were in; these new items are just for you."

Except for a few salons and specialty stores, it is difficult to find a salesperson who still practices the fine art of retail selling. Many stores are self-service or semi-self-service. Big-ticket items like furniture and entertainment units still require trained sales personnel who can explain the product's construction or technology. But, for the most part, the merchandise has to sing out from the walls, platform, or floor area on its own and make the shopper interested enough to buy.

In the late 1960s, the transition to fewer salespeople and less stock help began. As the inflation rate went up, the cost of inventory also increased, and merchants are now unable to keep large back stock. More merchandise is now out in front; less is out of the customer's sight. Merchants are bringing in a third less merchandise today than a few years ago, and they still have to make the store look full. Skimpy displays turn buyers off. In ready-to-wear stores, frontal merchandise display units are an effective way of stretching floor inventory and visually maximizing the impact of the items.

## Operations

Retail traffic takes its toll on furnishings, as does moving and shifting of merchandise and display elements. Merchants know they have to change their store's appearance regularly. But they do not want to have to replace items because they become shabby before the end of their useful life. If the acceptable life cycle for carpeting is 6 years, it should not be worn out in 3. If the counters are an 8-year item, the veneer should not be peeling off in 4 years.

Products that show fingermarks or scratches or that require frequent polishing or hand scrubbing should be avoided unless the store has a large maintenance budget and can afford the extravagance. Otherwise, every item specified should be carefully scrutinized from a minimal-maintenance viewpoint.

Merchants are very concerned that the designer know how employees operate "back of the house."

This includes the marking, receiving, and shipping of merchandise and the supporting systems for paperwork. Departmental wrapping and sales-check writing should be accomplished smoothly and not be a source of daily stress, especially during the busy end-of-the-year selling season. Elements such as office space, cafeteria, and locker rooms have to be considered early in the design program.

If the designer has never sold at retail, it is a smart idea to take the time to observe the sales staff. Dealing with customers, writing sales-checks, handling stock, and interacting with the other salespeople in a real-life situation need to be considered in the design of a functional environment. In laying out selling spaces, the designer has to be aware of what salespeople will and will not do physically to stock the department and get merchandise for customers. How far will they reach up or bend down on a day-in, day-out basis? Personal observation of these problems will make the solutions easier to develop.

# 5

# Basic Store Layouts

There are two basic planning guidelines for laying out a retail sales floor. Six basic plans can help the designer to carry them out. These are certainly not the only plans that can be developed, but they form the foundation on which others can be created.

*The guidelines*

· Use 100 percent of the space allocated.

· Do not sacrifice function for esthetics. Successful plans combine both to the fullest.

*Six basic plans*

· Straight
· Pathway
· Diagonal
· Curved
· Varied
· Geometric

## Straight plan

The *straight plan* is a conventional form of layout that utilizes walls and projections to create smaller spaces. It is an economical plan to execute and can be adapted to any type of store, from gift shops to apparel outlets, from drug and grocery stores to department stores.

Variety in the straight plan can be introduced by creating niches with the merchandise. To define transition from one section of the store to the other, displays can be placed to help lead customers. Elevate floor levels for a change of pace.

This plan lends itself well to pulling customers to the back of the store. In a bookstore, for example, special sale merchandise can be placed at the rear, with signage informing shoppers of the items and directing them in the right direction.

## Pathway plan

Applicable to virtually any type of store, the pathway plan is particularly suited to larger stores over 5000 square feet and on one level. The *pathway plan*, a good architectural organizer, gets shoppers smoothly from the front to the rear of the store.

This plan is recommended for apparel stores because of its ability to minimize the cluttered feeling which tends to discourage or disturb shoppers who do not care to fight their way to the racks in the back. This plan also focuses the shoppers' attention to other merchandise on the path. The designer can create designs off the path using the floor or ceiling as directional elements.

## Diagonal plan

For self-service stores, a *diagonal plan* is optimal. The cashier is in a central location, with sight lines to all areas of the space. Soft goods or hard goods stores, including drug and food stores, can take advantage of the diagonal plan.

Visually, the plan has an exciting and dynamic quality. Because it is not based on a straight line, it invites movement and circulation.

## Curved plan

For boutiques, salons, or other high-quality stores, the *curved plan* creates an inviting, special environment for the customer. It also costs more to construct than angular or square plans.

The curved theme can be emphasized with walls, ceiling, and corners. To complete the look, specify circular floor fixtures.

## Varied plan

For products that require back-up merchandise to be immediately adjacent (shoes and men's shirts, for example), the *varied plan* is highly functional. It is a variation of the straight-line plan with sufficient square footage allowed for box or carton storage off the main sales floor with perimeter wall stocking.

As shown in the illustration on page 44, the varied plan has a "bellows" effect, a tapering back or space delineation that focuses on a special-purpose area in the back. Service departments in stereo, jewelry, or hardware stores can be located in this narrow end. For a tobacco shop, it is a fine place for the humidor.

## Geometric plan

The designer creates forms with shapes derived from showcases, racks, or gondolas in a *geometric plan*. This plan is the most exotic of the six basic plans, and the designer can use wall angles to restate the shapes dominating the sales floor.

The geometric plan comfortably allows for fitting rooms without wasting square footage; this benefit makes the plan especially suitable for apparel stores. Also, it can nicely accommodate adjacent stock, making it an alternative to the varied plan for shoe stores and gift shops.

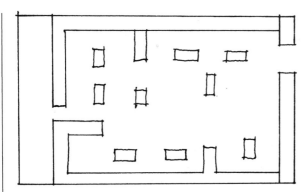

This straight plan uses walls and projections to create smaller spaces and is economical.

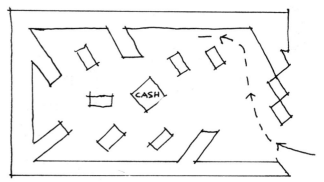

This diagonal pattern permits angular traffic flow and creates perimeter design interest and excitement in movement. The central placement of the cash-wrap permits security and vision.

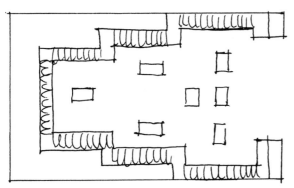

This varied plan illustrates added variety of forms which can work to a designer's advantage.

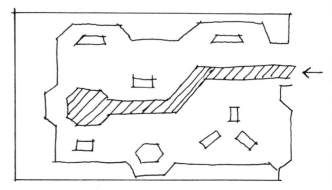

This pathway plan pulls patrons through the store to the rear without interruption by floor fixtures. The merits of such a layout are that the path can take any shape and that it creates a design pattern.

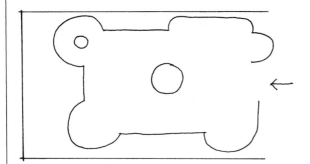

People respond to circular and curved shapes such as those shown here, which soften the angular and square plan.

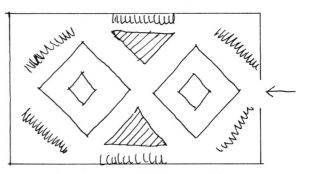

A geometric plan can establish interest without excessive cost, if the store's product can accept it. Ceiling and floors can be lowered or raised to create zones and departments.

**Alternate Plan Arrangements: Solving a Store Design Problem**

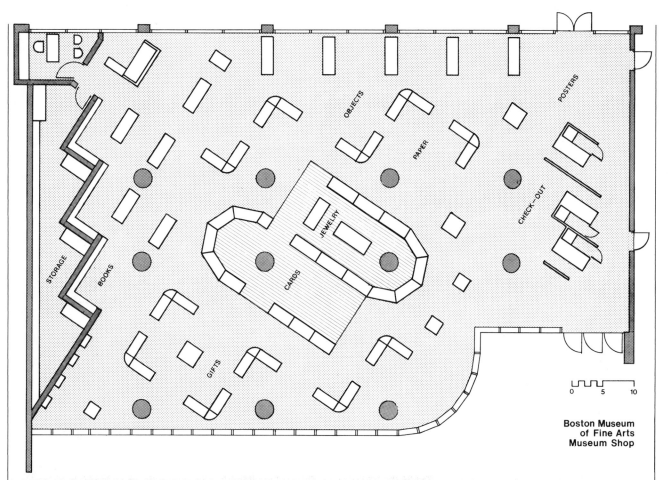

Boston Museum
of Fine Arts
Museum Shop

Many major museums have turned their former "gift shops" into miniature department stores, profitable for the institution and fun to shop in. Because these stores carry a wide variety of merchandise in a limited space, they are a challenging exercise in store planning. The new 6000-square-foot shop at the Boston Museum of Fine Arts, located in the new addition, is based on the diagonal plan. Checkouts, placed near entrances, are also angled. Cards and jewelry are located in the center of the space. Showcases and display units are angled around a partially mirrored column.

*Design for the addition:* I. M. Pei & Partners. *Design for the shop:* Charles E. Broudy & Associates. *Photo:* Charles E. Broudy.

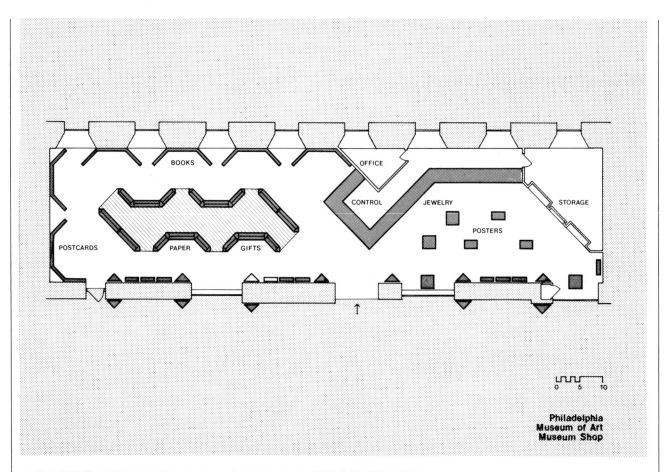

BOOKS

OFFICE

CONTROL    JEWELRY    STORAGE

POSTERS

POSTCARDS    PAPER    GIFTS

0    5    10

Philadelphia
Museum of Art
Museum Shop

The remodeled shop of the Philadelphia Museum of Art has been responsible for increased retail sales and for attracting new members to the museum. Working with a difficult 25- by 98-foot space on a lower level, the layout combines diagonal, pathway, and geometric plans. Best-selling posters are mounted close to the ceiling. In this position, they also draw attention to the jewelry showcases below. Fixtures in the book section (left, rear) are designed to allow customers to view front covers rather than only spines as in conventional book display units.

*Design:* Charles E. Broudy & Associates. *Photo:* Charles E. Broudy.

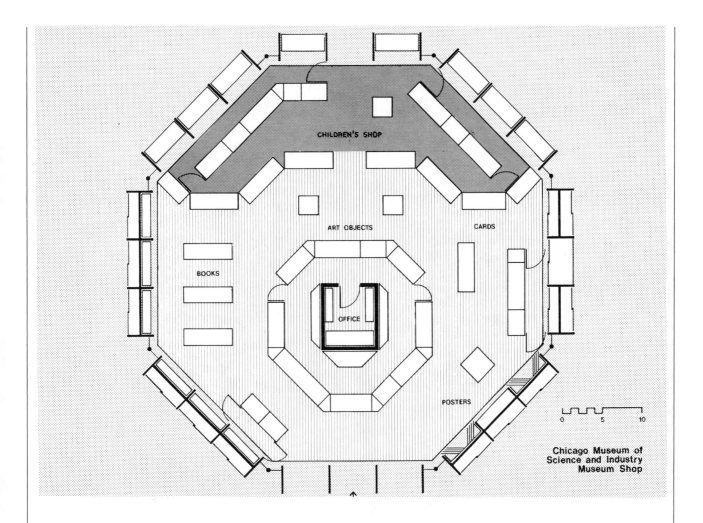

CHILDREN'S SHOP

ART OBJECTS

CARDS

BOOKS

OFFICE

POSTERS

Chicago Museum of
Science and Industry
Museum Shop

Chicago's Museum of Science and
Industry is the only permanent major
structure remaining from the 1892
Columbian Exposition. Today, it is one of
the most visited of U.S. museums. The
1981 remodeling program included a
new freestanding octagonal museum
store located in the central section of the
main floor beneath the central dome. The
freestanding shop shown at left is
defined by an overhead space frame.

*Design for the 1981 remodeling:* FCL & Associates,
Inc. *Design for the shop:* Charles E. Broudy &
Associates. *Photo:* Barbara Karant, Karant +
Associates.

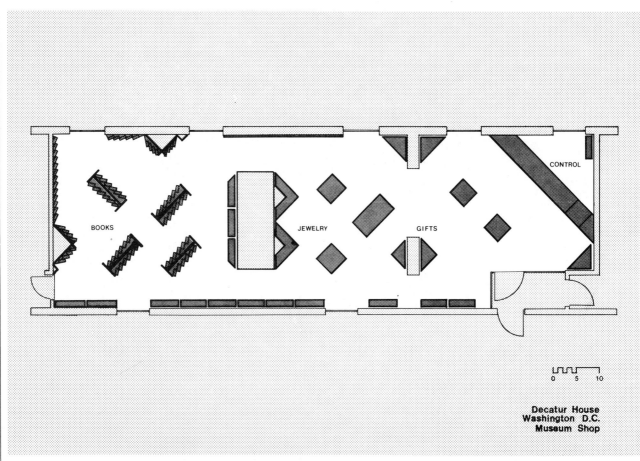

CONTROL

BOOKS

JEWELRY

GIFTS

0  5  10

**Decatur House
Washington D.C.
Museum Shop**

**When the National Trust for Historic Preservation purchased the Decatur House for its Washington, D.C., headquarters, a 30- by 96-foot space was remodeled for a museum store carrying expanded selections of books, jewelry, gifts, and accessory items. The straight plan has cashier and wrapping at the end near the main entrance.**

*Design:* Charles E. Broudy & Associates.

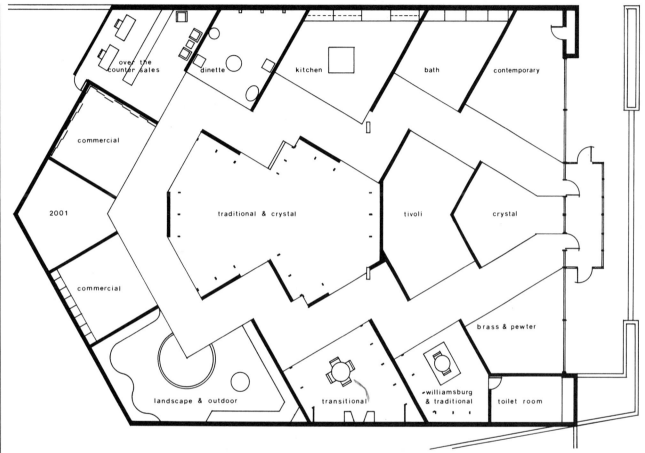

**In the geometric plan for the showroom of Lighting Designers, Inc., Rockville, Maryland, fifteen angled spaces present fixtures by functional and style groupings.**

*Design:* Charles E. Broudy & Associates.

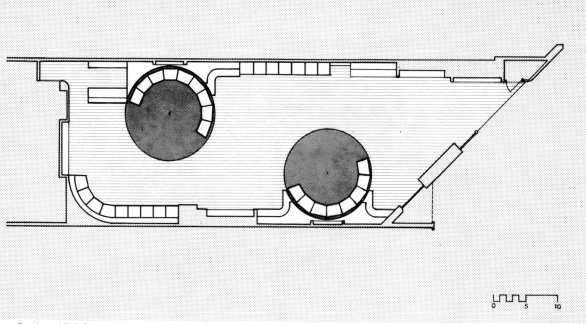

Hahn Shoes, Beachwood Mall, Cleveland, Ohio

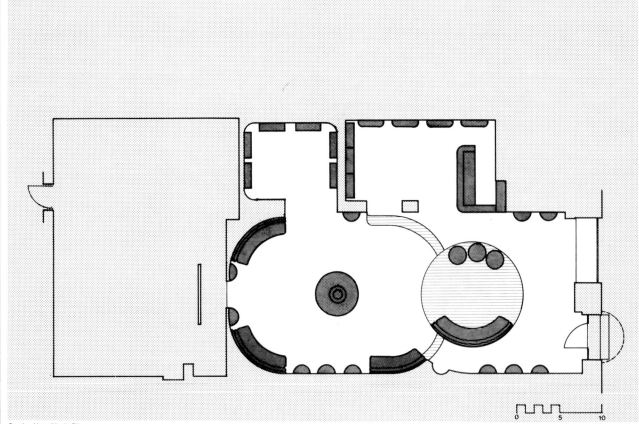

Cuoio, New York City

**Layouts for four shoe stores.**

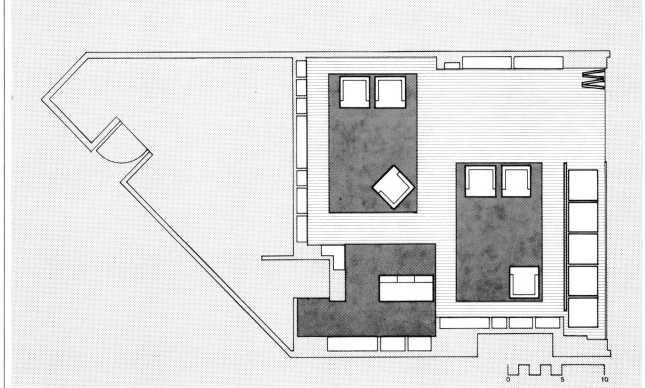

Johnston & Murphy, Galleria Mall, Houston, Texas

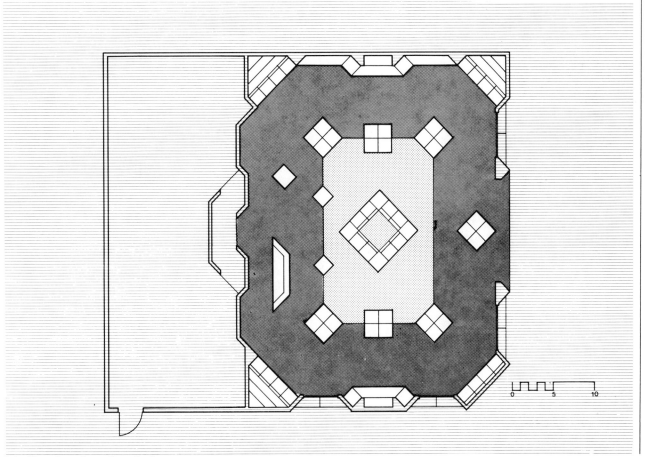

Irving Shoes, Susquehanna, Pennsylvania

51

# 6
# Exhibiting
# Merchandise

**D**isplaying merchandise to its best advantage In the retail world, "display" often has a double meaning: "to show off or exhibit" or "to hold or contain."

Merchants look favorably on the axiom that if it does not hold the building up or is not nailed down, it is for sale. A retail store is not a museum. Merchants want what the customer sees to be paid for and taken out of the store. Merchants may want a museum-quality environment, but they also want the goods to move—and as often as possible!

The designer should keep in clear focus that an exhibit space with suitable backdrop and lighting will be created to frame and highlight the product. But that product is not an archival object. Rather, it has a markup, a predetermined market to which it has been selected to appeal, and a designated "shelf life." It moves in, and it moves out.

*Analyze the merchandise* to determine its "appeals," the characteristics that will determine how it will be shown to the buying public.

*Made to measure* does not apply only to custom-made clothing. In retail store design, the term means creating the casework or fixtures that will fit the dimensions of the goods to be sold. In apparel stores, 85 percent of the total space on the sales floor is devoted to housing the merchandise on racks or shelves or in bins or freestanding units. The balance, 15 percent, is for back-of-the-house purposes. There is some variation in this ratio between types of stores, department store to small boutique. All units must show the merchandise to its best advantage— effectively lighted and framed. Often, these display-housing modules must have structural flexibility. These fixtures can be purchased (if

you can locate stock items) or custom-manufactured.

There has yet to be developed an easy-access, computerized databank to store the dimensions—length, width, and height—of the hundreds of thousands of items sold at retail.

So, to obtain efficient housing, the designer *must physically measure the sizes of the merchandise,* as it will be displayed on the sales floor and stocked either in the selling area or in back-up areas. This is an absolute requirement, whether the items are

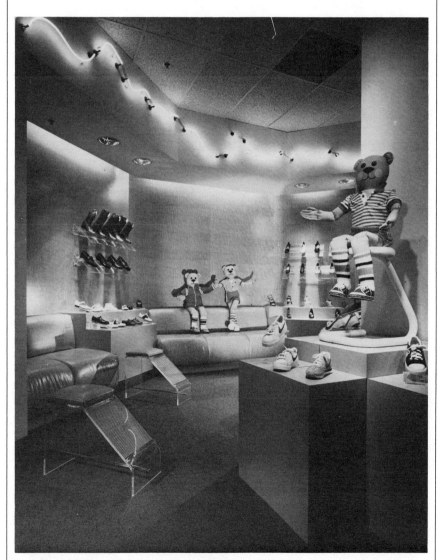

**At Bullock's in Beverly Center, an urban mall in Los Angeles, merchandise is shown in a theatrical environment created with lighting and a backdrop of fine materials. In the children's shoe department, colorful neon scribbles identify major merchandise in a fun way—pink for girls, blue for boys, green for shoes.**

*Design:* Walker Group, Inc. *Photo:* Toshi Yoshimi.

TYPICAL MERCHANDISE DISPLAY ANALYSIS

| | POSTCARDS | STATIONARY | TOYS/GAMES | GLASSWARE | JEWELRY | OBJECTS | TOTAL |
|---|---|---|---|---|---|---|---|
| SALES AREA (SQUARE FEET) | | | | | | | |
| Service | | | | | | | |
| Self Serve | | | | | | | |
| Plan of Space | | | | | | | |
| Siting Consideration | | | | | | | |
| MERCHANDISING | | | | | | | |
| Number of Items | | | | | | | |
| Seasonal Increase | | | | | | | |
| Item Pricing | | | | | | | |
| Sign Consideration | | | | | | | |
| MERCHANDISING SPECIFICS | | | | | | | |
| Wall Display-Accessible | | | | | | | |
| Wall Display-Above 80" | | | | | | | |
| Island Display-Accessible | | | | | | | |
| Secure Display, Under Glass | | | | | | | |
| Manufacturers' Displays | | | | | | | |
| STOCK | | | | | | | |
| Concealed in Floor Display | | | | | | | |
| Drawers/Doors behind Sales | | | | | | | |
| Stockroom/Backup Areas | | | | | | | |

TYPICAL MERCHANDISE DISPLAY ANALYSIS - GIFT SHOP (EXAMPLE)

| | POSTCARDS | STATIONARY | TOYS/GAMES | GLASSWARE | JEWELRY | OBJECTS | TOTAL |
|---|---|---|---|---|---|---|---|
| SALES AREA (SQUARE FEET) | 10% | 13% | 20% | 15% | 18% | 22% | 100% |
| Service | —— | —— | 10% | 20% | 60% | 25% | |
| Self Serve | 100% | 100% | 90% | 80% | 40% | 75% | |
| Plan of Space | LINEAR | OPEN | U-SHAPE | LINEAR | ENCLOSED | RANDOM | |
| Siting Consideration | NEAR CASHIER | REAR | MID-SHOP | PERIMETER | EASY VIEWING | NEAR FRONT | |
| MERCHANDISING | | | | | | | |
| Number of Items | 200 | 420 | 500 | 175 | 300 | 100 | 1695 |
| Seasonal Increase | HOLIDAYS | 600 | XMAS | 200 | 350 | 130 | |
| Item Pricing | ● | ON PRODUCT | ON PRODUCT | PARTIAL/SALE | ● | ● | |
| Sign Consideration | ● | ● | ● | BRAND NAMES | —— | —— | |
| MERCHANDISING SPECIFICS | | | | | | | |
| Wall Display-Accessible | ● | ● | ● | ● | ● | ● | |
| Wall Display-Above 80" | —— | ● | LARGER ITEM | ● | —— | ● | |
| Island Display-Accessible | ● | ● | | ● | —— | ● | |
| Secure Display, Under Glass | —— | —— | EXPENSIVE FRAGILE | EXPENSIVE | ● | ● | |
| Manufacturers' Displays | 50%/50% | —— | AUTO MODELS | —— | EARRINGS | —— | |
| STOCK | | | | | | | |
| Concealed in Floor Display | ● | ● | ● | ● | ● | ● | |
| Drawers/Doors behind Sales | | ● | ● | ● | 100% | ● | |
| Stockroom/Backup Areas | BOX STOR. | ● | ● | ● | —— | ● | |

postcards, books, blouses, shoes, men's shirts, overcoats, glassware, or pieces of furniture.

Each item in a store has a basic dimension and space size. The designer converts these size elements into housing and display for the products to create vehicles that provide the best setting to show the merchandise to its greatest advantage.

# Guidelines to creating sales-stimulating merchandise displays

### 1. Breathe new life into tried-and-true display methods

Reviewing catalogs from stock fixture manufacturers is a good jumping-off point to help the designer generate refreshing ideas. Starting with catalog items, use eye-catching materials to give additional dimension, a new design composition. The objective is to get the shopper to stop, look, and evaluate the merchandise. Here are a few ways to dress up a stock fixture:

- Add panels made of an interesting fabric or mirror, metallic, or wood material.

- Subtly play matte and reflective surfaces against each other.

- Build in lighting to give added emphasis to merchandise in bins, racks, or shelves. Use pinpoint lighting to give extra sparkle to glassware, jewelry, china, and silver.

### 2. Imagine yourself to be the merchandise on display

Ask yourself how you would like to be shown off to the best advantage. Would you not want to project your true image ("the real you")? Should not the setting make you stand out from your surroundings? Are you classic, elegant, or conservative, or are you trendy and avant-garde?

Analyze the merchandise in the same manner. Catch its mood and then project it. Recognize its personality—timeless or au courant—and create an appropriate environment.

Other than electronic items, most merchandise cannot talk for itself, so the setting you design will have to "talk" for the goods. Avoid chaotic backgrounds so the personality of the stock will not have an uphill struggle in competing for the shopper's attention.

### 3. Set the tone

What mood should customers perceive when they walk into the space? Soft elegance? Woody classic? Neutral greige? A lively "junior" environment? Pleasant and placid? Price-conscious discount?

One of the most challenging assignments in retail store design today is to give customers the impression that they are in a below-retail-price-level establishment without insulting them visually. Plain pipe racks and unshielded lighting fixtures talk down to customers.

**Ann Taylor**

**Little Daisy**

### 4. Coordinate the environment with the product's end use

The trend to retail computer stores by IBM, Digital, and other electronic producers has spawned a whole new school of retail design. Background colors, lighting, materials, and display fixtures—all have to be coordinated with the user-technology interface. High-technology, big-ticket merchandise must not intimidate the shopper. The setting has to invite the shopper into the space and establish a comfortable environment for product investigation.

### 5. Do not accept the status quo

Consider these design options:

a. Change levels of the major horizontal planes: the floor and the ceiling. Create forms with recesses, dropped-ceiling areas. Depress floor areas or elevate them. Customers do not mind a few steps, not more than three, to get from one part of the sales floor to another.

b. Use interesting hardware on casework.

c. Investigate unusual wall coverings: papers or fabrics or architectural materials like metal and wood tambours.

d. Create a spatial feeling. Use two- or three-dimensional art. Even on a tight budget, you can find suitable items that will lend character and dimension to the selling area.

A combination ceiling-hung lighting and display unit offers function and visual interest at Ann Taylor in Beverly Hills, California. A wooden double-layer overhead unit repeats the square shape of the elevated display platform at Little Daisy in San Francisco.

*Design:* Charles E. Broudy & Associates. *Photos:* Charles E. Broudy.

## 6. Assemble and organize merchandise in a sculptural manner

Consider enclosure or framing. A good basic idea is to use your floor plan as a geometric theme and then repeat the shape decoratively. Triangles, rectangles, circles, arches, squares, rhomboids—all can be translated into two- and three-dimensional effects for floor, ceiling, and walls. Create levels with your geometric forms with ziggurats, dropped-ceiling panels, abstract wall treatments.

Enclosing or framing the merchandise can be done with lighting, pedestals, platforms, screens, or freestanding display units. Look for solid-void and negative-positive relationships.

**The Swan Gallery in downtown Philadelphia utilizes pedestals, recessed glass shelving, and freestanding showcases to display art objects and handmade jewelry.**

*Design:* Charles E. Broudy & Associates. *Photo:* Vilma Barr.

**Staggered free-form wooden-block perches for displaying sports footwear.**

*Design:* Charles E. Broudy & Associates. *Photo:* Charles E. Broudy.

**This display system for Joan & David women's shoe salon in the Ann Taylor unit, Highland Park, Dallas, Texas, features angled clear shelving mounted between floor-to-ceiling supports.**

*Design:* Charles E. Broudy & Associates. *Photo:* Charles E. Broudy.

## 7. Define the accessibility the customer will have to the products

Will the merchandise be handled by the customer, or will it be viewed from afar or through glass? The determinant will be the level of service: full self-service, modified self-service, or full personal service.

## 8. Display systems should be flexible

Retailers like to say that they love flexibility. Sometimes a dramatic set-in-concrete idea is bypassed for a less awesome but more flexible arrangement.

Retailers also love to put out merchandise on tables and displays in the highest traffic spots. Store paths or aisles that are 6 to 8 feet wide can accommodate customer traffic. The rule is "Do not put anything in the way of the customer unless it is an attractive display!"

For an apparel retailer, Charles E. Broudy & Associates designed a three-way mirror on wheels. (Who decreed that mirrors must be fastened to a store's wall?)

**In the new Sears Food Preparation Shops, housewares are stacked in high-tech, wire-frame shelf units, hung from brackets attached to slotted wood space dividers, or suspended from the open-lattice ceiling.**

*Courtesy:* Sears Merchandise Group.

The oak-base pedestal showcase in the Philadelphia Museum of Art shop is portable. Polished chrome frames the glass enclosure, which has a two-part sliding top.

*Design:* Charles E. Broudy & Associates. *Photo:* Charles E. Broudy.

**(Far right) A custom-designed revolving wheel at H.I.S. Pantwheel, Westport, Connecticut, holds multiple pairs of pants. The unique display device makes full use of wall height in the long, narrow store.**

*Design:* Charles E. Broudy & Associates. *Photo:* Charles E. Broudy.

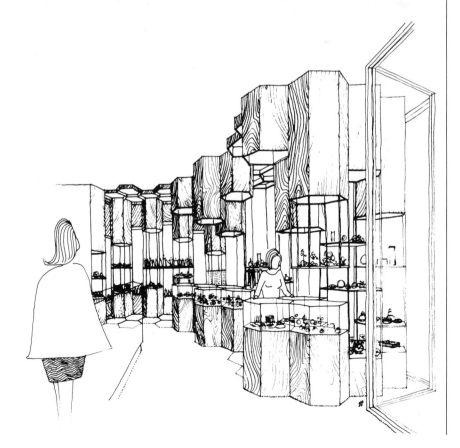

In the Honeybee chain of women's apparel and accessory stores, inspiration for the six-sided fixturing came from the natural honeycomb structure of a beehive.

*Design:* Charles E. Broudy & Associates.

# Retail display standards

## Cubes and bins

- For shirts, sweaters, pajamas, and other folded items; cards; books

- Freestanding; wall-mounted; counter base

## Shelving

- For artifacts and objects; shoe display

- Adjustable or fixed; enclosed or open; wall-mounted or attached to freestanding display units

## Freestanding display units

- For apparel, artifacts, and objects

- Apparel: T-stands, 4-way or quad stands, round racks, split round racks, slotted dividing walls

- Artifacts and objects: towers and étagères, pedestals, columns, tables; gondolas for self-service drug items, cards

- Special: slotted units for ties, belts

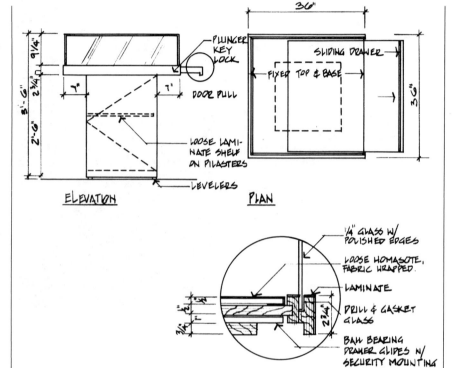

**Design for a freestanding pedestal jewelry case, used in the Philadelphia Museum of Art shop. (Compare the photograph on page 59.)**

*Design:* Charles E. Broudy & Associates.

**Design for a freestanding cube unit for such merchandise as sweaters and shirts.**

*Design:* Charles E. Broudy & Associates.

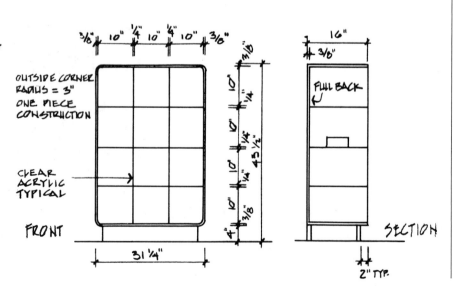

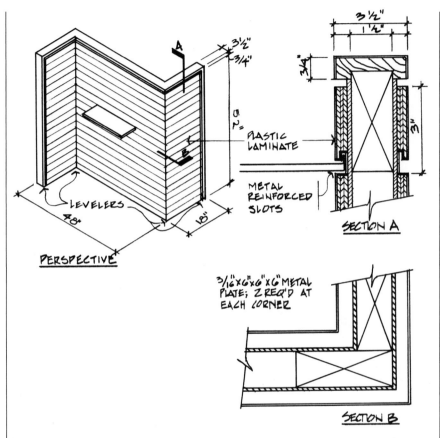

**Design for a Z-shaped floor unit with a slot wall to be used for displaying socks, ties, belts, handbags, etc.**

*Design:* Charles E. Broudy & Associates.

*Hanging devices*
- For apparel
- Horizontal bars; front-facing and side-facing wall-mounted fixtures

*Showcases*
- For accessories, cosmetics, jewelry
- Island; linear; self-service

*Special uses*
- Salesperson's stand-up work desk
- Cash-wrap counter

# 7

# Colors, Materials, and Finishes

Selection of the store's color scheme, surface coverings, and finishes is a part of the design process where the designer's creativity can show through. Inspiration sources are virtually limitless. The designer's exposure to art, music, travels, philosophy, psychology, architecture—all the inputs and impressions that mold the designer's style subconsciously contribute to the selections made.

Here, as in lighting selection, the designer's "signature" can be evident. Merchandise and client satisfaction come first; then the designer's "dimensional identity" can come through, subtly.

Anything goes that does not inhibit selling! And all materials are fair game as long as they work out together.

Find out your client's likes and dislikes. Eclectic? Timeless? High tech? Contemporary? Retail merchants have a high degree of "visual literacy." Indeed, color, line, and design as applied to the human form or to products for interiors or packaged for their store's shelves are very much a part of what they deal with every day. On buying trips or when attending conventions and trade shows, they travel to New York, Los Angeles, Chicago, Rome, Paris, Milan, and Hong Kong, and they make the rounds of new and remodeled stores. They return with ideas and suggestions (and often photos) for their store's designer to adapt or refine.

## Development of the color, materials, and finishes plan

• *Determining how much of the background will be covered by merchandise.* Will the materials be covered by shelving, cabinets, or hanging garments? Wall-mounted hang rods can cover two-thirds of a wall's height. Expensive materials behind the merchandise are not necessary because products cover much of the wall. Put your budget where it will have more impact.

• *Determining how much flexibility the store's plan allows for.* Will space allocated for an aisle during the summer be part of the department's sales floor at Christmas? Changes in materials should be planned with clear foresight into physical departmental shifts.

• *First costs versus life cycle costing.* Can the budget handle higher first costs for floor coverings, wall coverings, trims, and hardware in exchange for longer life? If it cannot, the designer and the store owner should establish wear priorities. Most merchants will not balk at replacing carpeting that is wearing out due to high traffic, but they do not want a carpet that looks shabby soon after installation. The designer should present the facts and the options and then make recommendations within the bounds of what the client can realistically afford to spend, given the projected income.

• *Materials as part of the security system.* Angled mirrors and wall-mounted mirrors contribute to the visual control of the store by allowing employees to monitor what would otherwise be blind spots in a store. Where an electronic surveillance device is placed near an entrance, designers should make sure that certain materials such as metals under consideration for use in this area will not interfere with its operation.

• *Safety concerns.* Floors at entryways and steps should be covered with slip-retardant material. Suppliers now offer an attractive array of textured products in cocoa mat, ceramic tile, sheet vinyl, vinyl tiles, and rubber. Materials specified for floors, walls, and windows should meet applicable flame-spread and smoke generation codes and building standards.

• *Early consideration of maintenance.* While the materials and finishes plan is still in its formative stage, submit a daily-weekly-monthly maintenance schedule of first-choice items for the client's review. In essence, the designer is practicing preventive medicine, to avoid the "Why didn't you tell me we'd have to polish the brass every other day?" retort that can stifle future commissions from the merchant. For example, painted walls need frequent repainting; most merchants favor fabric or paper with higher first costs and reduced care. Dressing room walls not covered by mirrors should have wood, plastic laminate, or vinyl covering.

• *Making substitutions.* Keep an open mind regarding product availability, particularly when you are in the midst of a fast-track job. Scurrying around to locate an acceptable substitute for original selections that have been discontinued, are out of stock, or have increased significantly in price is often high on the designer's least-favorite-tasks list. The designer should keep both the project's integrity and the time constraints for delivery in mind when substitutions must be made.

## Color psychology for store design

Color and lighting are two of the most influential factors in creating a store's distinctive personality and

A study in contrasts: contemporary urban sleek and vintage rural natural. The three-level Ann Taylor's 5th Avenue and 57th Street store in New York was created from a former two-story retail space. Merchandise departments ring the atrium, highlighted by a glass-enclosed elevator and curved staircase. Stainless steel handrails, columns, and trim contrast with parquet wood flooring, matte-finish painted drywall in muted shades such as mauve. The retail store of the French Creek Sheep & Wool Co. is located in a remodeled c. 1790 barn in Elverson, Pennsylvania. The rustic country setting for the merchandise features natural fieldstone walls, exposed beams, and plank flooring with braided or oriental area rugs.

ANN TAYLOR  *Design:* Charles E. Broudy & Associates. *Photo:* Norman McGrath.
FRENCH CREEK SHEEP & WOOL CO.  *Design:* Charles E. Broudy & Associates, *Photo:* Peter Olson.

adding to the salability of the merchandise.

"Color in an environment," according to store planner-designer and writer Dorothy Kamm, "defines space, indicates function, suggests temperature, influences mood and projects personality." Affecting customers' color preferences are current trends and geographical, national, cultural, and economic factors. Kamm's research indicates that low-income groups tend toward strong, prominent colors, while high-income groups prefer the neutrals and more diluted color schemes.

In a store composed of several departments or selling areas, it is not advisable to have abrupt changes or totally different color schemes adjacent to each other. Customers should not be conscious that back-

## Color Terminology

Keep basic color terminology in mind when developing the color scheme and considering materials and finishes.

• *Value:* a color's darkness or lightness

• *Tint:* a delicate color or hue

• *Shade:* the degree of darkness of a color

• *Intensity:* a color's brightness or dullness

• *Tone:* a color's degree or modification

• *Color wheel:* circular arrangment of 12 colors

• *Primary colors:* red, blue, and yellow (Mixtures of these are the origins of all other colors.)

• *Secondary colors:* orange (red and yellow); green (yellow and blue); purple (blue and red)

• *Tertiary colors:* combinations of primary and secondary colors produce tertiary colors such as yellow-green, blue-green, red-orange, red-violet

• *Complementary colors:* opposites on the color wheel

## Table 1 Using Color as a Selling Aid

| TYPE OF MERCHANDISE | COLORS OR COLOR THEMES | CONSIDERATIONS |
| --- | --- | --- |
| Men's apparel | Generally warm. Can borrow from gray flannel, blue pinstripe, herringbone, and tweed. Traditional colors such as brown, billiard green, wood tones. High-fashion colors. | Comfortable classic tones are cyclical, regularly return to favor. Brighter colors appeal to the youth market. |
| Women's apparel | Neutrals. | Women's fashions are bright and varied. Background should not conflict with merchandise and displays which should be made to stand out. |
| | Warm colors, including peach. | Flattering to skin and hair, particularly when seen in a mirror. |
| Children's apparel | Bright, primary colors. | Create a lively ambience. |
| Toys | Bright. | "Festive competition" works here. Bright and lively colored toys are enhanced by similar color scheme for fun atmosphere. |
| Jewelry | Cool or warm. | Create sparkle and clarity. For costly jewelry, give feeling of luxury. Enhance the product. |
| Books | Any color the designer wishes. | Keep the color plan simple so it will not compete with the jumble of book covers. Separate departments with contrasting color or colors. |
| Gifts | Neutral. | For varied merchandise. |
| | Punchier colors; complementary colors. | For merchandise with slower turnover and fashion cycle. |
| Shoes | Light colors for floors and walls. | Better for displays and for trying on merchandise in selling area. Dark or leather colors blend with many shoes and offer no contrast. |
| Fabrics | Neutral. | Colors should not clash or compete with colors and patterns of the fabrics themselves. |
| Electronics | Warm colors. | Contrast to hard-edge look or industrial look. |
| | Bright, bold colors. | Can be used because most of these products are small-scale. |
| Department store merchandise | Overall uniform scheme. | Gives feeling of unity, sophistication. |
| Discount store merchandise | "Jumpy" colors and textures; primary tones. | Convey a trendy, upbeat mood. |

ground colors are changing. Colors should nudge, rather than push, the shopper from one part of the store to another. Table 1 contains additional ideas on the impact of environmental color on sales.

Dorothy Kamm, in her article on the subject, draws from Faber Birren in typifying characteristics of color groups as follows:

- *Timeless color palettes*
  Neutrals—beige, cream, off-white, gray, greige, tan. Do not compete with merchandise; in good taste; can last many years.

- *Accent and jewel colors*
  Ruby, burgundy, emerald, hunter green, navy, turquoise, teal. Use sparingly; can be visually jarring to owner, and customers may tire quickly of very bright or dark areas used over large surfaces.

- *Cool color schemes*
  Gray, blue, blue-green, gray-green, blue-violet. Conservative and adaptable; good for home furnishings, men's wear; soothing, restful, and relaxing.

- *Warm color schemes*
  Red, orange, yellow. Friendly, cheerful; add excitement to an area; good for children's wear, active sportswear, housewares.

- *Pastels*
  Peach, mauve, lavender. Flattering to complexions; good for lingerie, jewelry.

**The entrance to the Houston Hat & Boot Co. store is wood-strip flooring, butting up to carpeting beyond. The cash-wrap–gift display island is made of the same wood and trimmed with brass. The store is in the King of Prussia Shopping Center, near Philadelphia.**

*Design:* Charles E. Broudy & Associates. *Photo:* Peter Olson

# Materials and finishes

Table 2 lists materials and finishes by "characteristics and considerations," and "recommendations." For a thorough discussion of floor-covering terminology, technology, and uses, the reader is referred to *Specifier's Guide to Contract Floor Covering*, available from Hearst Business Communications, Inc., FCW Division, 919 Third Avenue, New York, NY 10022.

**Table 2  Materials and Finishes for Retail Stores**

| Material | Characteristics and Considerations | Recommendations |
|---|---|---|
| **FLOORS** | | |
| **Wood** | | |
| Parquet | Often used set in mastic; checkerboard, herringbone patterns. | Can be a first-use, economical way to achieve the wood look. Can be glued down. |
| Straight boards | Hardwood | Will give an antique or "old floor" look. Effective in an accent area to set off an all-carpet floor. |
| Acrylic-impregnated wood flooring | Glue-down parquetlike treated wood; very low maintenance. | Good for large shops or shopping centers. Can withstand moisture. |
| Edge grain softwood | Very durable. | Expensive. Produces a deep, unique flooring look. |
| Marble | High gloss wears off quickly. Can be obtained $\frac{1}{4}$ in thick. | Easily maintained. Rich looking. |
| Terrazzo | Marble chips mixed with cement. | Expensive but long-lasting. Gives quality appearance. Good for aisles. |
| Granite | Available in $\frac{3}{8}$-in thickness; can be quick-set on subfloor. | Quality appearance combined with low maintenance. Appropriate for traditional and contemporary use. Good for heavy-traffic areas. |
| Flagstone | Can be used in grid or free-form design, single or multi colors. | Expensive. Gives a natural look. Effective even when used sparingly. |
| **Ceramic tile** | | |
| Quarry tile | Natural nonslip quality. | Good for aisles, corridors, wet areas such as food preparation spaces. |
| Glazed tile | Wear patterns can appear in heavy-traffic areas. Comes in a variety of colors. | Provides bright accent areas. Can be effectively used as a theme material to give a "continental" look. Walls and countertops are additional uses. |
| Integral | Good wearing quality. | Use for aisles, floors, and traffic areas. |
| **Carpet*** | | |
| Wool and nylon blend | Durable. | Best used for quality shops and salons. |
| Acrylic | Sturdy; less costly than wool and nylon blend. | Long-wearing, colorfast. |
| Nylon | Carpet glued directly to subflooring. | Long-wearing. Colors have improved in new generations. Avoid shiny pile. |
| Polypropylene | Moisture-resistant. Resists fading. | Not used as often as three types listed above. |
| Padding | Rubber and jute. | Used extensively for large areas. Gives softer, plusher underfoot feel. (Both forms of padding extend carpet life.) |
| **Special-purpose** | | |
| Area rugs | Antique or new orientals; patterned contemporary or solid movable rugs. | Effective over wood floors or neutral background carpeting. Creates quality atmosphere. |
| Entryway flooring: | | |
| Cocoa mat | Scrapes dirt off shoes. | Good appearance when new; replace when appears matted. |
| Slats | Permit dirt to fall through to trap below. | Necessity for stores in frost belt. Good investment for all other climates, especially for entryways that lead to other flooring materials. |

*Some synthetic carpeting needs stretching soon after laying.

| Material | Characteristics and Considerations | Recommendations |
|---|---|---|
| **FLOORS** | | |
| Carpet tiles | Easily replaced; owner should have reserve inventory of replacement tiles. | Good for heavy-traffic areas. Easier and less conspicuous to replace than patching broadloom. |
| Resilient | | |
| Solid vinyl | Wide variety of colors and textures available. Glue-down installation. Minimum maintenance required. | Well suited for heavy-use areas such as aisles, corridors. Versatile style palette, from high-tech to elegant. |
| Vinyl composition tile | Good selection of patterns and colors. Low maintenance. | Less expensive than solid vinyl. Long-wearing but lacks richness. Suitable for hard-use areas—discount stores, back-of-the-house spaces. |
| Asphalt | Low cost. | Less frequently specified as price spread between asphalt and other types of resilient flooring has narrowed in recent years. |
| **EXTERIOR WALLS** | | |

Even though freestanding stores are the most challenging to the store architect, commissions to design them are rather infrequent: one freestanding store for every 25 storefront projects is a reasonable estimate. The designer, then, has to communicate the store's personality to prospective customers primarily through the storefront. By using traditional or contemporary materials with flair and efficiency, the store's front can become the merchant's single most dramatic and effective "silent salesperson."

| Material | Characteristics and Considerations | Recommendations |
|---|---|---|
| Masonry | Limestone panels. Brick. | Has solid, quality appearance. Economical; available in many shapes and colors. Costly to ship long distances. |
| | Fieldstone, ledgestone. | For accent walls. Use regional materials. |
| Marble | Thin veneers will not give long use in harsh weather climates. | A rich, quality product that requires careful specification. Interesting and varied color selection. |
| Granite | Costly but durable. Veneers are becoming thinner. Low maintenance. | Limited colors but effective for traditional, classic stores. |
| Precast concrete insulated sandwich panels with exposed aggregate | Moderately costly, but reduce construction time. | Efficient material for large wall surfaces. Because material is manufactured, not natural, it works best with contemporary designs. |
| Anodized aluminum | Available with preinstalled windows and insulation. | Available in several price ranges and color ranges. |
| Stainless steel | Same as above. | Long-lasting and virtually maintenance free, material has austere, hard-edge look. |
| Porcelain enamel | On aluminum or steel base; prefabricated for window walls; or made in large panels with sealant joints. | Suitable to cover large expanses. Many colors to select from. |
| Cement plaster | Produced with insulation, gypsum wallboard, and metal studs. Cost efficient. | Scoring and jointing can easily create interesting slopes and shapes. Material is popular for covering large building expanses. |
| Glass reflective surfaces | A moderate-to-expensive prefabricated material. Colors are limited. | Most successful when used on a contemporary structure, as a visual integrator to reflect natural or artificial surroundings. |

*( Continued)*

**Table 2 Materials and Finishes for Retail Stores (*Continued*)**

| Material | Characteristics and Considerations | Recommendations |
| --- | --- | --- |
| INTERIOR WALLS AND PARTITIONS | | |

For dividing and defining interior spaces, the retail store designer is involved with:

1. Permanent walls—load-bearing or structural walls

2. Floor-to-ceiling partitions—divide one selling or nonselling area from another when merchandise or service is dissimilar or intimacy or privacy is desired

3. Freestanding partitions—dividers that separate spaces without blocking the view; should be easily relocatable and adaptable

To cover wall and partition surfaces, there is a plethora of choices, with more entering the marketplace every year. From smooth and glossy marble to textured brick and from glittery mirrors to velveteen, the store designer can match atmosphere, mood, and budget to available products. Investigate wall systems that permit metal store fixture standards on the wall with panels of mirror, fabric, plastic laminate, or wall covering between the standards.

| Material | Characteristics and Considerations | Recommendations |
| --- | --- | --- |
| **Permanent walls and floor-to-ceiling partitions** | | |
| Brick | Expensive. | Can be used in natural color or painted. Extends exterior experience indoors. Provides distinctive depth and texture. |
| Exposed concrete block | Inexpensive. | Split-face varieties and color can dress up this material. |
| Marble and granite veneer | Reinforcing produces larger blocks. Specify honed or polished finish. | Has distinctive richness. Popular for jewelry and other big-ticket item stores. Use to attain a varied wall texture. |
| Ceramic tile | Many sizes, textures, colors, and shapes for permanent installations. | Effective as overall background for housewares department or accents in other sales areas. Hand-painted scenic tiles can be focal points. |
| Plaster and stucco | Classic stucco, stipple, sand textures, and other imprints possible. | Carries out a warm climate theme. Deep texture can cover layers of previous finishes. |
| Sheetrock | Inexpensive basic interior material. | Joints need taping and proper spackling or they will show under glossy paint. Easily covered with paper or fabric. |
| Paint | Low cost and flexibility make paint the most used of all interior materials. Easily scuffed. | Merchandise and painted color background should not compete. Glossy and flat finishes create different backdrop effects. Painted treatments include supergraphics, stripes, stencils, contrasting panels. |
| Wood paneling | Modest to very expensive. Produced in boards or veneer. | Made in range of natural finishes or in lacquer colors. Can be natural barn look or elegant matched panels. |
| Plastic laminate | Colorful; easy to construct and maintain. Corners are vulnerable to chipping. | Good for dressing rooms, as a long-term substitute for paint, and in hard-use areas. |
| Wall fabric, wallpaper, and wall vinyl | Price ranges from low to high but maintenance is often very low. Proper background preparation needed on substrate for thin or expensive materials. | Enormous variety, but designer should consider budget and product availability before making final selection. |
| Mirror | Can be used clear, gray or bronze colored, or smoked. | Visually enlarges a space or "stretches" a wall. Important to visual security program. Sparkle and luster of clear or tinted mirror can enliven a drab space. |
| Stained and leaded glass | Great variety of colors. Custom or stock designs. | For dividers, accent areas in hard or soft goods stores. Lighting from behind adds to visual punch. |
| Etched glass | Can carry signage or decorative ornamentation. | Opaque or clear versions available. Most effective for "period" design themes. |

| Material | Characterisitics and Considerations | Recommendations |
|---|---|---|
| **INTERIOR WALLS AND PARTITIONS** | | |
| Slotwall | Slotted wood panel with metal or plastic devices to support shelves or hangers. | For self-serve display of apparel, shoes, books, gifts, tobacco products, etc. |
| Free-standing partitions | | |
| Grilles | Allow see-through effects. | Applicable to dividers of departments, and in some cases permit display and graphics to separate departments. |
| Compressed spring systems | Can support hangrods or shelving. | Good for housewares; permit a see-through wall housing shoes, apparel, and home furnishings, etc. |
| Homasote with wall covering | Flexible display divider; easy to pin merchandise directly to surface. | For paper products, apparel, and lightweight accessory and houseware items. |
| Wall cubes | Hollow glass or plastic cubes. | Shoes, hardware, small appliances, etc. placed in cubes make combination merchandise exhibit and space divider. |
| Stained, leaded, and etched glass | See listings under "Interior Walls and Partitions," above. | Panels |
| Plastics | Clear or opaque color. | Can be suspended on wires from the ceiling or organized within frames. Used to break up space in large selling areas such as furniture showrooms or department stores. |
| **CEILINGS** | | |

In retail stores ceilings offer another design dimension. In offices, banks, schools, and hospitals ceilings are a surface against which to bounce light or control sound. These aspects are certainly true in stores, but in addition, the designer can utilize materials, textures, and different height levels for stunning effects, or to restate a pattern used on floors or walls.

| | | |
|---|---|---|
| Acoustical tile | | |
| Exposed T-bar | Mineral or fiberglass panels, exposed metal track—2 by 4 ft or 2 by 2 ft. | Economical but "busy" ceiling. |
| Concealed spline | Textured mineral tiles in concealed spline, usually 12-in square. | Even, unbroken ceiling appearance. Use for more sophisticated applications. |
| Textured or scored | Scored panels in 2 by 4 ft, or 2 by 2 ft. Present linear and various geometric forms on surface. | Linear and grid-like in appearance. Use where ceiling interest is needed. |
| Luminous ceiling | | |
| Plastic | Plexiglass or acrylic in a variety of finishes and looks. | Can cause glare or shadowing from dust or dirt. |
| Tiffany type | Plastic, colorful, decorative; costly. | Strong, powerful appearance. |
| Egg crate | Metal or plastic; square or hexagon shapes. | Light can appear diffused. |
| Low brightness | Parahex or square-shape grids. Colors: silver, bronze, gold. | Good way to reduce glare of fluorescent lighting. |
| High-cell parabolic | Plastic or metal. | Creates a low glare, with various grid width openings. |
| Baffle ceilings | | |
| Insulated fabric | Foam board covered with fabric. | Helps conceal exposed lighting; has sound absorbent value. |
| Wood baffles | Wood-veneer plywood or solid wood. Color or natural. Gridlike patterns. | Good for remodeling; creates either woodsy or contemporary feeling. |

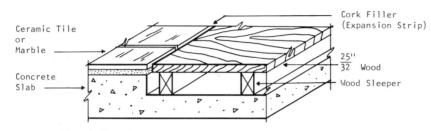

Ceramic Tile or Marble

Concrete Slab

Cork Filler (Expansion Strip)

$\frac{25"}{32}$ Wood

Wood Sleeper

**Ceramic tile or marble used with wood**

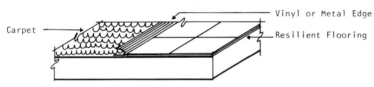

Carpet

Vinyl or Metal Edge

Resilient Flooring

**Carpet and resilient flooring**

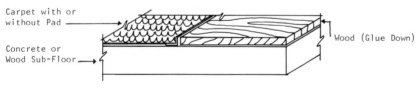

Carpet with or without Pad

Concrete or Wood Sub-Floor

Wood (Glue Down)

**Carpet and wood**

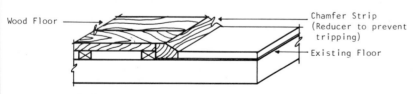

Wood Floor

Chamfer Strip (Reducer to prevent tripping)

Existing Floor

**Wood and existing flooring**

**Examples of dissimilar floors in retail environments. Store designers often utilize different flooring materials to indicate pathways or for visual interest. Careful detailing is important because of different subfloors, thicknesses, expansion and contraction qualities of materials, tripping dangers, worn edges, and cleaning and maintenance.**

**Exposed-brick interior walls, while costly when constructed new today, are often a found asset in rehab projects. This multilevel Morristown, New Jersey unit of Roots Clothiers was created from the remodeling of an existing colonial-style office building plus a new addition. At the meeting of the old and the new walls, the existing windows were made into oak-framed openings without creating any new brick penetrations. Felt-covered panels give added dimension to hanging garments. Pinned merchandise displays are easily changed.**

*Design:* Charles E. Broudy & Associates. *Photo:* Lawrence S. Williams, Inc.

Case study of colors, materials, and finishes selected for Dimensions, a 3400-square-foot men's apparel store located in Willow Grove Park, a 100-store enclosed mall near Philadelphia.

*Design:* Charles E. Broudy & Associates. *Photos:* Charles E. Broudy.

The entrance features illuminated black glass and brass sign, wood and glass doors, and a ceramic tile apron.

Doors swing open to reveal polished brass display fixtures; the flooring at the entry is parquet wood, leading to a carpeted area.

Polished brass pipe frame fixtures at Dimensions can be used to display hanging garments or accessories. Parquet flooring forms a pathway to rear showcases.

*(Right)* Plants are interspersed between oak display units at Dimensions. Carpet butts to parquet flooring; the dropped ceiling echoes angles of the flooring materials.

*(Below)* A display island at Dimensions projects strong geometric lines of wood and glass. Overhead lighting and the wooden pedestal focus attention on the mannequin. The carpet repeats the shape of the ceiling.

*(Top left)* Small items are displayed in a Dimensions case fabricated of antique brass and curved glass.

*(Top right)* A seating area in Dimensions is defined by overhead lighting and a colonnade-framed portal. Club chairs are upholstered in a neutral tone to blend with the carpeting. The color scheme is beige and dark green.

*(Bottom)* The spacious cash-wrap area also has gifts, toiletries, and other impulse items arranged in an organized point-of-purchase display. Pale oak wood contrasts with dark-green felt wall covering. Additional lighting is provided in the wood-faced valance.

# Bibliography

Kamm, Dorothy: "Chroma-Zones: The missing Link in Sales Evolution?" *Visual Merchandising*, December 1982, pp. 69–71.

Telchin, Charles S., and Seymour Helfant: *Plan Your Store for Maximum Sales and Profit*, National Retail Merchants Association, New York, 1969, pp. 93–107.

# 8

# Lighting

Retail store lighting is not a space lighting problem; it is a merchandise lighting problem. Thus lighting should be designed with a solid sales orientation. Customers do not want to "buy" lighting effects; what they are interested in is the merchandise.

A good electrical and lighting plan echoes the floor plan. The lighting plan supports the merchandise and the store's traffic patterns. When the designer develops the store layout, the lighting plan will begin to evolve as part of the creative process. As the designer begins to express in the plan what it is the merchant wants to achieve and as the main elements of the design are established, the lighting techniques will be integrated into the visual package. After the layout is approved by the client, the designer will refine the lighting plan.

Lighting can help to make a store successful. How well the lighting is handled can set the store—and the designer—apart. In the field of retail store design, designers have built fine reputations and successful practices on their lighting design talents as well as the more traditional architectural and planning skills. The methods by which the designer can add sales appeal to the merchandise by lighting effects while staying within the constraints of the project's budget (and the applicable energy codes), mean a great deal to clients and prospective clients.

Lighting is one area of store design where the visually savvy merchant-client will normally give the designer only a few broad instructions.

· Unlike floor coverings, which merchants do not seem to mind replacing after they become worn by heavy traffic, lighting fixtures are regarded as a more permanent part of the selling area, and store owners do not want to change them every few years.

· The store owner does not want goods returned because the lighting rendition on the sales floor made the merchandise look very different after the customer got it home.

· The merchant wants an effective lighting plan and an efficient one. In a 20-department store, the client will probably tell you not to come up with 20 different lighting plans. Remember that flexibility is one of the keystones of a successful store plan. A collection of independent lighting parts trying to function as a unified sales supportive tool would defeat this. For most stores over 10,000 square feet, develop an overall lighting design, and then augment and supplement it within the departments. Lighting is an extremely malleable as well as precise design tool: A store planner can highlight, sculpt, signal, wash the walls, or subdue—all within the frame of an overall plan.

For many types of interior lighting use, there are accepted ranges of user-light-level requirements and illumination solutions. For banks, offices, schools, or hospitals, the tasks performed are repetitive. Workers' task lighting needs are analyzed, and acceptable ranges are selected to provide sufficient, glare-free lighting. The level of light required to perform these tasks is well documented and, for the most part, accepted by design professionals.

No such widespread accord exists for retail store lighting. There are far more variables in a retail establishment than in almost any other type of interior use (restaurants is the other major nonstandard category). There are very few "standard" solutions for lighting retail stores because nearly every retail project is unique. The merchandise mix, trading area, customer profile, and mood to be communicated are rarely the same, except for some "formula" chains.

Just about the only constant in retail stores lighting design is that *the initial impact is important*. The eye adjusts to the light level even before it begins to transmit to the brain signals about the merchandise. Light is the quickest and most direct form of nonverbal communication. Consider the impression of a store with bright (100 footcandles or more) overall illumination, unbaffled, and all fluorescent, versus an interior with accent lighting complementing the merchandise, architectural detail defined by lighting, and discreet overall (ambient) lighting. Both have their place in today's retailing sphere, and they reflect two vastly different selling philosophies.

"Lighting is the most important decorative item in the store. It is as important an element in a store as it is in the theater. The quality of lighting can make or break merchandise."— Geraldine Stutz, president, Henri Bendel (see Chapter 16). *(Top left and bottom left)* At Dimensions, The Bellevue Stratford Hotel, Philadelphia, a multilevel illuminating column cap creates design interest and provides flattering light for vignette and open merchandise displays. *(Above)* In Quails, Woodbridge, New Jersey, a lighting beam reinforces the floor pattern and fixture layout. *(Top, opposite)* In the Philadelphia Museum of Art shop, an overhead fluorescent lighting system was custom-designed to illuminate displays and visually tie together display units of different heights.

*Design:* Charles E. Broudy & Associates, *Photos:* Charles E. Broudy.

# Developing the lighting plan

The designer should start working on the lighting plan before and after the following elements have been determined:

- Merchandise handled

- Market profile (appeal to discount shopper, family, haute couture buyer, etc.)

- Store area

- Size and shape of departments

- Ceiling height

- Colors and materials for walls, ceilings, floors and fixtures

- Type of display windows (closed or open back)

An effective lighting plan will satisfy these eight purposes:

1. *Motivate the customer to purchase:* A successful lighting plan heightens the sense of excitement and discovery. It should work in tandem with the floor plan and background materials to "set the stage" for the merchandise to attract the shopper.

2. *Put the light where the merchandise needs it:* If the merchandise cannot be seen, it cannot be sold. *Light the merchandise!* Do not give the same intensity to the walls or floors. The designer has to visualize the lighting plan with the merchandise *in place.*

3. *Divide up the merchandise area.*

4. *Help to direct the shopper to the merchandise:* Does management want the shopper to linger or to move on? Will shoppers be able to orient themselves quickly to the various merchandise locations?

5. *Minimize structural deficiencies:* Lighting can help designers solve unusual space problems (see discussion in "Refinements" section, following).

6. *Give accurate color rendition to merchandise and flatter customers:* Improving color-rendering properties and efficacies[1] have been principal objectives of lamp manufacturers for several years. New fluorescent and metal-halide lamps have color-rendering properties considered equal to or better than incandescent lighting. Improvements have also been made in high-pressure sodium lamps (see Table 1).

7. *Make shoppers and employees feel comfortable:* Glare contributes to employees' eye and general

---

[1]*Efficacy* refers to the efficiency of lamps (bulbs and tubes). Efficacy is lumens (of light output) per watt (of electrical power requirement), not including ballasts.

physical fatigue. For customers examining merchandise, glare can represent an obstacle in the selection process.

8. *Avoid boredom:* All-over use of fluorescent lamps will give a flat look to the space and the products. Fluorescent, though economical, lacks sparkle and dramatic punch. Mixing incandescent with fluorescent is a popular solution.

# Selecting lamps and lighting fixtures

There are thousands of lamps and lighting fixtures to choose from, and they all produce illumination.

To help narrow the field, the designer should decide what kinds of lighting the merchandise needs: overall lighting, framing, or highlighting. Consider first costs but also evaluate operational cost, maintenance, and longevity.

Determine what light quality is needed for a specific application:

- *General lighting:* includes lighting systems, such as luminous ceilings

- *Linear lighting:* usually fluorescent, running down the center of the store, or along the perimeter

- *Directional lighting:* spotlighting, adjustable track, recessed adjustable heads

**Table 1   Color Rendition Comparison**

| Source | Benefits | Design Considerations |
|---|---|---|
| Natural light | Sales appeal. Customers like to see colors in daylight. Adds spatial and design interest. Skylight can introduce natural light to tne center of the store. | Fading of merchandise, carpet, furniture from ultraviolet rays; windows limit hanging space for garments or shelf space for packaged goods and food. Balance of heating-cooling load has to be considered. |
| Incandescent | Provides accurate color rendition; flexible; most easily controlled and directed. | Higher energy consumption; shorter life; increased maintenance. |
| Fluorescent | | |
| Cool white | Economical. | Cold and unflattering; not recommended except in special cases where color rendition does not add to salability of product. |
| Cool white, deluxe | Good for fabrics, natural materials. | Simulates north light. |
| Warm white | Suitable for selling and nonselling areas such as offices, credit department. | Provides warm tone. Test effect on products to be illuminated so color rendition is accurate. |
| Warm white, deluxe | Flatters complexion; creates warm environment. | Blends well with incandescent. |
| Ultralume 3000 | Approximates standard incandescent lamp. | Higher first cost. Good color rendition on many products. |
| Multireflector lights | Cost-efficient: low voltage reduces energy use for operation. | Higher first cost; requires special housing with transformer; sometimes can be used in place of standard incandescent; may not be as optically correct; good for spotlighting, track, and recessed applications. |
| HID (high-intensity discharge) | Energy-efficient; powerful; good for high-ceiling spaces. | Specify color-corrected lamps from major suppliers for metal halide, high-pressure sodium, mercury. |

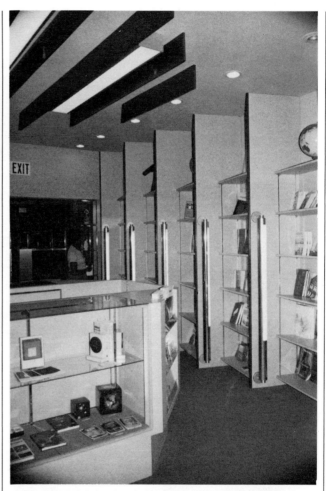

Mixed sources for ambient and merchandise lighting: Natural light from a skylight, recessed incandescent down lights, and shielded fluorescent strip lighting make a bilevel Ann Taylor store in Highland Park, Dallas, Texas, work.

*Design:* Charles E. Broudy & Associates. *Photo:* Charles E. Broudy.

Vertical task lighting for shelf displays. Tubular lighting is mounted on extension of dividers between shelf displays. A partial shield directs light to merchandise and avoids glare in customers' eyes at the Museum Store, The Franklin Institute, Philadelphia.

*Design:* Charles E. Broudy & Associates. *Photo:* Vilma Barr.

· *Point:* narrow light beams focused on particular displays

· *Baffled light:* moderate a direct light source; baffles can be made of metal, wood, plastic or fabric

· *Specialty lighting:* neon, sparkle lights, rear screen, showcase, cove lighting

The luminous ceiling is an accepted solution for overall lighting, but it is not the only answer for the whole floor area. A store under 500 square feet may need task and merchandise lighting only. Medium-size and larger stores require ambient as well as task and specialty lighting. Some discount stores operate on ambient lighting only.

In some areas where lower intensity is desired or a contrast is appropriate, surface-mounted or recessed fixtures can be successfully integrated.

Valance lighting, usually fluorescent, should illuminate the front of the merchandise. There should also be sufficient light when the garment or item is removed from the wall hang rod or shelf.

A variety of lamps, including low voltage, are available as track lighting. Track lighting is flexible and punchy.

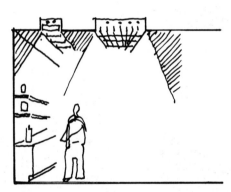

Ambient lighting with fluorescent can be skylight-type with plastic lens, or it can be low-brightness with an egg-crate baffle. High ceiling areas can also be lit with HID, mercury, or metal halide.

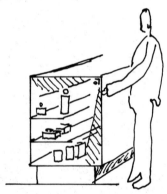

Normally integral with the showcase's metal structural frame, showcase lighting can be a fluorescent or a "T" type of incandescent.

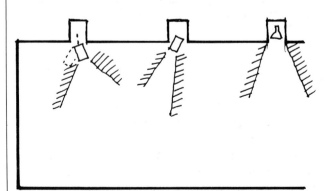

(Left) Fully extended 360-degree swivel; (center) partially extended 360-degree swivel; (right) retracted, fully recessed. Recessed "Indy" lights retract and are multiposition lighting fixtures.

# Refining the lighting plan

Decide how much importance to give the lighting as part of the design scheme. For example, to accent a canopy or a wall, the designer may use tiny star lights (also known as Tivoli lights) or neon. Soft cove lighting at the ceiling line or in the ceiling, either around the perimeter or down the middle, can draw shoppers to the sides of the store or to the back.

## Solve unusual space problems

1. Expand or retract space. To retain the lighting plan's flexibility and provide highlights as needed, fixtures that are recessed into the ceiling and can also be pulled out and swivel 360 degrees are effective.

2. Make the small store seem larger and the large store more intimate. Lighting projected on walls and ceiling brightens a space and will make a small store seem bigger. To create an intimate feeling in a large store, use pendant lights, either fluorescent or incandescent; they will form an implied ceiling.

3. Make low ceilings seem higher and high ceilings appear lower. To heighten a ceiling, use wall-washing up lights on a light color surface. Conversely, pendant lights which project illumination downward will make a ceiling appear lower. Do not use fixtures that throw light sideways.

4. Make a narrow store seem wider and wide store look narrower. To visually stretch the walls, project light or wall wash a light color or a reflective surface. To make a store appear less wide, use dark colors on the walls and direct sources of light on objects with a narrow-beam pattern.

## Flatter the merchandise

Does the merchandise glitter? Will the colors be affected by light, or fade? Is the merchandise perishable? Is the merchandise prepackaged, and will the packages hang or be stacked on the selling floor? Consider shadows from the packages.

## Flatter the customers

Areas near mirrors need special care. Overhead lighting can make a customer look ghostly white or green-tinged. For apparel stores, lighting that imparts a healthy, peachy complexion is most flattering. Reduce the appearance of wrinkles on people and apparel by projecting light from the front, not overhead. Color rendition of the lamps should be closer to an incandescent color than cool fluorescent.

# Window lighting techniques

To attract foot or vehicular traffic, retail stores have display windows that face out onto a street, mall level, parking area, highway, or walkway. There are two basic types of display windows: closed back and open back.

Store designers are not frequently called upon to actually create the lighting for particular displays, but they should be aware of the more popular forms of window lighting and give visual merchandisers sufficient outlets, power supply, and structural supports for them to do their job.

- *Closed back:* Behind the glazing, the display area is enclosed on three sides and creates its own environment. The theory is that without peripheral distractions, the attention of passers-by will focus on the merchandise displayed. Many New York merchants along Fifth Avenue and Madison Avenue favor this approach, believing that the surroundings outside the window present enough distractions and competition for the pedestrian's attention and that a pure show window offers a welcome visual respite.

- *Open back:* The other approach is to permit the interior of the store to be visible through the window. Proponents of the open-back window believe that the merchandise, movement, color, and illumination of the store's interior are attractions in themselves and augment the goods displayed in the window.

**Pendant-style incandescent lights create an intimate effect and define the seating area at Boyd's, an upper-price men's apparel store in Philadelphia. Perimeter lighting is fluorescent.**

*Design:* Charles E. Broudy & Associates. *Photo:* Robert Harris, Berry & Homer Photographics.

**Stretching the width of a store with form and light. At H.I.S. Pantwheel, Westport, Connecticut, white-painted wood baffles conceal fluorescent bulbs from view and create ceiling interest.**

*Design:* Charles E. Broudy & Associates. *Photo:* Charles E. Broudy.

### 1. Track lighting

This form of window lighting is the most popular and is today's mass version of theatrical lighting. Tracks can be mounted horizontally or vertically. Most frequently specified lamps are 150-watt spotlighting and low-voltage pin spots.

Overhead track lights can cause apparel to appear wrinkled. To offset this effect, horizontally focus lights on a vertical track. Footlights that shine upward can counterbalance down lighting. Tracks and individual floor-mounted lights that beam illumination up to mannequins create a special romantic effect.

### 2. Stage lighting

C-clamps, Kleigl lights, or barndoor louvers can be adapted to store windows. They provide particular emphasis and direct light, and they can produce very sophisticated, traffic-stopping window scenes. Window designers like the high-tech look of curly cords attached to many stage-lighting fixtures and sometimes leave them exposed as a design element.

### 3. Combination lighting

Windows that display a large quantity of small items, such as calculators, tape recorders, or cameras, best project their wares with an even, high-footcandle level. Fluorescent and incandescent in combination will produce from 100 to 300 footcandles.

### 4. Pin spots

High-power, high-output pin spots can focus a 6-inch- to 12-inch-diameter circle of light. Merchandise such as jewelry or small art objects as well as apparel benefit from judicious pin spot lighting. Framing projectors create many shapes, including rectangles and squares.

### 5. Filters and colored lamps

Entire displays can take on a specific hue—warm or cool—by use of gel filters placed over incandescent bulbs or by replacing white lamps with colored ones.

# Exterior lighting

A retail store will face out onto either the natural environment and daylight or the built environment and artificial light in a mall or building interior.

For freestanding stores or stores in a strip center or along the street, the store designer has very few creative limitations other than those of good taste and applicable codes for exterior lighting. Stores located in malls or within multiuse buildings have restrictions which must be closely adhered to. Here, lighting is mostly a matter of window and signage illumination.

### 1. Store exterior facing a natural environment

Illumination beginning with the twilight hours gives the store designer the best opportunity to be creative with lighting. For stores facing a street or in a strip center, there is usually only one side of the building which will benefit from sales-oriented lighting design. A freestanding store may have other facades which face the parking area or walkways. Lighting in the parking areas also falls within the designer's scope of responsibility. Lighting from bollards or lamppost lighting or other soures is involved here.

For the front facade, lighting should complement the main signage carrying the store's name. If the sign itself is not illuminated, the designer should use the sign as the focal point and light with ground-mounted floods or from lighting mounted above and/or below the sign.

If the building exterior has an interesting texture, use lighting to emphasize it: wood, brick, stone, and stucco all respond to HID (high-intensity discharge) lights, waterproof high-output fluorescent lights, and spot lighting with a variety of types of lamps.

Create your own evening and nighttime images with color, either as an all-over wash or for accents.

To emphasize architectural details such as arches over doorways or windows or an awning or canopy, use sparkle lights. Small, usually white bulbs have a festive, quality look when used with care and moderation.

### 2. Store exterior facing a built environment

Before the designer plans the lighting scheme for a store that faces onto a mall or building interior, the landlord or rental agent must be consulted to find out what can be specified. Some will allow a limited range of highlighting if the signage is not illuminated. Others will permit concealed or recessed lighting whether or not the sign is illuminated.

Some landlords do not permit neon lighting. Most reject blinking or flashing lights.

Calculate the amount of public space illumination provided by the building owner or shopping center operator, and then determine how much more punch and personality your client's store needs. Some mall stores do not have an "exterior" at all; they are fully open during business hours from party wall to party wall, and a rolling metal divider is pulled across the front after closing. For other stores with more traditional fronts, the designer can sculpt shapes for windows and doorways and then concentrate the illumination to emphasize this dimensional technique.

## Consulting engineers and lighting designers

The store designer can call in lighting and electrical specialists to review the design or assist in preparing contract bid documents.

· A lighting designer with extensive retail store design experience can make suggestions or help you to refine your design.

· A consulting electrical engineer can perform the following services: prepare lighting budgets; prepare plans and specifications for emergency and exit lighting; prepare plans and specifications for security lighting systems, fire alarm and burglar alarm systems; and handle plans and specifications for telephone-intercom systems and credit card and cash register systems. The circuiting planned by the engineer will fulfill the lighting design's requirements, including staggered rows of lighting, dimmer control, and energy efficiency.

· Many store designers still design their lighting fixtures and layouts to achieve the design effect they desire. An electrical engineer should be consulted for technical review.

## Conserving energy through lighting

Lighting consumes about 5 percent of the nation's energy. According to energy engineers, lighting is the easiest and least expensive energy-eater to tame. The new science of lighting energy management "considers the quality and quantity of light needed for productive work performance, for interior and exterior building safety, and to identify areas and create retail displays to attract the passersby," advises lighting consultant E. A. Wareham, III, PE, a proponent of lighting energy management.

See Tables 2 and 3 for comparisons of various lamps.

**Table 2  Lumens per Watt of Various Light Sources***

| Type of Lamp | Small | Middle | Large |
|---|---|---|---|
| Low-pressure sodium | 135 | 145 | 180 |
| High-pressure sodium | 90 | 105 | 120 |
| Metal Halide | 67 | 75 | 93 |
| Fluorescent | 66 | 74 | 70 |
| Mercury | 25 | 51 | 51 |
| Incandescent | 14 | 20 | 24 |

*Notes:

1. Since many variations in light bulbs are offered that alter efficiency in lumens per watt—e.g., color of phosphors, reflectors, and surface coatings—the table provides averages of typical lamps in each category.

2. The values indicated by this table do not take into account drops or increases in output as a result of typical luminaires. The efficacy (lumens per watt) of low-pressure sodium drops somewhat from the 180 values when the lamp-luminaire system is considered.

*Source:* Donald Leibowitz, *Guide to Efficient Lighting,* State of New Jersey, Division of Purchase and Property, Trenton, 1982, p. 12.

**Table 3   Lamp Characteristics Compared**

| Characteristics | Incandescent (including tungsten halogen) | Fluorescent | Mercury vapor | Metal halide | High-pressure sodium | Low-pressure sodium |
|---|---|---|---|---|---|---|
| Wattages normally available | 6 to 1500 | 4 to 219 | 40 to 3000 | 100, 250, 400, 1500 | 100, 150, 250, 400, 1000 | 35, 55, 90, 135, 180 |
| Efficacy (lumens per watt, lamp only) | 14 to 25 | 55 to 92 | 20 to 63 | 65 to 100 | 80 to 130 | 125 to 183 |
| Life (hours) | 750 to 12,000 | 9000 to 30,000 | 16,000 to 24,000 | 1500 to 15,000 | 10,000 to 20,000 | 18,000 |
| Light control | Very good to excellent | Fair | Very good | Very good | Very good | Very good |
| Relight time | Immediate | Immediate | 3 to 5 minutes | 10 to 20 minutes | 1 minute | 1 minute |
| Color rendition | Very good to excellent | Good to excellent | Poor to very good | Poor to very good | Fair | Poor* |
| Comparative fixture cost | Low because of simple fixtures | Moderate | Higher than incandescent and fluorescent | Generally higher than mercury vapor | Highest | Similar to metal halide |
| Comparative operating cost | High because of relatively short life and low efficacy | Lower than incandescent; placement costs higher than HID because of greater number of lamps needed; energy costs generally lower than mercury vapor | Lower than incandescent; replacement costs relatively low because of relatively few fixtures and long lamp life | Generally lower than mercury vapor; fewer fixtures required, but lamp life is shorter and lumen maintenance not quite as good | Generally low; fewest fixtures required | Lowest; fewest fixtures required |

*Although color rendition is poor, monochromatic yellow provides greatest three-dimensional acuity and fog and mist penetration.

*Source:* Donald Leibowitz, *Guide to Efficient Lighting*, State of New Jersey, Division of Purchase and Property, Trenton, 1982, p. 17.

# Case studies in retail store energy management[2]

## Case study 1. Sloan's Supermarkets, New York City

In an effort to reduce energy consumption, Sloan's Supermarket chain in New York City removed two lamps from most of their stores' four-lamp fluorescent fixtures. According to the executive vice president of the chain,

Energy conservation is important to us, especially when you consider that we pay about 10.3 cents per kilowatt-hour for electricity. We attempted to cut back by removing two of the 75-watt fluorescent lamps from most of our eight-foot fixtures. (Each Sloan's Supermarket uses 75 to 150 F96 fluorescent luminaires.) We kept them that way for a while, but I wasn't satisfied with the results.

While energy conservation is important, marketing is important, too, and we believe that using energy to support our marketing efforts represents a wise, cost-effective use of energy. Accordingly, we returned to four lamps in each fixture, but we didn't use the same 75-watt lamps as before. Instead, we installed high-efficiency 60-watt fluorescent lamps. These cut energy consumption and costs by about 20 percent, yet reduced light output by an amount so small the difference is virtually imperceptible.

Immediately after we returned to four lamps in each fixture, store sales took off, providing us with a gross sales increase of from 10 to 15 percent. We did nothing else in the stores during this period, so I can attribute virtually all the increase in sales to the new lighting.

## Case study 2. McRae's Department Stores, Jackson, Mississippi

In early 1977, the McRae's Department Stores chain, headquartered in Jackson, Mississippi, began a lamp retrofit program designed to save 1.8 million kilowatthours per year. One of the key strategies of the program has involved reliance on 75-watt and 120-watt ellipsoidal reflector (ER) lamps as replacements for 150-watt R40 floods, both in deep-baffled downlight and track-mounted "can" fixtures. The 75-watt ER lamps produce about the same amount of light as 150-watt R40 floods because of the lamp's design.

The light beam is focused about 2 inches ahead of the lamp face, thus getting more light out of the fixture and onto merchandise without the in-fixture losses associated with R40 flood distribution. Initial tests showed the ER lamps to be so effective that 75-watt versions were slated for use in some of those cases where it was felt that 120-watt lamps would have been needed. The chain expected to save more than 700,000 kilowatthours per year based on the ER conversions alone.

[2]*Source:* National Lighting Bureau.

**Case study 3. J. C. Penney**

The J. C. Penney chain found that lighting needs varied on a seasonal basis. Keeping all lights on at maximum level at times provided too much light, wasted energy, and detracted from the appearance of displays. To correct this problem and permit fine-tuning of its lighting, the chain converted to specially designed dual-level ballasts for its mercury-vapor fixtures. As a result, by adjusting one of the ballast wires, the power being supplied to 400-watt lamps changed to 300 watts, and that to 250-watt lamps changed to 190 watts.

Ballast manufacturers can generally accommodate other requirements when larger orders are involved. The newest developments in the ballast field include electronic ballasts for use with fluorescent lamps and miniaturized ballasts used with the fluorescent and metal-halide lamps available or about to be introduced for direct installation in incandescent sockets.

**Case study 4. Safeway Stores, California**

Safeway has installed energy control systems that turn off rows of fluorescent fixtures in a uniform manner during periods when less light output is sufficient. These occur during stocking periods, or when they can take advantage of daylight during particularly clear days.

Each system consists of a transmitter mounted on the lighting panelboard and receivers connected to fixture ballasts. The transmitter can be controlled manually, by a time clock, or by a computer. When less light is needed, the transmitter's signals are sent to receivers over existing lighting circuits. No expensive rewiring is needed.

According to the chain's energy management director, the first installation—in a 20,000-square-foot Stockton, California, store—paid for itself within a year.

**This display in Higbee's Department Store at the Randall Park Mall in suburban Cleveland saves space and gives each chair a high degree of visibility. Fluorescent lamps concealed in vertical channels provide backlighting. Recessed spotlighting in the ceiling highlights the front of the display.**

*Courtesy:* General Electric Co. (Nela Park).

## Retail Store Illumination*

To the retail store owner and manager, well-planned lighting increases sales and productivity; effects security and safety; and reduces errors and energy consumption. Lighting systems are designed from four basic aspects: quality, quantity, cost, and energy consumption.

Since the purpose of store lighting is to sell merchandise, the engineer must know the merchandise characteristics—texture, color, finish, size, and shape. Using concentrated filament sources highlights the most important merchandise features. For example, texture is a very essential quality and should be highlighted from an angle and not from a flat source, which could reduce the attractiveness of the material.

### INTERIOR LIGHTING

The Illuminating Engineering Society (IES), based in New York, has established the following seven categories of retail store lighting areas: circulation, merchandising, display, sales, showcase, service, and self-service.

The *circulation area* can be near the store entrances or inside the store and generally requires low lighting levels of from 20 to 35 footcandles.

For *merchandising areas,* lighting is the most effective means of directing attention in the field of view. The recommended level is three to seven times the amount of light required for circulation areas. The brightness of ceilings, columns, and other architectural features around the merchandising area should be relatively lower. Self-service stores require more illumination than do full-service stores.

In many stores, *sales areas and display areas* are the same, and the lighting serves both purposes. Lighting design in the sales area is determined by the type of merchandise and how it is arranged. Feature displays contribute sparkle and drama. At normal eye level, they may be properly illuminated with two to three times as much light as other displays. Elevated displays farther from the normal field of view require three to five times as much illumination as their surroundings to attract attention.

The lighting level in *showcases* begins at 100 footcandles. A general guideline is that showcase lighting should be twice the store's ambient lighting. (Example: ambient lighting = 60 footcandles; showcase lighting = 120 footcandles.) Wall cases should be treated the same as counter showcases and should be illuminated from top to bottom. The lighting level at the bottom should not be less than $\frac{1}{10}$ that of the top.

A *self-service retail store* requires more light in merchandising and display sources than does a *full-service retail store* because shoppers must see more quickly what they want to buy. Merchandise occupies most of the selling area, and the general lighting should be somewhat uniform, 150 to 200 footcandles. In stores where sales personnel assist shoppers, 60 to 120 footcandles is sufficient.

The lighting engineer can suggest a fixture layout that will raise the illumination levels in merchandise areas higher than those in the traffic zone. Light sources should be shielded from direct view to avoid glare.

### OUTDOOR LIGHTING

The brightness level for a structure depends on the level of illumination in the neighborhood and the color of the building's surface. Typical values for exposed concrete facades are between 5 and 10 footcandles. To prevent possible annoyance to pedestrians or motor traffic, the lower portion of the building should have less illumination.

Both high- and low-height fixtures are used for parking lots. Light from low-level units is below eye level, and there is little glare into a person's eyes. This type of lighting will require more units than a system with taller light standards. For most outdoor retail store parking lots, high-level lights utilizing high-intensity discharge (HID) lamps are recommended.

*Technical consultant for this section: Leonard R. Korobkin, PE, Gamze, Korobkin, Caloger, Inc., Engineers, Chicago, Illinois.

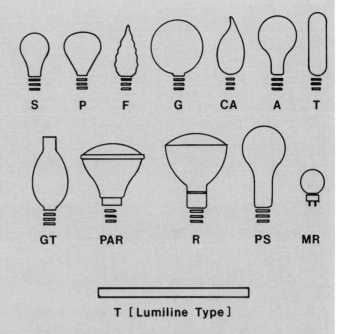

T [ Lumiline Type ]

### Bulb Shapes of Incandescent Lamps

| Bulb shape | Meaning |
| --- | --- |
| A | Standard |
| CA | Candle |
| F | Flame |
| G | Globe |
| GT | Globe tubular |
| MR | Multireflector |
| P | Pear |
| PAR | Parabolic reflector |
| PS | Pear straight neck |
| R | Reflector |
| S | Straight side |
| T | Tubular |

*Source:* Donald Leibowitz, *Guide to Efficient Lighting,* State of New Jersey, Division of Purchase and Property, Trenton, 1982, p. 8.

### Table 4   Lighting Levels for Outdoor Spaces

| Parking areas | 1 to 3 footcandles |
| --- | --- |
| Pedestrian entrances | 2 to 5 footcandles |
| Driving and ramp areas | 5 to 10 footcandles |

### RECOMMENDED PRACTICES TO CUT LIGHTING COSTS AND CONSERVE ENERGY

1. Prepare a cost analysis. In one section, list original cost of material and labor, controls, and wiring. In another section, include operating cost of power consumption, air conditioning load, maintenance, relamping, etc.

2. Select luminaires based on proper lighting distribution for the application. The efficiency of a luminaire is one indication of the quality of its design.

3. Establish a lighting maintenance program that includes periodic cleaning and relamping.

4. Use energy-conserving fluorescent lamps where possible. Most save about 15 percent of the electrical energy used by standard lamps.

5. Fluorescent and HID ballasts made for the higher-voltage, 277-volt service are now in use in retail stores. Where

## GENERAL LIGHTING LAMP/BALLAST CHARACTERISTICS

| Type of Lamp[1] | Wattage Range | Initial Lumens per Watt Including Ballast Losses[2] | Average Rated Life (Hours) |
|---|---|---|---|
| Low-Pressure Sodium | 18-180 | 62-150 | 12,000-18,000 |
| High-Pressure Sodium | 35-1,000 | 51-130 | 7,500-24,000+ |
| Metal Halide | 175-1,500 | 69-115 | 7,500-20,000 |
| Mercury Vapor | | | |
| Standard | 40-1,000 | 24-60 | 12,000-24,000+ |
| Self-ballasted | 160-1,250 | 14-25 | 12,000-20,000 |
| Fluorescent | | | |
| Standard | 20-215 | 63-95 | 9,000-20,000+ |
| Self-ballasted | 8-44 | 22-50 | 7,500-18,000 |
| Incandescent | 60-1,500 | 13-24 | 750-3,500 |

Notes:
1. Data are based on the more commonly used lamps and are provided for comparison purposes only. Actual results to be derived depend on factors unique to the specific products and installation involved. Consult manufacturers for guidance.
2. Lumens (of light output) per watt (of power input) is a common measure of lamp efficiency (efficacy). Initial lumens per watt data are based upon the light output of lamps when new. The light output of most lamps declines with use. The actual efficiency to be derived from a lamp depends on factors unique to an installation. The actual efficiency of a lighting system depends on far more than the efficiency of lamps or lamp/ballasts alone. More than lighting efficiency must be considered.

*Source:* E. A. Wareham III, "Focus on Interior Ambient Lighting," *Buildings,* April 1983, p. 80.

codes permit and 277 volt is available, operational savings result from reduced wiring and distribution equipment costs.

6. Use a single larger incandescent lamp instead of two or more smaller lamps.

7. Use long-life-rated lamps.

8. Use higher-power factor ballasts.

9. Install diffusers which provide special light distribution coverage.

10. Install timers and photocells to turn off lighting when areas are not in use.

11. Provide selective switching and, where applicable, local control of lighting.

12. Apply light-reflective finishes for walks and other surfaces.

13. Investigate auxiliary relays for lighting that interface with computerized energy management programs.

### BIBLIOGRAPHY

"Electrical Construction and Maintenance," *Actual Specifying Engineer,* various issues from 1971 to 1983.

*Energy Audit Workbook for Retail Stores,* U.S. Department of Energy, Washington, D.C., 1978.

Leibowitz, Donald: *Guide to Efficient Lighting,* State of New Jersey, Division of Purchase and Property, Trenton, 1982, p. 8.

*Lighting Handbook,* Illuminating Engineering Society, New York, 1971.

*National Electrical Code Handbook,* McGraw-Hill, New York, 1981.

"Recommended Practice for Electric Power Systems in Commercial Buildings," *IEEE Standards 241-1974,* Wiley, New York, 1974.

Traister, John E.: *Practical Lighting Applications for Buildings,* Van Nostrand Reinhold, New York, 1982.

Wareham, E. A., III, PE: "Focus on Interior Ambient Lighting," *Buildings,* April 1983, p. 80.

Don't illuminate the top of the merchandise. Do illuminate the front.

Don't aim light at the customer. Do use baffles or louvers.

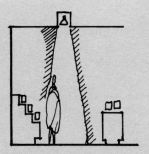

Don't illuminate the floor, unless it is a carpet store display.

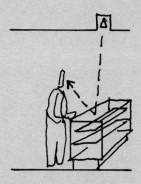

Don't create glare on glass showcases. It would hinder the customer's view of the merchandise inside.

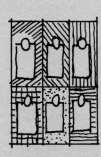

Do understand how fluorescent lamps affect color rendition. Refer to manufacturers' charts.

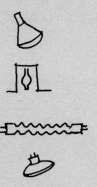

Do consider energy consumption when selecting fixutres.

Do conceal source lamps to prevent glare.

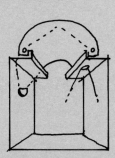

Do use lighting to sculpt or highlight the important features of the space and the merchandise.

**Dos and Don'ts of Retail Store Lighting**

# **B**ibliography

Dorsey, Robert T.: "The Potential for Energy Conservation in Lighting," *Lighting Design & Application*, July 1978, p. 25.

Leibowitz, Donald: *Guide to Efficient Lighting*, State of New Jersey, Division of Purchase and Property, Trenton, 1982.

National Lighting Bureau: *Lighting Energy Management in Retailing*, Washington, D.C., 1981.

Undercoffer, Diana G.: "Bullock's Beverly Center," *Visual Merchandising and Store Design*, April 1983 pp. 30–31.

Wareham, E. A., III, PE: "Focus on Interior Ambient Lighting," *Buildings*, April 1983, pp. 76–81.

# 9
# Systems and Energy[1]

The golden rule of HVAC (heating, ventilating, and air conditioning) for retail stores is: "Systems should not be seen, should not be heard, should not be felt, and should be tucked away in space left over after the designer has completed the store layout."

To effectively apply this rule to a retail facility, the HVAC engineer should have basic information on the business operation: the type of merchandise to be sold, the caliber of employees, business hours, and the customers who will be attracted to the store. Along with the architectural designer's concepts, these factors will guide the mechanical designer. In addition, the merchant should relate the projected energy budget to anticipated gross sales, project lease terms, and preliminary plans for operating and maintaining the equipment associated with the system. The owner's definition of comfort and periods when the store will be shut down must also be known.

From this information, the mechanical designers can determine the system's degree of sophistication and the quality of the equipment that will comprise the system. For example, a merchant with knowledgeable maintenance personnel and a long-term lease can consider a more sophisticated system that offers more energy options, will require fewer replacement parts, and will be more cost effective over the life of the lease.

The architectural designer sets the plan, specifies

---

[1]Technical consultant for this chapter: Leonard R. Korobkin, PE, Gamze, Korobkin, Caloger, Inc., Engineers, Chicago.

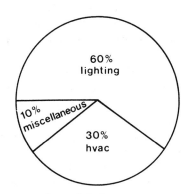

**Average energy use in a retail store.**

*Source:* National Lighting Bureau.

**Table 1  Design Criteria**

|  | Outdoor | Indoor |
|---|---|---|
| Summer condition | 95° Fdb | 76° db |
| Winter | −10° Fdb | 70° F |
| Critical solar attitude | August 21 | 62° |
| Wind speed and direction |  |  |
| Summer | 8 mi/h, SW to NE |  |
| Winter | 11 mi/h, W to E |  |

the materials, and advises the engineers on (1) what space is available for the HVAC prime mover equipment and (2) what space is available for the energy distribution equipment and the preferred terminal equipment. With the store designer's input, the mechanical designer must assemble information to answer the basic questions in the next section.

## Determining the store's requirements

1. What type of retailer is this design to serve—jewelry, apparel, food, furniture, etc.?

2. What is the total size of the store, and what are its physical limitations?

3. If the store is located within an existing shopping center, what are the landlord's design criteria? What services will the landlord furnish? For example, the owner of a shopping center near Chicago lists the criteria in Table 1 which the engineer must address in the design of tenant space. The landlord further states that primary distribution supplied in or near tenants' premises is available for use with the tenant's variable-air-volume box and reheat coil at certain temperatures and pressure conditions. The landlord also controls the noise level of the system by limiting the level of sound emitting from the equipment.

4. If the space is in a shopping center or building complex that does not furnish the primary and secondary energy utilities, what fuel source is available, where is it available, and how can it be used in the design?

5. Where will the store be located if not in an enclosed shopping mall? The HVAC design will depend upon anticipated seasonal conditions. For example, a heated entrance vestibule is a potential requirement for stores in cold climates.

6. Does the tenant control his own environment after closing hours? This has become an important question for some retailers, such as candy and perishable food store operators, who require a certain level of heating or cooling after hours to maintain their merchandise. Most shopping centers with central plants shut down their primary air-conditioning systems after hours, thus requiring tenants to provide separate cooling sources for their products.

7. Is the proposed space to be located in an independent building with an existing HVAC system that served the previous occupant? If documentation is available, the engineer must verify the drawings on site. Otherwise, he will be required to go through the painstaking task of sketching the system in place. Usually, some or all of the existing systems can be used by the new occupant at considerable cost savings.

8. Is chilled- and hot-water piping provided? If so, the engineer is restricted to a system which can employ these services.

Major tenants occupying spaces over 100,000 square feet in centers and malls may have the option to design their own energy plant, complete with boilers, pumps, and chillers. Most large national retailers have standard design parameters for HVAC. Stand-alone buildings also allow the mechanical designer to compare the full range of options and recommend those which best fit the structure and the type of retail business.

# Some frequently specified HVAC systems

### Variable air volume

This system—basically intended for ventilation and cooling—has been used in many cold-climate installations. If heating is required, independent radiation such as baseboard or duct-mounted heaters are used to achieve desired room temperatures. These systems tend to be found in larger stores or as part of a shopping mall system and, in fact, are the most flexible and cost-effective.

For large, freestanding stores, refrigeration equipment (compressors, condensers, and cooling towers) can be sized for 80 to 90 percent of the instantaneous load, resulting in capital and operating cost savings. The tenant who uses this system in a small shop as part of a large shopping center may not enjoy some of the primary equipment benefits, but he may have the advantages of lower first cost and operating costs, and controllable operation.

### Central chilled–hot water

This system is basically intended for larger stores and large shopping centers (mall or nonmall). It has many of the advantages of a VAV system, such as flexibility and cost effectiveness, and is appropriate to all climates. But since it needs local air-handling systems, including controls, outside air intakes, exhaust fans, coils, and piping, the total overall construction costs may be greater than those of VAV systems. Still, from the financial aspect, as well as physical convenience considerations, chilled-water–hot-water distribution systems are often preferred.

### Combined heating and cooling roof-top system

When first cost is the overriding factor in the design process, the building owner will usually choose this option. The heating and cooling equipment are housed together in a single unit located on the roof above the area to be served. The number of units will depend upon the size of the interior area to be affected.

Some designers will employ interior duct work extended from the unit for a more even distribution. Or they may choose no duct work, limiting the distribution to a point source.

These systems can be used for all store sizes in any climate. When considering this system, the owner must be aware of its disadvantages, such as shorter operating life, higher operating costs, higher maintenance costs, limited accessibility by store personnel, and lack of flexibility (Table 2).

## Table 2  HVAC Systems for Retail Stores

| Type of system | Climate | Size and type of retail structure | Advantages | Disadvantages |
|---|---|---|---|---|
| Variable air volume/ primary air | Warm | All sizes: shops, large stores, shopping centers | Low capital costs; low operating costs; flexibility; local control | Dependent on local plant (in shopping center) |
| Variable air volume/ primary air/with reheat addition | Warm/mild/ cold | Same as above | Same as above | Same as above |
| Double duct/hot and cold duct/primary air | Warm/mild | Same as above | Flexibility; local control; lower first cost for smaller tenant | Same as above |
| Central chilled–hot water plus air-handling units | All | Same as above | Local control; low first cost; flexibility | Same as above |
| Same as above with reheat radiation | Cold/mild | Same as above | Same as above | Same as above |
| Air-handling units, internal and external, with by-pass boxes | All | Same as above, plus stand-alone stores | Low first cost with rooftop unit; local control; flexibility | Additional heat required |
| Combined roof-top furnace and air-cooled condenser (gas or electric) | All | Same as above | Low first cost | Higher operating and maintenance costs; shorter life |
| Separate hot water boiler (oil or gas), air-handling unit and radiation, chiller | All | Same as above | Basic system; longer life | Higher first cost |
| Internal furnace and roof-mounted air condenser | Cold/mild | Same as above | Same as roof-top unit, but a slightly higher first cost | Same as roof-top unit but with better accessibility |
| Internal package unit, gas-fired duct heaters | Cold/mild; without duct heater, warm | Same as above | Same as above | Same as above |

# Maintenance and operational suggestions for retail stores

1. Lower thermostat during heating season; raise thermostat during cooling season (5 degrees from design).

2. Make monthly energy consumption and cost data available to manager or engineer so that they can evaluate and compare them against the previous month's usage.

3. Automatically lower heating or raise cooling temperatures during last half hour of business day.

4. Keep all doors and windows shut if heating or cooling is in operation.

5. Provide a temperature control training program for manager and staff that will give them a thorough understanding of how the HVAC systems were designed to operate and be maintained.

6. Install and use programmed digital heating and cooling thermostats.

7. Control building electrical load demands to avoid excessive peak periods.

8. Keep surfaces of radiator clear of merchandise for efficient operation.

9. If hot water heating is used, monitor water temperature for the level that will satisfy heating needs.

10. Inspect oil heaters to assure that oil temperatures are being maintained according to manufacturer's or oil supplier's recommendations.

11. Check temperature control systems for proper regulation.

12. If boilers are used, shut them off in spring and fall when air conditioning is running.

13. If two boilers are installed, use one boiler as lead, and only bring other boiler into operation as required. The lead-lag position of boiling should be changed regularly.

14. Inspect smoke stacks for products of combustion; make burner adjustments if necessary.

15. Check and repair oil leaks at pump glands, valves, or relief valves.

16. Monitor stock temperatures to determine when boiler should be internally cleaned.

17. Run boilers on low fire during spring and fall.

18. Regulate amount of combusion air during winter.

19. Keep heat transfer surfaces of all electric heating units clean and unobstructed.

20. Keep air movement in and out of the electric units unobstructed.

21. If central A/C system does not have a hot deck or reheat coil, set thermostat at 78° F in summer.

22. With a multicompressor and chiller installation, operate one unit at full load rather than both at part loads.

23. Operate only those pumps needed to maintain flow volume.

24. Shut off secondary hot water pumps located in air-handling units during spring, summer, and fall when heating is not required.

25. Inspect fans annually and clean if necessary.

26. Turn on self-contained units such as window or through-wall units only when needed.

27. Inspect tension and alignment of all belts, and adjust as necessary.

28. Where applicable, lubricate motor bearings and all moving parts as manufacturer recommends.

29. Keep condenser coils clean. Keep inlets screens clean. Keep cooling towers clean.

30. In summer, when outdoor temperature at night is lower, use outside air for cooling. Readjust outside air dampers for summer and winter use.

31. If the HVAC design employs reheat coils for summer use, try to operate satisfactorily without them.

32. Make sure filters are clean.

33. During winter, try to operate with a minimum of outside air.

34. Set a schedule to operate exhaust fans only when needed.

35. Keep VAV boxes in adjustment.

# Bibliography

*Energy Audit Workbook for Retail Stores*, U.S. Department of Energy, Washington, September 1978.

# 10

# Support Spaces

The four basic types of supportive functions carried out in nearly every store are merchandise movement, customer services, staff functions, and operations and building functions.

Most of these are referred to as "back of the house" because they are normally out of customers' sight. One exception is the cash-wrap station where cash or plastic credit cards are exchanged for goods, receipts prepared, credit is checked, and purchased items are packed into bags or boxes for the trip home. Other activities are often performed at the cash-wrap desk, including clerical tasks.

Space given over to off-the-floor storage of merchandise stock has been steadily shrinking over the past decade. What had been back-up stockrooms have been recycled into sales areas. There are three reasons for this trend:

1. *High cost of inventory:* Debt servicing on unsold inventory can bite deeply into merchants' profit margin. They prefer to place frequent reorders rather than pay interest on borrowed funds for slower-moving goods or goods not close to the selling floor.

2. *Lack of trained help:* For the most part, the days of the professional salesperson who truly "waited" on a customer are gone. If the merchandise is not on the selling floor, some clerks are reluctant to check a back stockroom or holding area to find an item.

3. *Impact of merchandise density:* "Boxed" goods, such as housewares, small appliances, and sound reproduction equipment, can be stacked to make their own pedestals and display bases. This shows the customer a depth of selection, offers display flexibility, and cuts down on storage space.

*The store designer should identify the required support spaces before the sales space is allocated.* (See Table 1.) In working up the overall program for the project, space needs of the four basic types of functions should be considered as givens. It may take a store planner just 5 or 10 percent of the total project design time to do layouts for the support spaces, depending on the store's size and complexity. An omission or major miscalculation, however, can cause hours of redrafting.

A small soft-goods store can devote an average of 15 percent of its total gross floor area to support functions, including receiving and shipping, stock, toilet room, and general storage. Shoe stores and shoe departments can have 50 to 70 percent stock and 30 to 50 percent sales floor. Shoe profits are generated by the amount of stock on hand: The more they have, the more they can sell. The number of seats on the sales floor is not so critical a factor.

Service-intensive stores often give more gross space over to support. Boyd's, a 70,000-square foot upper-priced men's store in downtown Philadelphia, devotes half of its total space in the adjacent older buildings it owns to various support activities. To house their 40 tailors and 20 pressers, Boyd's needs approximately 5000 square feet.

Most opportunities for creative design of support spaces occur when the store planner solves storage problems. Space-saving devices, unique bins and shelving, or a rack system offer technically feasible and economical solutions that may be esthetically pleasing as well. Some examples are:

- A "Pantwheel" that displays folded pairs of jeans on a revolving display selector measuring 5 feet wide by 4 feet deep by 9 feet high (the height is used to maximum). This omits the rack storage room by housing more merchandise in a store.

- An adaptation of equipment found in dry cleaning stores, a movable hanging device, utilizes dead space below the roof and above the ceiling.

- A triple-tier hanging apparel device which enables a person to reach the merchandise from the floor without a ladder or step stool.

## Receiving

Most medium and large stores will tell the planner the system and the equipment preferred for initial merchandise handling. Or the designer could be asked to research the vendors of this equipment and come up with recommendations. Manufacturers and distributors of warehouse equipment will supply catalogs; some will devise a layout at no cost, while others will charge a fee.

## Shipping

Transfers from a main receiving facility and shipments between units in a multistore chain require sturdy movable equipment. For one chain's intrastore shipment, the planner custom-designed a shipping system. Merchandise was picked up by the trucker at the end of the day. The

**Table 1   Support Spaces in Retail Stores: For Customers, Staff, Operations, and Building Functions**

| Area | Considerations | Functional and design requirements |
|------|----------------|-----------------------------------|
| CUSTOMER SERVICES | | |
| Cash-wrap desk | Often in customers' view; multipurpose: for writing, cash handling, packing merchandise. | Outlets and wire management for cash register, phone, credit check-charge input; storage for sales books, bags, and boxes, etc. |
| Wrapping station | May be seasonal or permanent. | Storage bins for boxes, bags, wrapping material; holding area for sends; phone outlet. |
| Return desk | May be seasonal or permanent. | Holding area for returned items on shelves, bins, or movable carriers (may need to be secured); storage area for credit books and other supplies. |
| Fitting rooms | Trend to smaller, tighter spaces; average range: 12 to 18 sq. ft. | Lighting flattering to skin tones; materials and finishes that are simple, attractive, durable; may need security control—locks on doors of dressing rooms to prevent entrance by other than legitimate customers and staff; control desk at entrance to group of fitting rooms. |
| Credit offices | Privacy to make applicants feel comfortable. | Basic office environment for lighting, desks, chairs, counters, files; outlets for phones, computer terminals; employee storage of coats and valuables; cash handling and security for customers who pay bills by cash or check in this area. |
| Layaway and alteration pick-up | Medium to large stores need separate spaces; smaller stores can set aside part of back stockroom. | Storage for hanging and boxed goods; may need security for merchandise, cash handling; surface for writing and wrapping merchandise; phone outlet. |
| Repair service | Same as above. | Same requirements as layaway-alterations, plus work station if repair of jewelry, china, watches, etc. is carried out on premises. |
| Community rooms | For larger stores, shopping centers, and malls. | Appropriate acoustics, lighting, seating, based on owner's intended uses. May include serving kitchen. |

| Area | Considerations | Functional and design requirements |
|---|---|---|
| **CUSTOMER SERVICES** | | |
| Parcel checking | For security or as service to customers carrying briefcases, luggage, parcels. | Storage bins or spaces; counter with storage for tags, receipts; phone outlet. |
| Toilet rooms | Check local codes for size, separate male and female, separate personnel and employee, special food store codes. | Locate near plumbing; check codes for venting and air handling, handicapped requirements. |
| **STAFF FUNCTIONS** | | |
| Toilet rooms | Same as above. | Same as above. |
| Lockers and checking areas | For security and employee convenience. | Storage bins and spaces; attendant desk; storage for tags and receipts; athletic-style lockers for coats and personal items; seating for changing of shoes. |
| Office | For merchandising staff; for accounting staff. | For departmentalized stores, buyer's office usually in or near department; can be 6-by 6-foot cubicle with desk, chair, file; accounting can be near credit office; outlets and wire management for phones, office machines, computer terminals; safe; cash drawers. |
| Lunchroom | Recommended for stores in areas where restaurants are remote. | Tables and chairs; vending machines are optional. Large stores may run their own employee cafeteria. |
| Lounge | Employee rest area; can also be used for informal meetings. | Chairs, tables; cot or equivalent (health code). |
| Training rooms | For medium and large stores. | Tables, chairs; instructional aids; cash register; storage space for sales books and other supplies; phone outlet. |
| **OPERATIONS AND BUILDING FUNCTIONS** | | |
| Elevator | Self-service. Departments and corresponding floors should be listed above door opening. | Cab interior can be fitted with display system for ads, posters, even television. |
| Escalator | Requires valuable sales floor space but is a very efficient people mover. Customers are visually exposed to merchandise and displays as they ride. | Owner must evaluate budget versus benefits to determine the absolute need for this conveyance. |

(Continued)

**Table 1  Support Spaces in Retail Stores: For Customers, Staff, Operations, and Building Functions** (*Continued*)

| Area | Considerations | Functional and design requirements |
|---|---|---|
| OPERATIONS AND BUILDING FUNCTIONS | | |
| Dumbwaiter | An efficient and low-cost material mover. Size of objects to be transported is important factor. | Takes up relatively small amount of space. Can be manually or electrically operated. |
| Heating and cooling | See Chapter 9, "Systems and Energy." | |
| Telephone service | From a wall-mounted panel board to a separate room. | Contact phone company as early as possible in the planning stage. |
| Trash and garbage | Type of refuse: clean—paper goods and boxes; hazardous—glass, plastic, spray cans. | Trash-garbage room near exit; trash compactor, bailer; dumpster is outside, sometimes screened with optional roof covering. |
| Janitor's closet | Medium and large stores. | "Slop sink" with plumbing connection; storage for mops, buckets, cleaning preparations, polishes, and cloths. |
| Supply room | Separate or space in general "back room." | Storage for extra lamps, bulbs, air-conditioning filters. Merchandise-related supplies, such as sales books, tickets, bags, boxes, wrapping paper, etc. Small stores may keep seasonal displays and signs here. |
| Display/carpentry/sign making | Medium and large stores. | Storage and equipment for building of window and sales floor displays; spray painting; fabrication of backdrops and platforms; outlets and ventilation for fabricating equipment. |

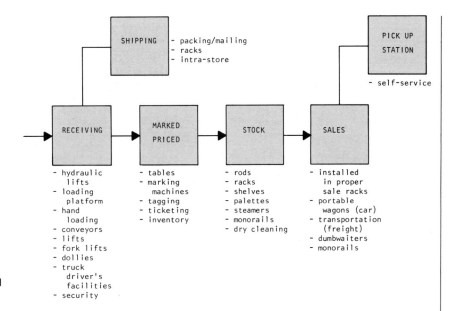

**Merchandise movement in a typical retail store.**

trucker had a key that unlocked a storage vestibule from the outside at the destination store. Containers were unloaded and stored in the locked vestibule overnight. In the morning, employees would unlock the vestibule from the inside (the store side) and wheel the containers into the store.

## Marking and pricing

Factory or warehouse supply houses offer a large selection of steel equipment suitable for retail marking and pricing. Basic components are a flat table, with options such as drawers and storage shelves with files and doors below. For small jobs, simple millwork or carpentry can be priced out to compare costs or fit an oddly shaped space.

## Stock

As was discussed before, the apparel retailer has drastically reduced the size of stockrooms. Formerly, in medium and large stores, hanging merchandise or boxed goods were unloaded and stored in depth on rods or shelves. Now the merchandise is "held" out of sight of the selling floor and then moved directly onto the sales area on racks and carts and put out for display. Facilities to prepare goods creased from shipping and handling—steam irons or pressing machines and sometimes commercial dry cleaning equipment—is needed by the retailer.

For gift shops, a work space to clean glassware or other items is often provided. Shoe stores need an area for touch-up dyes, stretchers, pads, etc.

Merchandisers of boxed goods

have cut down on stockroom aisle space with movable shelving units that ride on tracks or trolleys. These units are similar to those used for office file storage and can be operated either manually or electrically to slide apart for loading or unloading of merchandise. Shoes adapt well to this system.

## Sales

In multilevel stores, transporting the merchandise from one level to another can be accomplished either by freight elevator in medium and large stores or by manual or electrically powered dumbwaiter in smaller stores.

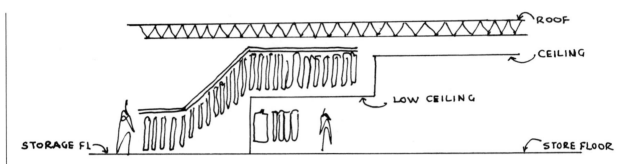

Track-mounted conveyor allows storage of garments in spaces near roof that are normally not easily accessible.

A pull-down hang rod retracts after use. The device utilizes space above normal reach.

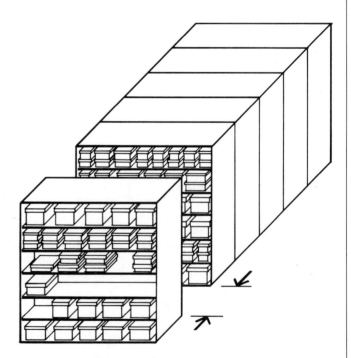

Aisle space in stockrooms is reduced by using movable shelving racks that ride on floor tracks. Units move apart individually to permit access from either side.

# Pick-up station

In home furnishings retailing, both discount and better-quality merchandise is being sold from furniture "warehouse" stores. The warehouse is adjacent to the showroom, and customers can back into a pick-up station dock and take their purchases home with them. Heavy-duty steel storage racks support several levels of furniture in the warehouse. A forklift picks the furniture selected off the shelf and takes it directly to the customer pick-up area.

(*Top*) **A typical cash-wrap station designed for the Ann Taylor chain of women's apparel stores. The space below the counter is fitted to hold bags, boxes, tissue paper, salescheck books, labels, etc. The surface above the wrapping counter is provided for customers' check writing.**

*Design:* Charles E. Broudy & Associates. *Photo;* Charles E. Broudy.

(*Bottom*) **Escalators are often the largest single support item for operations and building functions in shopping centers and individual stores. Customers can view merchandise and displays as they ride.**

*Design* for The Gallery at Market East, Phase I: Bower & Fradley. *Courtesy:* The Rouse Company.

# 11

# Security

Warning posted in Forbidden Planet, a science-fiction store in Manhattan: ''Shoplifters Will Be Disintegrated.''

Merchandise shrinkage is a $24-billion-a-year problem to American retailers. To get an idea of just how big a headache that is, $24 billion is equal to the entire amount U.S. industry spends annually for manufacturing plants and equipment to produce consumer goods, and 20 percent more than the entire Medicare budget for 1984.

Estimates on where merchandise goes that is not legitimately paid for put shortages from customer and employee theft at 65 percent, with human and bookkeeping errors responsible for the balance. Shoplifting costs each U.S. household over $300 per year. In Chicago alone, retailers estimate that they are losing more than $300 million per year to shoplifters.

Stores put aside reserves out of their cash flow and potential profits to cover losses. Inventory shrinkage has risen to an estimated 2.5 percent of sales, continuing an upward trend begun in 1975. In 1980, inventory loss among major retailers sampled in a National Retail Merchants Association (NRMA) survey ranged from 1.3 to 5.6 percent. A 2 percent level is acceptable; at 3 percent, shrinkage hurts profits. A loss of even 1 percent, common at many supermarkets, can put a sharp dent in profit margins, which usually total only 1 percent of gross sales or less.

Research performed by Sears, Roebuck & Co. indicates that there are about the same number of male shoplifters as female and about the same number of juveniles as adults. The giant retailer found that clothing is the No. 1 item shoplifted from its stores, followed by jewelry, cosmetics, hardware, and children's wear. The NRMA adds electronic games, records, and clocks to this list. These departments are termed "high-shrinkage" areas, meaning that compared to an average shrinkage rate of 2.2 percent (based on sales), these areas are rating losses as high as 6 or 7 percent.

## Planning for protection

Faced with such sobering merchandise shrinkage statistics, the store planner should plug in merchandise protection factors as soon as the sales area plan is contemplated. *Blind spots* on the sales floor, that is, sections that are blocked from employee surveillance, can lead to problems.

There are four major security consideration areas:

1. Merchandise protection on the sales floor
   a. Visual surveillance
   b. Physical hindrances
   c. Mechanical protection equipment
2. Back-of-the-house merchandise protection
3. Currency protection
4. Building protection

The rules of thumb that can be applied to designing protection plans are:

· Control store entrances.
· Know where the patrons are.
· Protect the merchandise from theft.

## Merchandise protection on the sales floor

### Visual surveillance

The trend to more self-service and fewer salespeople has been a factor in the rise of losses due to shoplifting. Salespeople's presence throughout the department is a proven deterrent to pilferage. However, with few trained full-time salespeople and more dependence on part-time help with no loyalty to the store, retailers are relying on other means to thwart theft (Table 1).

A few stores still have suffcient professional sales

## Table 1 Dos and Don'ts of Visual Surveillance

| Do | Don't |
| --- | --- |
| In small stores and in departments of larger stores, place cash-wrap where the fitting rooms and entrances can be seen. | Do not put a fixture in the middle of the floor higher than 4 ft 6 in, an average short person's sight line. Supermarkets and drug stores often create product displays 6 ft and higher. |
| Create openings in partitions on sales floor. Place convex mirrors for visibility in hard-to-see places, like corners or down hallways. Use full-size mirrors that can be angled for apparel sales floors. | Avoid spaces that force a difficult plan, like a Z shape, dog leg, or broken-back plan. Do not add a second entrance that will be open during business hours from a parking lot or from the street unless mechanical devices or a guard can be employed. |

**The entrance to Higbee's Department Store at Randall Park Mall in suburban Cleveland invites customers and projects store identification along with a sense of safety and security. For facade lighting, metal-halide and high-pressure sodium lamps are good choices because of their high efficiency and long life.**

*Courtesy:* General Electric Co. (Nela Park).

help to monitor much customer activity visually. At Boyd's, an upper-price Philadelphia men's store in a high-security-risk downtown location, a greeter assigns a salesperson to each customer as they walk in.

In midsize and larger stores, uniformed, jacketed security team personnel are placed at escalators and along heavy-traffic aisles. Some stores even have dogs along with guards at entrances and on the sales floor. The plainclothes store detective to apprehend shoplifters has long been a part of stores' loss-reduction efforts.

### Physical hindrances

· In shopping center open-front stores, *control the width of openings* by merchandise displays, plants, and signs.

· For apparel stores with several fitting rooms out of direct sight control, consider a *check station* for an employee who monitors the number of garments taken in for try-on, either by numbered voucher or some other system.

· Another fitting room control technique is *locks on fitting room doors*. Fitting room doors are opened by salespeople for legitimate customers. Securing them between uses prevents shoplifters from entering unmonitored fitting rooms, hiding mer-

chandise in bags or other carriers, or on their person, and making their way out of the store.

· Build fitting rooms with *floor-to-ceiling partitions between rooms*. This practice prevents shoplifters who work in teams to pass garments over or under partitions. The trade-off here is an extra load on the HVAC system.

· Be aware of *potential hiding places for electronic article surveillance (EAS) tags* illegally removed in fitting rooms. Resourceful thieves who have figured out how to remove plastic tags or metal strips without damaging the merchandise have stashed them behind partition-mounted mirrors or under a chair or shelf with gum or other adhesive. Keep surfaces smooth or seal off dead spaces with mastic.

· Specify locks for display cases for merchandise holding jewelry, small electronic items, or high-price items like expensive handbags to prevent "grab-and-run" thieves. The effectiveness of this technique depends on how conscientious the salespeople are in relocking the case after each use.

· "Smash-and-grab" attacks on glass showcases can be curbed by specifying *impact-resistant glazing*, made of a layer of polycarbonate plastic sandwiched between two outer layers of regular glass. According to the manufacturers, the glass can lit-

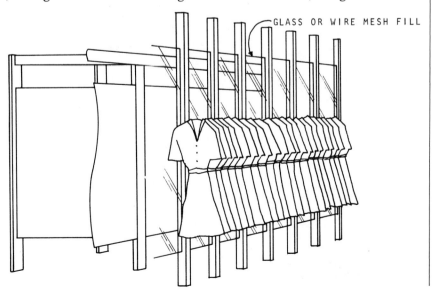

GLASS OR WIRE MESH FILL

**A dressing room security wall of glass or wire-mesh fill protects garments hanging on the other side of the partition.**

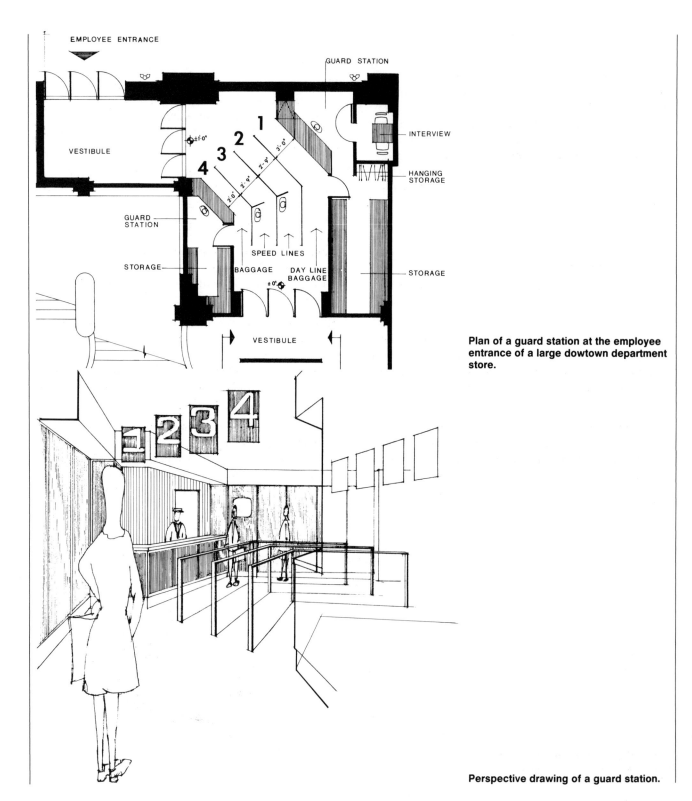

Plan of a guard station at the employee entrance of a large dowtown department store.

Perspective drawing of a guard station.

erally stand up against anything thrown at it, including bricks, hammers, and burning blowtorches.

· "Hit-and-run" thefts, when the burglar grabs an armful of usually expensive clothing off a rack or scoops up jewelry or small electronic equipment from a countertop and rushes out the door, has been met with *cable lock systems* for hanging garments, *lock-equipped T-stands*, and *hidden switch-pins* for countertop items.

· Mannequins with expensive accessories are being enclosed *behind glass cases* to eliminate pilfering from the displays. Most mannequins on the sales floors are not fully accessorized.

· New point-of-sale cash registers and information systems are equipped with a *button to summon security officers* when a salesperson suspects shoplifting.

· *Closed circuit television* enables a monitor to record a theft in progress to use as evidence for prosecuting a suspect. Some stores use *ersatz TV cameras*, which move to "scan" the area and have a blinking red light but have no recording mechanism, as visual deterrents to would-be shoplifters.

· Provide *safes and vaults* for stores selling furs, jewels, artworks, or other costly merchandise that have a history of high theft appeal. They can be either built in, floor to ceiling, or freestanding.

· *Baggage check areas* for store personnel, a traditional method of controlling employee theft, has been joined in recent years by *parcel check* for shoppers. Patron parcel checking takes additional space, personnel, and fixtures, but store owners who have installed such systems believe parcel checking helps to prevent their profit margin from walking out the front door.

### Mechanical protection equipment

Electronic article surveillance (EAS) systems, with their identifying plastic tag or metal strip, are considered by retailers to be the most effective devices used on the selling floor. According to a survey by the accounting firm of Arthur Young, nearly half of department stores contacted used such devices; 19 percent of mass merchandisers do; and 29 percent of specialty stores employ them.

*How EAS operates.* Two electronic pedestals with an electronic signal passing between them are placed at the store or department entrance. Goods are fitted with plastic tags or metal strips. If someone walks between the pedestals with the tag still in the merchandise and thus interrupts the signal, it bounces back, setting off a signaling device such as a buzzer, alarm, or tape recording that advises the person that they are carrying a still-tagged item.

Signals are generated electromagnetically and may range throughout the radio frequency (RF) spectrum up to ultra-high frequencies (UHF) or even microwave. Security directors and loss-prevention officials say that safety and reliability of the signal types are about equal. (See the list of EAS equipment makers at the end of this chapter.)

Because of the tagging device, microwave systems are suitable only for soft goods. For hard goods, retailers can choose between systems employing metallic strips and those in which an electronically impregnated label is attached to the merchandise. These labels look much like ordinary pressure-sensitive labels. Two types of metallic strips are currently available: one which is always on and one which can be activated and deactivated.

*Mechanics and costs of EAS.* For a 5000-square-foot apparel store, EAS costs for start-up and the first year of operation will range from $2500 to $5000. Costs drop significantly thereafter, to between $500 and $1000. Tags cost 50 to 75 cents each. Pressure-sensitive labels cost between 4 and 8 cents each. Service contracts range from $250 to $350 per year.

At one major East Coast department store chain where 1.4 million tags are used annually, tagging costs are $100,000. The operation is done at one receiving location rather than at the individual units. Another retailer cites high labor costs at the unionized warehouse (7 cents per garment) and prefers tagging at each store for about 1.5 cents per garment.

Items selected for tagging are those which are associated with a high incidence of theft or which generate a high profit. Landover, Maryland-based Giant Foods tags 3 percent of all items carried, including health and beauty aids and meats. The cost for an average system is $30,000 with a one-year payback predicted.

*Electronic banking.* Supermarkets cash more checks for individuals than banks do. Banks and supermarkets both know that transferring money is faster and cheaper than paper checks. It now costs retailers about 45 cents to cash each check: for food stores with already small profit margins, savings in this area can affect the bottom line.

Automated teller machines (ATMs) offer the promise of fewer bad checks and lower handling costs. In 1980, about 200 such machines were in operation in supermarkets. Three years later, there were 1500 more machines in supermarkets to verify checks and serve as branch banking facilities. So far, most of the supermarket banking activity has been in the Midwest.

One Iowa chain, Dahl's, has electronic cash registers as well as ATMs. Customers at the checkstand pass a debit card through a magnetic-strip reader to verify that sufficient funds are on hand. They then enter a secret identification number on a keyboard, and the transaction is recorded at the register.

# Back-of-the-house merchandise protection

*There is a good chance that merchandise will disappear before it even gets to the sales floor if there is not tight inventory control and surveillance from the moment it is delivered to the store.* Protection from the loading dock on is as important as the measures just discussed for sales floor security. Electronic equipment, furs, jewelry, liquor, pharmaceuticals, and cigarettes are particularly prone to theft from delivery areas. The store planner and the owner can plan off-the-sales-floor protection by several methods.

1. *Merchandise check-in:* Manually or electronically recorded stock counts as a record of receipts.

Shortages through manufacturer-vendor error or loss in transit can be caught here.

2. *Segregating and locking delivery areas:* After unloading merchandise from trucks into a delivery vestibule after store hours, the goods are secured by locked doors which can be opened only from the store side by employees with keys. Stores often provide truckers with toilet rooms and drinking fountains in the vestibule space.

3. *Locked mesh cages in stockrooms:* High-risk merchandise is separated from other goods, segregated in floor-to-ceiling mesh cages and locked. This deters dishonest employees and others who find their way back into the stock area.

4. *Electronic surveillance:* Functioning closed circuit television cameras monitored by a member of the security staff can be cost effective because of the density of the stocked merchandise. Electronic monitoring equipment from companies like Honeywell and IBM transfer impulses to a panel so that an operator can be alerted when a door is illegally opened. These same panels can be combined with life safety indicators and HVAC controls.

5. *Insurance-approved construction:* The design of a new warehouse or other storage facilities or the remodeling of existing storage spaces can be affected by insurance rates scaled by different types of construction. Input from an insurance expert in the research stage of the design can favorably influence insurance premiums. Payback for following prescribed insurance-approved construction guidelines can be earned in 5 years.

# Currency protection

At cashier stands, grab-and-run thieves who reach around to scoop up cash in register drawers are being countered by thick clear plastic hoods placed around three sides of the registers. Customers can still see the sale rung up. The hoods allow enough space for clerks in front of the registers to deposit cash and make change but protect the cash from a would-be robber's leaning over the counter and plucking the money from the drawer.

Cash should never be counted in the open on the sales floor—only behind closed doors. A money counting area in the office, with an optional counter height surface, is a good idea. The executive in charge will either deposit the cash in a night depository or put it in an office safe for pick up by a security transfer company the following day. Metal containers on the exterior of the store will allow after-hours pick up by the transfer company.

# Building protection

Police files can produce numerous cases of determined thieves who have hacked their way into a store through masonry walls, gypsum and metal stud partitions, and chopped their way through the roof. Clever intruders can turn off alarm systems and side-step electronic beams. Retail outlets, like banks, can implant the best of what protection technology currently has to offer. Often they work; sometimes they do not.

A few decades back many retail stores displayed an outline of silver tape around windows and doors. If the glazing was broken, the wire contained in the tape would set off an alarm.

Tape has largely been replaced by electronic sensors and ray beams. The silver tape outline has given way to an inconspicuous wired disk, sensitive to vibration.

Glazing is the building envelope's weak security link. Bullet-proof, riot-proof, and brick-proof glass that withstands shattering and is made from the same kind of tough, clear polycarbonate midlayer used for impact-resistant display cases is expensive but a good investment. Merchants who have never been "hit" are more casual about protection measures. Those who have been hit want protection against merchandise loss and also against the annoyance of being awakened by the police in the middle of the night reporting a shattered store window and missing inventory. Gates, grilles, and wire

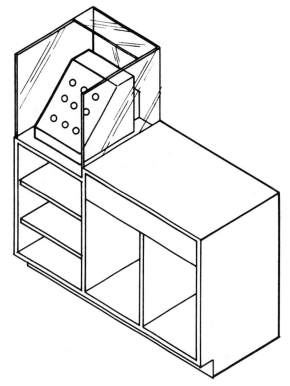

A cash register is protected by a clear plastic hood at a cash-wrap station.

across glazing, while not esthetically desirable, will keep burglars out.

Some small stores in urban areas keep front doors locked. Customers are admitted by an electronic buzzer and lock release. A foot treadle hooked up to a buzzer or bell that signals the owner when a patron has entered the store is a less drastic front door security technique. Large retail establishments have one or more night security guards.

Inside the store, ray beams can be installed across aisles and skylights. Night-lights discourage illegal entry and allow police patrols to view the store interior. Time clocks can be set to automatically regulate after-hours illumination of windows, sales floor, and stockrooms. The designer has the choice of 24-hour lights that are rechargeable battery units or incandescent or fluorescent lights. Their placement should be planned along with other lighting so they coordinate with the specified fixtures for ambient or display illumination.

A safe environment, a highly visible landmark, parking convenience, and ease of finding one's car were the goals for parking lot lighting at Heinen's Supermarket in Mayfield Village, Ohio. High-pressure sodium lamps were specified for this installation. Clusters of lamps mounted on high poles permit broader coverage, reduced glare, and fewer poles.

*Courtesy:* General Electric Co. (Nela Park).

The store's lighting checklist should include appropriate lamps and fixtures for storerooms, loading docks, security lights, and post lights. For the exterior, high-intensity discharge (HID) systems are both energy-efficient and design-effective. These lamps have a high light output relative to wattage input combined with compact size. According to General Electric Company's Nela Park lighting application specialists, to produce a maintained level of 5 footcandles over a large area, the following approximate watts per square foot using these lamps would be:

| | |
|---|---|
| Lucalox (high-pressure sodium) | 0.1 |
| Multi-vapor (metal halide) | 0.15 |
| Mercury vapor | 0.22 |
| Incandescent | 0.54 |

# Security hardware makers

### Manufacturers of EAS systems
Checkpoint, Thorofare, New Jersey
Knogo Corp., Hicksville, New York
Sensormatic, Deerfield Beach, Florida

### Manufacturers of security fixtures or components[1]
This list of manufacturers is not complete since most fixture manufacturers incorporate some security measures into their lines.

Barrett Hill, Inc., New York, New York
Berg of Northwest, Portland, Oregon
Cal-Tuf Glass Corp., South Gate, California
Capitol Hardware Mfg. Co., Chicago, Illinois
Columbus Show Case Co., Columbus, Ohio
Daniels Display Co., Inc., San Francisco, California
George Diack, City of Industry, California
Sid Diamond Display Co., Inc., New York, New York
Dom Security Locks, Maspeth, New York
Edron Fixture Corp., New York, New York
Grande Mfg. Corp., Irvine, California
Kenstan Enterprise Inc., Huntington Station, New York
Lafayette Display Fixtures, Brooklyn, New York
Levin Fixture Corp., Burlingame, California
Magic Glass, San Francisco, California
Manhattan Store Interiors, Inc., Brooklyn, New York
Noris Metal & Display Case Co., Brooklyn, New York

[1]*Source: Visual Merchandising*, October 1982.

**A high-efficiency, nonglare security illumination system at the rear of the 14,900-square-foot Ken Schoenfeld Furniture store, Bellevue, Washington, utilizes five wall-mounted 70-W high-pressure sodium lamps. Each compact fixture provides the equivalent illumination of a conventional 175-W mercury-vapor lamp.**

*Design:* Baylis Architects. *Lighting design:* Engineered Electrical Systems. *Courtesy:* GTE Lighting Products.

Otema Store Fixtures, Markham, Ontario

Plexiframes, San Francisco, California

Leo Prager, New York, New York

Rax-Unlimited, South Gate, California

Russell William Ltd., Columbia, Maryland

SGM Corp., New Brunswick, New Jersey

Scandus, Inc., Palo Alto, California

Securax, Inc., Fort Worth, Texas

Sound Product Design, San Rafael, California

Spacemaster Corp., Melrose Park, Illinois

Target West Supply & Display, Inc., Los Angeles, California

VM Designs, Inc., Burbank, California

The NRMA has published several studies and guidelines on shrinkage and ways to curb it. Among these is the booklet, *Apprehending and Prosecuting Shoplifters and Dishonest Employees*, available to nonmembers for $9.75 and to members for $6.75 per copy. It can be ordered from the NRMA Book Order Department, 100 West 31st Street, New York, New York 10001. Statistics on shrinkage, reported in the organization's annual "Financial and Operating Results of Department and Specialty Stores," may also be purchased by writing to the same address. For more information, contact the NRMA at the above address or call 212-244-8780.

# Bibliography

Barmash, Isadore: "Retailers Losing Theft Battle," *The New York Times*, May 27, 1981, pp. 25, 36.

"Cuts of $10.3 Billion in U.S. Programs Cleared by House," *The Wall Street Journal*, Oct. 26, 1983, p. 6.

Harper, Laurel A.: "Shopfitting for Shoplifting," *Visual Merchandising*, October 1982, pp. 100–106.

*Lighting Application Bulletin:* General Electric Co., Nela Park, Cleveland, Ohio, pp. 6, 16.

"List of Manufacterers of Security Fixtures or Components," *Visual Merchandising*, October 1982, p. 106.

McGinley, Laurel: "Consumer Prices Increased 0.5% in September," *The Wall Street Journal*, Oct. 26, 1983, p. 2.

O'Neill, Robert E.: "First National Safeway," *The New York Times*, May 15, 1983, p. 15.

————: "Watch the Goods, Not the Customer," *The New York Times*, May 15, 1983, p. 15.

"Pros and Cons of Electronic Tagging Devices," *Shopping Centers Today*, May, 1983, pp. 56–58.

Tannenbaum, Jeffrey A.: "Business Bulletin: Briefs," *The Wall Street Journal*, Nov. 3, 1983, p. 1.

Wattley, Philip, and Michael Tackett: "Shoplifting Rise Startles Retailers—And the Customer Pays," *Chicago Tribune*, July 20, 1982, Sec. 1, p. 9.

Commercial Center

San Francisco SMSA

# 12

# Construction: New; additions and alterations; adaptive reuse; multiple stores and chains

Retailers are prodigious builders and rebuilders. There is sound reasoning behind this: Successful merchandising depends on having the right store in the right place with the right goods.

According to the National Retail Merchants Association (NRMA), the decision to open a new store is made after "a careful study of the market, both in geography and demographics, and an evaluation of what is presently available to the potential customer in merchandise assortments, price lines and services." A storekeeper will remodel or expand, the NRMA notes, "to meet the growth pattern of the area." Here are some examples of recent announcements of retail construction plans.

**Some examples of current retail building types: A single-level strip center for office and retail utilizes regional styling and materials at the Commercial Center of Miami, located on the Golden Glades Expressway. The dual-level neighborhood center in the San Francisco SMSA is a classic contemporary brick structure. Still-sturdy older structures can be revitalized for mixed retail, office, and residential use. Three- and four-story buildings on River Street in Troy, New York, underwent rehab in August 1983.**

COMMERCIAL CENTER   *Photo:* Matilde Batista-Ballee. *Courtesy:* Real Estate Research Corporation.
SAN FRANCISCO SMSA   *Photo:* Helen Holden. *Courtesy:* Real Estate Research Corporation.
RIVER STREET   *Photo:* Robert Miller. *Courtesy:* Real Estate Research Corporation.

### Dayton Hudson Sets $2.5 Billion Budget for Next Five Years[1]

Chicago—Dayton Hudson Corp.'s president, Kenneth A. Macke, said the retailer plans $2.5 billion in capital spending over the next five years, with 75% of the outlay earmarked for opening more than 400 stores. That would represent more than a 35% expansion.

Mr. Macke said that nearly 85% of the total will be applied to

[1]*The Wall Street Journal*, Dec. 2, 1983, p. 4.

River Street

Target, the Minneapolis-based company's discount chain, and Mervyn's, its family-apparel business.

Target, which has 205 stores, will add 58 more. Mervyn's, with 109 stores, will build 126 more. Dayton Hudson operates 1,083 stores in all.

In addition to the new construction in the capital budget for 1984 through 1988, the company will invest in store renovations, new distribution and operation facilities and further computerization.

### Rehab to Turn Auto Agency into Retail Shops[2]

Renovation is underway on a former North Side automobile dealership that will transform the property into a 27,000-square-foot specialty shopping center.

The $2 million development at 5300 N. Broadway, called Broadway Festival, will accommodate 11 to 14 retail stores and is expected to be ready for occupancy by early 1984.

"Recycling, where we can make an old building serve the community in new ways, is typical of the development we're doing around the country," said Donald P. Novack, president of Vistar Financial Inc., one of the two California firms responsible for the project. Novack said census figures showing a 25 percent growth in the area's population from 1970 to 1980 drew the company to the development.

### Hillside Shopping Center to be Reopened as Updated Mall[3]

After a fast-track, $3 million renovation, Hillside Shopping Center is scheduled to reopen Thursday as "Hillside Shopping Mall."

A steel "space frame" has been erected along the 600-foot-long canopy of the mall and topped by a 45-foot-high open steel structure in a stylized "H" form. Dropped ceilings throughout the 165,000-square-foot center court were eliminated, and arched skylights were put in over a new fast-food court.

The center's brown brick exterior was coated with an off-white concrete. New lighting was installed in the parking lot and on the new exposed-steel facade. New signs have been designed for inside and outside the renovated mall.

In addition to the food court, interior work has included the closing of two mall entrances and conversion of retail space to create 67 stores, ranging in size from 330 to 9,000 square feet, an increase of 5 from the original 62 stores.

### Emerging Trends in Real Estate: 1984[4]

Some of the greatest retail investment opportunities involve buying well-located but older and somewhat obsolete centers and then remodeling and remerchandising them. In fact, in 1981 and 1982, roughly half (46%) of the gross leasable area added nationwide was expansion of existing centers.

Almost all department store chains have embarked upon ambitious programs of existing store modernization and remerchandising. Greater emphasis is being placed on soft goods, and even modestly priced stores are making a renewed pitch for trendy upscale shoppers. Macy's plans to open 11 stores and remodel 10, capitalizing on its new image as one of the best merchandised and most tuned-in department stores.

Many of the regional malls built in the late '50s and early '60s are being upgraded. For example, Topanga Plaza in the West San Fernando Valley is adding a three-level Nordstrom store, reconfiguring space to create a 12 unit food court, and redecorating the entire bilevel concourse. Even more dramatically, the 163rd Street Mall in Miami has been enclosed with a teflon-coated, fiberglass fabric roof and heavily retenanted.

# Managing the retail construction job

For smaller stores, the client decision maker, owner, writer of checks, and merchandise manager are likely to be the same person. The retail designer has a one-on-one relationship with the owner-manager of the store.

In larger companies, the designer will be talking to a committee of executives and specialists who are responsible for various areas of the firm's operations—finance, promotion, merchandising, engineering and maintenance, administration, visual merchandising, and security, among others. Whether the client firm is formal and conservative or friendly and freewheeling, a designer can be sure that the design drawings will undergo many, many changes. *Leave nothing to memory!* Distribute copies of meeting notes. Keep a log of telephone conversations and discussions relating to the design and construction phases. And, of course, get all drawings initialed and dated by the client.

The designer and the client should review and

---

[2]*Chicago Tribune*, November 13, 1983, Section 16, p. 2D.

[3]*Chicago Tribune*, November 13, 1983, Section 16, p. 2B.

[4]RERC Real Estate Research Corporation, Chicago, 1983, p. 16.

understand the various types of contractor agreements. Contractor selection for a retail job is like any other construction project. A discussion of "Frequently Used Types of Construction Agreements for Retail Stores" appears at the end of this chapter. A copy of this synopsis for the client's use will be helpful if the client is unfamiliar with contracts in the building industry.

Sometimes the designer is requested to use, for example, the small store owner's brother-in-law who has his own contracting firm. "He'll do a good job for us . . . been in the business for years," you are assured. It may indeed work out just dandy for you and the success of the job. In any event, remember that this contractor is coming into the job with a certain rapport with the owner that may well relieve you of a number of headaches down the line. A contractor who has a good relationship with the owner is an asset to the job.

Relative or not, it is the designer's responsibility to alert the owner or the owner's representative of any problems. The owner and the designer will work together to find a compromise and rectify the situation. Through the often-trying construction phase, the designer should maintain good relations all around. The project will suffer if the designer's ire with the contractor's performance shows. Maintain a good disposition.

Quality control is monitored by the designer and the owner or the owner's representative. Start by setting the standards for excellence from the contractor and the subcontractors. Quality is hard to find today, at any price. Establishing standards is a good starting point, however, especially if you have not worked with the general contractor (GC) or the major subcontractors before.

# The retail construction package

This package includes:

1. Basic building, including HVAC, electrical, plumbing, sprinkler, and elevator work

2. Perimeter, partitions, drywall, wings, soffits, bulkheads, and valances

3. Fixtures that slip into the walls and floor fixtures that are removable and portable (racks, tables, gondolas, display stands)

4. Carpet and wall coverings (optional)

For a large store or retail complex projects, outline drawings are prepared showing the basic building shell, partitions, stairways, elevators, and drywall. Fixtures, curtain walls, or specialty lighting are not shown here, as well as portable or unattached items.

For freestanding floor fixtures, prepare an illustrated fixture "bible" showing all the store fixtures for the particular job: shelves, bins, racks, rods, and movable floor cases. This can be in booklet form or on large drawings.

Larger stores have experienced people in-house who are assigned as liaisons for the duration of the construction phase and may also act as construction managers. They often have their own systems of specifying and bidding. If this is the case, they will break down the four basic construction packages just listed to suit their operation. Sometimes even signs and furniture are let as a separate contract.

For small jobs, it is not unusual to put all four packages together and give it to the GC. Many GCs who work for retail stores do their own custom woodworking, metal, and glass. Or they can choose to subcontract them out.

# Schedules and time contraints

Construction schedules based on our experience and investigation are shown in Table 1.

Few, if any, other types of buildings are as closely linked to the annual calendar and seasonal events as are retail stores. If humanly possible, merchants want their new or remodeled store open for the year-end holiday selling season, and for good reason. Stores can do up to 40 percent of their annual gross in the 5 weeks before Christmas.

JOB SCHEDULE

| JOB # | 123 | ARCHITECT | CHARLES E. BROUDY & ASSOC. P.C. |
|---|---|---|---|
| NAME OF JOB | XYZ STORE | CONTRACTOR | JONES CO. |
| ADDRESS | 1001 G ST, NYC | START DATE | 12.5.83 |
| DATE | 12.2.83 | COMPLETION | 3.2.84 |

| TRADE | SUB-CONTRACTOR | 12.5 | 12.12 | 12.19 | 12.26 | 1.2 | 1.9 | 1.16 | 1.23 | 1.30 | 2.6 | 2.13 | 2.20 | 2.27 |
|---|---|---|---|---|---|---|---|---|---|---|---|---|---|---|
| CONCRETE FLOOR | J. WILLIAMS | ▨ | | | | | | | | | | | | |
| DRYWALL | D. BROWN | | | ▨ | ▨ | | | | | | | | | |
| CARPENTRY | JONES CO. | | ▨ | ▨ | | | | | | | | ▨ | | |
| CEILING | ABC CO. | | | | | | ▨ | ▨ | | | | | | |
| GLASS & STOREFRONT | ADAM INC. | | | | | | | ▨ | ▨ | | | | | |
| CABINET & FIXTURES | FRANK CO. | | | | | | | | | | | ▨ | ▨ | |
| HARDWARE | SMITHE LTD. | | | | | | | | | ▨ | ▨ | | | |
| PAINTING/WALL COVER | HIGH N' DRY | | | | | | | | | | | | | |
| CARPET/FLOORING | JENSEN & BROS. | | | | | | | | | | | | | |
| HVAC | H. HALL & SONS | | | | ▨ | ▨ | | | | | | ▨ | | |
| PLUMBING | SMITH BROS. | | | | ▨ | ▨ | | | | | | | ▨ | |
| ELECTRIC | CENTRAL ELEC. | | | | ▨ | ▨ | ▨ | | | | ▨ | ▨ | | |
| SPRINKLER | AAA SPRINKLER | | | ▨ | ▨ | | | | | | | | | ▨ |
| LOOSE STORE FIXTURES | FRANK CO. | | | | | | | | | | | ▨ | ▨ | ▨ |

A job schedule, prepared by the store designer, for a 3-month construction project. Subcontractors are indicated by the weeks they will be needed on the job.

**Table 1  Typical Design and Construction Times**

| Size of store in square feet | Design time from signing of design contract to beginning of construction | Construction time from commencing construction to opening date |
|---|---|---|
| 2,000 | 6 weeks | 6–8 weeks |
| 20,000 | 3 months | 4 months |
| 50,000 | $6\frac{1}{2}$ months | 4–5 months |
| 100,000 | $7\frac{1}{2}$ months | 6–12 months |

This period will often make or break the profit picture. Other important seasons are spring (especially Easter) and fall (especially back-to-school).

It is more the rule rather than the exception for small- and medium-size jobs to have very little lead time. Do not anguish over the fact that the owner should have signed you up a month earlier. Start compressing time, rev up the creative motors, and get your suppliers and the contractor to cooperate. A small store can be designed in 3 weeks and built in 5 to 6 weeks.

For large stores of 100,000 square feet and over, a 6-month construction timetable is not impossible, but it is very tight. Considering the amount of interior work, this phase could take up to a year to complete.

Fast-tracking the design and construction phases takes skill and determination but can be the difference between meeting and missing an opening deadline. To shave the timetable, develop the fix-

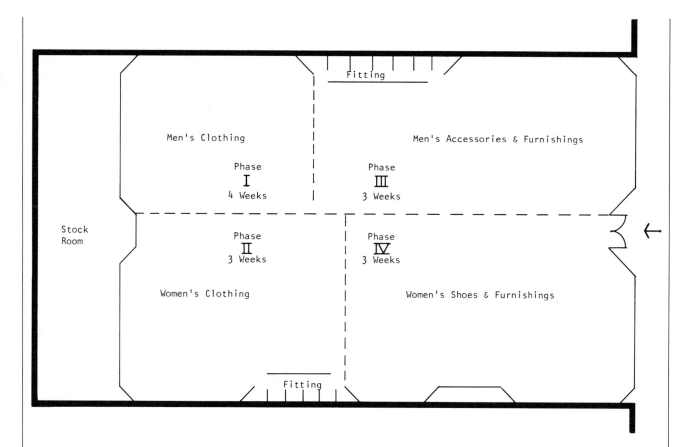

**Layout diagram of phased construction for a 10,000- to 20,000-square-foot men's store.**

ture design and perimeter design while the shell is under construction. Fixtures have a long lead time for design, fabrication, and installation. Set up communication between the GC and fixture sub (if different) so that they are working on parallel, rather than divergent, tracks.

Other items that have long lead times are elevators and escalators, special hardware and lighting, and roof skylights.

Plan a realistic schedule. But be equally realistic that the schedule will probably go off course. There are myriad reasons: a strike; the delivery truck was hijacked; the boat didn't come in; there is a shortage of materials; the fixture shop got too busy to handle the job. Or somebody didn't pay the sub on time. *Don't panic!!* Remember, the contractor's

value to a client is expediting capability. The objective is to keep the job running, sometimes, it may seem, in spite of itself.

When plotting the construction schedule for a remodeling job, make sure you allow for the store to remain open for business. Few retailers will close entirely for even one day. Tell the contractor at the beginning of the job that it will be done in stages: on one area of the store while the others will continue to operate. Help the contractor plan the scope of work from the outset.

A typical solution was prepared for Boyd's,[5] an apparel retailer in St. Louis, where space was condensed from 30,000 square feet to 20,000 square

---

[5]Boyd's, St. Louis, is not affiliated with Boyd's, Philadelphia.

feet. The space was divided into quadrants—the contractor worked on 25 percent of the store at one time, while three quadrants stayed open to serve customers.

For a long narrow store of nearly 10,000 square feet, the space was divided down the middle for construction remodeling. First one side was closed down while the other was worked on. After the installation of the new fixtures, wall coverings, lighting, etc., the building crew moved over to the opposite side. Certainly, the store staff had to live with some degree of chaos during this period, but the doors were kept open and the facility produced revenue.

This type of phased construction is not the most economical: The trades have to be brought in two, three, or four times, rather than once. Be sure that the contractor figures this expense into the price, and ask for a breakdown of the bid.

With the contractor, agree on procedures for dust protection and dust and trash removal. Design a construction enclosure that is both functional and attractive. Have some fun graphically with the "pardon-our-appearance" theme. Include an allowance in the budget for an enclosure that will contain the dust, noise, and general disruption.

It is wise to photograph the job before, during, and of course after construction. Progress shots should be taken from the same vantage points and dated. Black and white film is satisfactory for the construction shots.

## Substitutions

Substitutions are the bane of the designer's existence during construction. The manufacturer of the fabric or the floor covering in the selected style does not make it any more; there was a revolution in the country of the origin of the upholstery fabric for the shoe department seating; the contractor tells you that even though you approved the shop drawings or the sample cuts, it is impossible to get the items made up in time to meet the schedule.

Why, you ask, did the contractor lead you to believe that the products you specified could be delivered as promised? There may indeed be legitimate causes behind the problem. On the other hand, be aware of the contractor who took the job at a loss, hoping to make up the profit by pressuring you to accept more expensive substitutions.

Whatever the cause for a substitute product, it must perform and look just as right as the original, or you will have an unhappy client or owner's representative on your hands. Checking into the availability of substitutions is one of the designer's most unpopular tasks: It slows you and the job down. The most serious types of substitutions involve building materials like the facing or the roofing. If the product is behind the walls and covered up, like duct work, the situation may be more quickly resolved.

Rely on your own judgment wherever possible, and keep the owner advised of the situation. Occasionally, circumstances surrounding a substitution may force you to make a decision alone that others should help you make, ideally. Let your clients or the owner's representatives help you with the final approval. Tell them, "I recommend that you accept a substitute for these reasons, . . ." and then look at the options with them.

## Renovate or buy new fixtures

There are two major considerations:

1. Is the cost to renovate considerably less than buying new? Accurate estimates should be obtained from several contractors both ways.

2. Even if the cost of renovating is less than buying new, will the renovated fixture have a comparable life cycle to the new fixture, and will it be as esthetically desirable? If it fails either of these two tests, the fixture should be bought new.

Some effective techniques for upgrading original showcases are as follows:

1. Keep the basic unit intact, and change the color by spraying or by applying new wood or metal laminate.

2. Change the ends of the unit by applying mirrors or wood or plastic laminate.

3. Change the lighting, and refit the interior of the unit with a new material.

The fabricator will often take the item out of the store to work on in his or her own shop. Exceptions occur when the item is critically fitted to the wall.

Bid each item or group of items before awarding the contract. The bid will sometimes depend on how busy the fixture contractor's shop is when the bid comes in: If the shop is not busy and the fabricator wants the work, the bid may be low; if the bid is

high, the shop is busy and the fabricator does not need the work (Table 2).

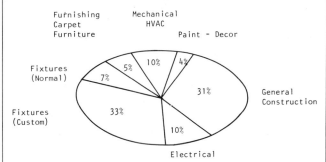

**Approximate cost breakdown for a 10,000- to 20,000-square-foot men's store.**

| Table 2 | Typical Costs: 2000- to 4000-Square-Foot Apparel Store in an Enclosed Mall* | |
|---|---|---|
| **Trade** | **Comments** | **Cost** |
| Building permits | These vary in all communities. Check with landlord or city hall. | Range from $500 to $2000 |
| Concrete slab | Most landlords require this; some do not. | $2/sq ft |
| Storefront | There are many variations, from an open front with sliding door or rolling gate to a complicated door and window design. | Low: $300/linear ft<br>High: $750/linear ft |
| Walls and partitions | The landlord usually provides studs on the perimeter walls. Drywall tape and spackling. | 1 side: $1.50/sq ft<br>2 side plus stud: $3.50/sq ft |
| Ceiling | 2- by 4-ft suspended panel ceiling is least expensive. Concealed spline or drywall is more expensive. | 2 by 4 feet: $1.50 to $2.50/sq ft |
| Floor covering | Carpet (most common).<br>Wood parquet.<br>Ceramic tile.<br>Marble. | $2 to $3/sq ft<br>$5/sq ft<br>$7.50/sq ft<br>$10/sq ft |
| Painting and wall cover | Painting is most economical.<br>Wall cover ranges from inexpensive to very expensive. | $0.30/sq ft<br>$1 to $2/sq ft |
| Heating, ventilation, and air conditioning (HVAC) | Cost depends on the landlord's criteria and can vary. | Approximately $6/sq ft |
| Electric and lighting fixtures | The service is presumed delivered to the premises, and a meter socket is required. Lighting with a mixture of fluorescent and incandescent including wiring. | $5/sq ft |
| Store fixturing | Varies according to the type of store. | Low: $15/sq ft<br>Mid: $25/sq ft<br>High: $40/sq ft |
| Signing: front | Illuminated can be plastic-faced box or individual letters. Nonilluminated is less costly. | Low: $1000<br>High: $3000 |
| Stockroom fixtures | Shelving, hang rods, tables. | $3/sq ft unless complex fixtures are needed |

*Prices vary in all parts of the United States and the world. Labor conditions and shipping also vary.

# Adaptive reuse

Many handsome, viable older buildings and complexes have been reclaimed and literally given new leases on life by adaptive reuse for shops or shopping centers or for mixed-use occupancy. In the past 15 years, there have been some stunning successes by developers and other entrepreneurs who had the foresight to look beyond the grime and shuttered windows and see the value of what the building could be. An abandoned chocolate factory and cannery in San Francisco; outmoded food distribution centers in Boston and New York; deserted railway stations in Pittsburgh and St. Louis; and an empty post office in Washington, D.C., are among the successful projects that preserve America's architectural heritage while turning a profit for owners by offering retail, restaurants, and other services to consumers. Federal tax benefits have encouraged many owners to pursue this type of building. Many features of older properties can be turned into dominant design elements.

**The $70 million renovation of the fifteenth-century Italian-style Plankinton arcade in downtown Milwaukee created Grand Avenue in Milwaukee's downtown. A second arcade was part of the 1982 project; the original arcade was a 1915 Holabird & Roche design. The Grand Avenue has 845,000 square feet of retail space and 125 shops, including two large department stores at either end. Many previously unknown structural relationships between adjacent buildings were revealed only after construction had begun.**

*Developer:* The Rouse Company. *Design:* Elbasani, Logan & Severin Design Group. *Photo:* Linda Goodman. *Courtesy:* Real Estate Research Corporation.

**Silver's, Detroit, rehabbed a 1898 McKim, Mead and White bank into a retail store and headquarters building. The building is faced with marble inside and out, and accented by arched windows, Ionic columns, arched colonnades, and bronze decorative grillwork. Silver's Design and Planning Dept. created 25,700 square feet of showroom and retail space on the main floor, and 4400 square feet on the lower level for the firm, which handles office furniture, gifts, and home accessories. Selling areas on the main floor were floated in the central space. New casework was designed to harmonize with original building materials, utilizing bronze mirror surfaces and polished brass trim.**

*Design:* Silver's, Inc., Design and Planning Dept., Keith Sipperley, AIA, project manger. *Photo:* Glen Calvin Moon.

**Exterior of Silver's. The adaptive reuse of the structure produced over 30,000 square feet of retail space on two levels and offices on a third.**

*Design:* Silver's, Inc., Design and Planning Dept. *Photo:* Glen Calvin Moon.

## Walls

· Exposed stone: Cleaning and repointing enhances appearance.

· Exposed brick: Cleaning by sand blasting, power wash, or chemical restoration adds to appearance.

· Existing arches and bearing walls: These features create interest and excitement as store dividers. Odd shapes and protrusions challenge the designer's inventiveness to come up with results that will house merchandise and enhance traffic flow.

· Wood: Paneling, wainscots, and moldings can be stripped to base material.

*Ceilings*

· Rough-hewn, old wood beams can add to the charm of a space when they are restained, sanded, or sand blasted.

· Old pressed-tin ceilings can enhance a retail environment.

· Arched brick or exposed-concrete ceilings add to the feeling of height in the store and can lead to innovative lighting solutions.

· Moldings of wood and plaster expose interesting details.

*Floors*

· Wood floors of all types, such as wide hardwood and softwood planks and thick wood blocks found in former manufacturing plants, can be sanded and stained, and bad boards can be replaced.

· Old ceramic and marble tiles can be restored for an overall surface or as contrast to carpeted areas.

*Other features*

· Lighting fixtures, bars, and back bars can be recycled.

· Old signs have much character and can be used as artifacts.

· Stained glass windows add charm to period buildings.

# **M**ultiple stores

There are many design advantages in working on a prototype for a chain of stores:

1. The volume of buying power can earn a discount on multiple projects by general contractors, fixture suppliers, and makers of carpeting, lighting fixtures, furnishing and furniture, signs, wall coverings, doors, hardware, etc.

2. Special detail and designs of interior and exterior items can be ordered because of the size of the

**The Sears, Roebuck & Co. unit in the Kentucky Oaks Mall in Paducah, Kentucky, is located near the New Madrid Fault. The 90,000-square-foot structure required extra bracing and rigid connections because of the earthquake risk. Lights, piping, and duct work are heavily reinforced. The rubber roof, a time- and cost-saving feature, can be patched like an auto tire's innertube. The single-story, steel-framed store is faced in white, textured brick.**

*Design:* Gassner, Nathan & Partners/Architects & Planners, Inc. *Courtesy:* Kroll Enterprises, Inc.

order. Many manufacturers will produce custom designs for a large-volume order.

For instance, if you were including a special door, handle, and glass treatment, the cost goes down if you order it in quantity. The same applies to most of the materials. Some stores order enough for 10 stores a year in one lump sum.

Sometimes owners use different designers in regional areas of the country. They think they may get (1) better service closer to home, and (2) different ideas and concepts for their overall national program. Styles of design may vary more in the Southwest or Northwest than those in Midwest or East.

On the other hand, reuse of proven ideas may be more cost efficient because the wheel doesn't have to be invented each time. Owners can reduce expenses because the design fee can be negotiated on an individual basis since much of the similar schematic and preliminary work is repeated (Table 3).

# Frequently used types of construction agreements for retail stores

## Lump-sum (stipulated-sum) agreement, American Institute of Architects Document A101, 1977

This form is the most frequently used because it virtually assures the owner and the financing institution that there is a design and cost established before construction. It is the preferred legal contract when there is competitive bidding.

When the architect has accurately drafted the plans and specifications, this contract is the easiest to administer for all concerned. Payment is usually determined monthly by visitation inspection by the architect.

Extras or change orders, if required, can be written and approved, either by AIA or Associated General Contractors (AGC) standard forms.

## Cost-plus agreement (fixed-fee or percentage), American Institute of Architects Document A111, 1978

This agreement is used when the scope of the work is hard to define, when many changes are expected during construction, or when the owner wants construction to begin prior to the completion of construction drawings and specifications.

The cost includes items of office and field overhead, rental rates for equipment, labor costs, and other agreed-to items.

The fee is generally an approved profit or fixed fee or a percentage of the cost.

A guaranteed maximum cost should be established when the scope of the work is fairly well defined. This puts a cap on the project. An incentive provision which affords the contractor an opportunity to share in the savings if the cost plus fee is lower than maximum is frequently used.

## Fast track

For owners who want to speed up the traditional pattern of construction, the fast-track agreement can be both time- and cost-efficient. The agreement is based upon the still-uncompleted preliminary designs, HVAC, structural plans, etc., furnished by the architect. From the incomplete drawings, the contractor estimates the cost of construction for the items, and a contract is agreed upon by those concerned. Subcontractors suggest economical approaches to construction situations, and the contractor and the architect utilize these ideas for the contract price.

A fast-track contract requires give and take on the part of the involved parties, but the result is a faster design-construction schedule.

## Design build

A single organization has the responsibility to handle the project from beginning to end. Advantages to the owner are speed of construction and reduction in the uncertainties of cost. However, the roles of designer and contractor are combined, and the usual checks-and-balances system is bypassed. This is a potential disadvantage to the owner because the

## Table 3  Design and Construction Checklist for New and Remodeled Stores

| Area or Service | Considerations |
|---|---|
| **STOREFRONT** | |
| Show windows | Type and size. |
|   Platforms | Fixed or portable. |
|   Backgrounds | See-through or enclosed. |
| Bulkheads above storefront in interior malls | Drywall. |
| Vestibule | |
|   Type of HVAC | Size and location. |
|   Floor | Nonslip or removable grille. |
|   Walls | Glass or maintenance-free; see-through or solid. |
| Entrances | |
|   Entrances and doors | How many and where? Consult building code. |
| Awnings | Sun coverage or cosmetic. |
| Canopies | Metal or plastic; sun and customer protection. |
| Exterior lighting | Security and ornamental. |
| Demising strips for separation of stores | In strip centers or malls. |
| Signs | Location and type. |
| **INTERIOR** | |
| Walls | Some are load-bearing in old buildings. |
| Partitions | Freestanding or permanent. |
| Blocking within partitions | For hangrail, shelves, etc. |
| Partition materials | Gypsum, or other. |
| Curtain walls | Suspended or projecting valances. |
| Doors, hardware | Location, type use, color. |
| Ceilings | Acoustical or smooth, painted or not. |
| Special ceiling detail | Drops, rises. |
| Floor finish | Material, thickness. |
| Depressions in floors | Change in materials. |
| Base | |
|   Cove | Vinyl. |
|   Wood | To match floors. |
|   Carpet | With cap cove or straight. |
|   Marble or other natural stone | How fastened to wall. |
| Stairs | |
|   Customer | Ease and comfort of movement from place to place. |
|   Service | Building code compliance; back-of-house uses. |
| Fixtures | |
|   Perimeter | Wall-type or departmental dividers. |
|   Freestanding | Loose, portable type. |
|   Specialty | Unusual display units. |
| Back-room Storage | |
|   Furniture | Seating, tables. |
|   Shelving | Wallhung, individual, floor-mounted. |
|   Hanging | How supported. |
|   Equipment | Marking, tagging tables, repair bench. |
| Lunchroom | Employees' use. |
| Toilet rooms | |
|   Flooring and base | Type of material. |
|   Walls | Paint, wallcover, ceramic tile. |

**Table 3   Design and Construction Checklist for New and Remodeled Stores (*Continued*)**

| Area or Service | Considerations |
| --- | --- |
| Toilet partitions and baffles | Metal or plastic laminate. |
| Fixtures | Toilet, lavatories, urinals. |
| Accessories | Towel, waste, soap dispensers. |
| Drains | For overflows. |

**PAINTING AND DECORATION**

| | |
| --- | --- |
| Clearly define scope for walls, ceilings, curtain walls, fitting areas | Specify flat, semigloss, or gloss paint or wallcovering. |
| Preparation of surface | Spackling, sanding, sealing. |
| Display window interiors | Material selection. |
| Nonselling areas | Specify where required. |
| Toilet rooms | Type of finish. |
| Trim and doors, frames, exposed metal | Clearly specify for paint or wallcovering. |

**RECEIVING AND SHIPPING**

| | |
| --- | --- |
| Loading platform | Doors, levelers. |
| Bumper | Truck bumpers. |
| Climate-control enclosure | HVAC retained at truck loading dock. |
| Mesh enclosure | For see-through storage. |
| Conveyors | Materials-handling equipment. |
| Forklifts | Provide for storage and maintenance space. |
| Slick rails | Pipe rail overhead to move hanging merchandise. |
| Overhead automatic carriers | Dry cleaning–style movers. |

**VERTICAL CONVEYANCES**

| | |
| --- | --- |
| Elevators | |
| Structure | Structural design of openings and support. |
| Hoistway | Masonry or gypsum walls. |
| Mechanical room and equipment | Provide adequate space. |
| Penthouse | Sometimes not required. |
| Glass enclosure screen | For glass-enclosed cabs or freestanding elevators. |
| Type | Hydraulic or electric. |
| Cab design | Material finishes and ceiling. |
| Doors and jambs | Painted or nonferrous metals, such as stainless steel. |
| Controls and signals | Up and down; pushbutton. |
| Escalators | Allocate proper space and size in preplanning. |
| Dumbwaiters | Electric or manual. |

**ELECTRICAL SYSTEM**

| | |
| --- | --- |
| Service | Adequate incoming electric power. |
| Meters | In malls, landlord submeters the smaller stores. |
| Panel boards | Provide adequate space and location for proper function. |
| Transformers | In small malls, stores are sometimes required to have these. |
| Time clocks | Usually for HVAC system and sign and window light. |
| HVAC wiring | Power to supply equipment. |
| Outlets, receptacles | Wall or floor. |
| Location | Provide for task and portable types for future use. |
| Type | Flush wall and floor use; underfloor conduit. |
| Equipment | Special-use motors and display equipment. |
| Signage | Required for illuminated signs. |

(*Continued*)

131

**Table 3   Design and Construction Checklist for New and Remodeled Stores** (*Continued*)

| Area or Service | Considerations |
| --- | --- |
| Cash registers | Proper wiring for complex registers. |
| Telephone | Panel board receptacle; check for other communication uses. |
| Intercom | Very important for large store. |
| Sound system | Includes piped-in music. Ceiling or wall speakers connected to microphone, radio, or recording equipment. |
| Equipment requiring electricity | Provide spares in panel boards or future equipment conduit. |
| Contactors | Various types—one switch can turn off lighting or equipment. |
| Bells, chimes | Doorbells, annunciators, and call systems. |
| Lighting fixtures | All fixtures: general, ceiling spot, display type, etc. |
| Emergency lighting | Provide for illumination of exit pathways. |
| Fire alarm system | Detection of fire. |
| Smoke detection equipment | Can prevent loss of life by smoke. |
| Computers | Many are being used, from personal size on up. |
| Tailor shop | Sewing machines and pressers. |
| Energy-saving devices | Timer switches and body-actuated devices. |
| **HEATING, VENTILATING, AND AIR CONDITIONING** | |
| Air-conditioning equipment and system | Type of air-cooled or water equipment and equipment locations. |
| Heating system | Heat from lights can be recovered and reused. |
| Ducts and insulation | Carefully specify size and location, especially vertical and horizontal runs. |
| Diffusers and grilles | Coordinate reflected ceiling plans. |
| Exhaust systems | |
|     Display window | Heat from lights builds up in enclosed windows. |
|     Tailor shop | Pressing equipment needs ventilation. |
|     Restaurant | If food is prepared, exhaust is required. |
|     Beauty shop | Often vented. |
| Control systems | Investigate types of controls applicable to a store's needs. |
| Equipment wiring | Underfloor conduit may be needed to handle remote equipment. |
| Energy-saving devices | Consider long-life lamps and lighting fixtures as well as devices. |
| **PLUMBING** | |
| Gas and water meters | Location of utilities. |
| Water supply | Availability and location of source. |
| Piping locations | Check on concealed locations and insulation. |
| Waste and sewage system | Learn location and size of pipes. |
| Water treatment system | Determine the capability of the community's system. |
| Fixtures | Check on water-saving units. |
| Maintenance room | Place drains, controls, and valves in this area. |
| Water heater | Large tank or local instantaneous heater at sinks. |
| Water softening | May be required for municipal water or well water. |
| Drinking fountains | Public and employee use. |

| Area or Service | Considerations |
| --- | --- |
| Store equipment | Determine if plumbing hookup is required. |
| Toilet rooms | Determine number of rooms needed and fixtures for each; provide for handicapped. |
| Tailor shop | Often requires steam piping. |
| Restaurant | For food-service equipment specifications, coordinate with consultant. |
| Employee cafeteria | Food and water services, vending machines. |
| Floor drains | Some wet areas, such as flower shop. |
| Roof drains | Some buildings have large piping. |
| Storm water drainage | For parking and entrance areas. |
| Hose bibbs | For exterior purposes, such as grounds keeping; interior sanitation; and flower and food shops. |
| **SPRINKLER SYSTEM** | |
| System, wet or dry | Depends on geographic location. |
| Fire alarm tie-in | Alarm system design allows for this. |
| Fire extinguisher | Provide sufficient locations for fire code. |
| Hose cabinets | Sometimes are built into the wall. |
| Siamese connection, exterior | Permits water hoses to pump water into building. |
| **SECURITY SYSTEMS** | |
| Burglar alarm, exterior | Perimeter protection at roof openings, doors, windows. |
| TV cameras | Building and patron surveillance. |
| Electronic customer surveillance | Use of detection equipment, usually at entrance. |
| Glass area | Large glass areas have sensors attached. |
| Sprinkler alarm | Activated when sprinkler discharges water. |
| Safe or vault | Fireproof for safekeeping of money. |
| Door buzzers and remote releases | Control doors and access to protected areas. |
| **OTHER ITEMS** | |
| Furniture | Consider location and type required such as shoe store seating. |
| Parking lot | Location, maintenance, and size. |
| Incinerators | Check environmental codes. |
| Dumpsters | Trash containers, exterior. |
| Balers | Paper and cardboard can be baled to save space. |
| Rubbish room | Some large stores and malls require one. |
| Landscaping | Visually enhances interior and exterior spaces. |
| Maintenance areas | Some stores need a workshop or repair area. |
| Cutting and patching for remodeling | Walls, ceilings, and floors that have had holes cut in them for mechanical and structural purposes should be detailed to avoid raw look. |
| Guarantees and warranties | Owner should collect and file contractors' and machinery contracts. |

contractor could be less attentive to materials and details; if the owner is not knowledgeable in these areas, he could be disappointed with the final product.

### Construction manager

A single organization is answerable to the owner for on-time and on-budget delivery of the finished product. The construction manager (CM) can be either:

1. *Architect:* As a CM, the architect expedites the work of a single general contractor or prime contractors of key trades.

2. *Consultant:* CM firms specialize in expediting and coordination of the construction process.

3. *General contractor:* Scheduling and project management is handled by the general contractor by an agreement similar to the cost-plus-fee arrangement.

# Bibliography

Cushman, Robert F., and William J. Palmer: *Businessman's Guide to Construction,* Dow Jones Books, Princeton, 1980, pp. 181–182, 187, 220–223, 226–227.

"Dayton Hudson Sets $2.5 Billion Budget for Next Five Years," *The Wall Street Journal,* Dec. 2, 1983, p. 4.

*Emerging Trends in Real Estate: 1984,* RERC Real Estate Research Corporation, Chicago, 1983, p. 19.

Myler, Kathleen: "Hillside Shopping Center to Be Reopened as Updated Mall," *Chicago Tribune,* Nov. 13, 1983, Section 16, p. 2B.

*Planning for New or Remodeled Stores,* National Retail Merchants Association, New York, 1979, pp. 3, 8, 13.

"Rehab to Turn Auto Agency into Retail Shops," *Chicago Tribune,* Nov. 13, 1983, Sec. 16, p. 2D.

*Repair & Remodeling Cost Data, Commercial/Residential,* Robert Snow Means Company, Kingston, Mass., 1983.

# 13

# Signage and Graphics

There are two types of signs for retail stores: exterior and interior. Both convey information. The primary purpose of exterior signage is to attract traffic. Interior signage acts as a "silent salesperson," directly adding to the point-of-sale influences aimed at the shopper.

The signage phase of a retail store design project differs markedly from signage done for a hospital, institutional building, office building, or apartment building. In these types of buildings, signage does not sell anything; its primary functions are to identify spaces and guide the user. Because signage is directly linked to a store's central activity—the movement of merchandise—the signage and graphics program is more time-consuming and more challenging.

For either interior or exterior signs, the designer has the opportunity to create graphic excitement. Feel free to present new ideas to the client even if they have little or no precedent. The merchant will tell you, probably after first hearing, if you should develop your concepts further. Signage is a strong adjunct to retail store architecture.

If the designer hestitates to get involved in the signage program, the void will be filled by the client's visual merchandising people. The problem with this is that the designer is giving up control of a vital part of the job. The designer always has the bigger plan of the overall store in mind.

## Exterior signage

The purpose of signage on a retail building exterior is for recognition— to draw traffic inside. A retailer's outside signage is as much advertis-

J. C. Penney

Dominick's

Penn Fruit

**The retail store designer has a wide choice of exterior signage styles and types: flat or dimensional, modern or traditional, illuminated or not, subtle or aggressive. The choice should work with the storefront architecture, restate the store's merchandising policies, and appeal to targeted customer groups. Examples of pinned-off individual letter signs are shown at J. C. Penney, San Francisco, and Dominick's, Skokie, Illinois. A pinned-off box sign with a plastic face and lighting behind it is at Penn Fruit, Philadelphia.**

J. C. PENNEY    *Photo:* Helen Holden. *Courtesy:* Real Estate Research Corporation.
DOMINICK's    *Photo:* Joan Papadopoulos. *Courtesy:* Real Estate Research Corporation.
PENN FRUIT    *Photo:* Charles E. Broudy.

Illumination for exterior signs can be built into the letters themselves, or come from above, behind, or below.

This freestanding, dimensional Ghirardelli Square, San Francisco, sign forms an arch, with illumination designed into each letter.

*Photo:* Helen Holden. *Courtesy:* Real Estate Research Corporation.

A plastic-faced box sign, illuminated from behind, at Thriftway, Philadelphia.

*Photo:* Charles E. Broudy.

**Two examples of punched-through plastic letters and illuminated sign box.**

**Higbee's, Beachwood Place, Cleveland.**
*Courtesy:* The Rouse Company

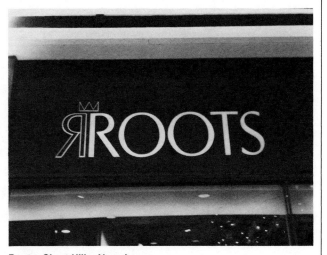

**Roots, Short Hills, New Jersey.**
*Photo:* Vilma Barr.

**Signs on freestanding buildings can be illuminated by special ground-mounted fixtures made for that purpose. Roots, Morristown, New Jersey.**

*Design:* Charles E. Broudy & Associates. *Photo:* Lawrence S. Williams, Inc.

### Table 1  Retail Store Signage and Graphics

| Type | Characteristics and considerations | Recommendations |
|---|---|---|
| **EXTERIOR** | | |
| **Wall** | | |
| Pinned off | Pin mount; individual letters. | Sophisticated; for quality store. |
| Direct mounted | Screw mount to wall. | Easy installation. |
| Rear illuminated | Neon tube creates glow on wall; letters are in silhouette. | Quality appearance; background wall material should be receptive to light halo. |
| Front illuminated | Plastic-faced or exposed neon. | Individual letters; metal sides. |
| Box sign | Fluorescent tubes behind plastic face in a metal box. | Economical; easy to change sign face. |
| **Canopy** | | |
| Illuminated letter | Individual letter mount; metal, plastic. Push-through letter. | Surface applied. Glowing letter is more elegant. Usually used on quality stores. |
| Box sign | Neon or fluorescent; behind plastic face. | Economical. |
| Neon | Individual, distinctive. | Not applicable on all types of stores. |
| **Pylon or tower** | | |
| Freestanding | Illuminated; heights vary. Flashing or blinking lights are usually not permitted. | Used for highway recognition, for shopping centers or larger stores. Sometimes lists tenants. |
| **Hanging** | | |
| Wood | Carved wood often with gold leaf lettering. | Used when a traditional, antique, or casual appearance is desired. |
| Metal | Wrought iron, often with scroll work. | Identifies a craft shop or tradesperson. |
| Glass applied | Glue-on or rub-on letters for show windows; cutout letters of thin plastic or plaster. | Changeable signage for show windows. |
| Awning | Canvas or metal; graphics can be painted. | A lightweight and semipermanent device to unite multifacade stores. Stripes, patterns or solids are appropriate. |

ing as identification. It is one of the first design elements the customer sees. For small retailers with a limited advertising media budget, exterior signage is a very good way to keep the store's name in front of the buying public.

Most stores with highway frontage are conservative, even bland, square or rectangular structures. The store's personality may often be in the signage. Graphics here can be bold and quickly perceived and still be in good taste. The design must be simple: It has to be read at 55 miles per hour by the driver as well as the passengers.

Stores that face out onto an enclosed mall also have "exterior" frontage. Mall developers set guidelines for the individual store's signage, so consult the tenant's criteria for dos and don'ts. (Also see Chapter 14, "Shopping Centers and Malls.")

*Both exterior and interior signs can be permanent, or changeable.* Table 1 describes the types of signs that can be used to carry out an effective program. (Also see pages 144–145.) There are two other techniques that can be useful:

1. Rather than use one large sign to draw attention to the store, use multiple small signs. The store

sign can be interpreted in materials and type-faces compatible with the building's design. An impression of quality is established; the message gets across, but it is more subdued than a single oversize sign.

2. For urban areas or in certain centers where canopies or awnings extend over the sidewalk or walkway, reinforce the store's identity with signage that is at a right angle to the facade. The store's name on the awning or canopy will attract pedestrians across the street; the right-angle signs will do the same thing to

| Type | Characteristics and considerations | Recommendations |
|---|---|---|
| Banners | Fabric or canvas. May have plain or patterned background. | Can be temporary or long term. Can be changed seasonally. |
| INTERIOR | | |
| Departmental and directional signs or graphics | Can be suspended from ceiling or valance mounted. Illuminated or nonilluminated, depending on effect to be created. Directional arrows and signs should not confuse customers. | In department stores or large stores, identification signs should be properly located for easy reading. A variety of surface backgrounds and types of letters create and extend the mood of the environment. |
| Name brand or product category | Can be placed above merchandise on a valance or suspended from above. Designer logos can be used. | Can be temporary or permanent, depending on the store's policies. Surface background is important if names will change. Letters can be cut out of any material that is appropriate for the solution. |
| Directories | In large stores and department stores, directories are needed to help customers get to the proper merchandise or service area quickly and easily. | Directories can be wall- or floor-mounted, or suspended from ceilings. Maps may also be employed; most are rear-illuminated. |
| Photomurals | Large photo enlargements (prints or transparencies) are used to encourage patrons to buy toiletries, lingerie, jewelry, etc. | These photos may be black and white or color, front-illuminated or rear-screen color transparencies. |
| Point of purchase | Table-top graphics and displays play a large part in retailing. They range from TV monitors of fashion shows, to nameplates, to mirrors custom-fabricated with a trade name. | Cosmetics, jewelry, sporting goods, foods, children's apparel, shoes. |

shoppers walking in front of the store.

## Fabrication

There are many quality sign fabricators around the country who will help you develop your sketches. They will do shop drawings for you which you and your client will approve. Reputable fabricators are skilled in sign materials technology; they know how to bend metal, understand lighting, can suggest suitable plastics, and will erect the finished sign.

Neon is a specialty for some sign shops. They are familiar with skills involved in bending the glass tubes and getting the correct neon color. Many craftspeople are working with neon now, and the designer should be assured that they know the technical aspects of the lighting, such as the correct ballast to use.

## Sign ordinances

Most communities have them. Sign ordinances most commonly control size; in a few cities, quality is also addressed. The Philadlephia Art Commission must approve the size, style, color, and illumination technique before a major sign can be installed in certain districts. The designer may encounter nearly as many hearings for signage as for the zoning permit. Presentations to groups may involve samples, photos with the new sign superimposed over the existing structure in the case of a remodeled store, elevations, and detail drawings. Such presentations may take place at night, particularly in small communities that do not have a full-time commission. If the approval hearings drag on and the designer is spending time beyond the regular contract agreement, he or she should be reimbursed on an hourly or per diem basis.

## Table 2   Dos and Don'ts of Retail Signage and Graphics

| Dos | Don'ts |
| --- | --- |
| In dark areas, provide for light on the sign or internal illumination. | Don't be too tricky with typeface or graphics that will prevent instant recognition. Keep it to the point, and make it simple to read. |
| When using removable letters, make sure the sign background is a hard surface, so the sign can be removed and a new one installed without a "ghost effect" remaining from the original sign. | Do not specifiy a highly reflective surface or background that will distort the sign or allow readability from only one viewing location. |
| Do consider baked-enamel, porcelain enamel, or metal that is available in many colors, to introduce variety into the palette. | Do not use a grade of plastic for the face of a sign box that will wave or "oil can." |
| For stores in shopping centers and malls, maintain storefront criteria. Many developers provide manuals, explicit instructions, and information regarding signs and graphics on the exterior of the stores. | On exterior signs, do not specify threaded screw mountings that will rust. |

**Banners are a bright and inexpensive way to announce retail activity inside without disturbing classic architectural facades. The building now housing Urban Outfitters faces Philadelphia's Rittenhouse Square. The store's nylon banners are replaced every 3 to 5 years, according to art director Nancy Burpee.**

*Photo:* Vilma Barr.

Awnings shelter shoppers on the outside from rain and sun, and protect merchandise in the show windows from ultraviolet ray damage. A store name can be carried on both the front and the sides of an awning. Both fabric and metal are appropriate materials for awnings and canopies. The new Swan Gallery awning blends with those of older shops.

*Design for Swan Gallery:* Charles E. Broudy & Associates. *Photo:* Vilma Barr.

Bright white letters are applied directly to glass window walls of Crate & Barrel's Cambridge, Massachusetts, store. The building, formerly occupied by Design Research, now has offices above the retail levels.

*Design:* Benjamin Thompson & Associates. *Photo:* Vilma Barr.

141

# Interior signage

The sign program should include:

- Hanging signs
- Supported signs
- Holders
- Dividers

The main purpose of signage inside a store is to help sell merchandise by talking about it. The second function it can successfully perform is direction, that is, informing shoppers where they are, what is for sale in that area, how to get to other areas, and what they will find when they get there. The directional aspect is especially important in medium-size stores (10,000 to 50,000 square feet) and large stores. People intensely dislike the feeling of disorientation. The second worst thing a merchant can hear about a store is that customers can't find what they are looking for, even though it was advertised, displayed in the window, etc. (The worst thing to hear about a store, as was noted in an earlier chapter, is to pay for a store design that was ruined when the merchandise was brought in.)

With retailers paring costs to maintain profitability, signage has taken over selling duties once carried out by clerks. "Many Stores Abandon 'Service with a Smile,' Rely on Signs, Displays," a *Wall Street Journal* article (see Bibliography) headlined. "They Reduce Staff as Costs Rise, Able Help Vanishes, Shoppers Seek Discounts."

That's why companies like Sears, Penney and Montgomery Ward & Co. can cut sales help to pare expenses and still argue that they are improving service. Penney's David F. Miller says his company has maintained "a pleasant

**Overhead-mounted back-lit transparencies give strong identification and drawing power to a cosmetics section.**
*Courtesy:* Sears Merchandise Group.

shopping experience" for customers by turning to "improved packaging, store layout and design, merchandise arrangement and signs" instead of hiring more salespeople. Productivity, as measured by sales per employee-hour, has risen, yet some customers find "that no one has talked to them before they got to the cash registers."

Target discount stores attempt to make up for the lack of floor people largely through signs and displays. Signs are used for everything from specifications for television antennas to reminders to pull carts through checkouts. Displays, such as one showing tires on sale, advertise the merits of the merchandise.

**A curved design theme is repeated with strong graphic elements across a cash-wrap station, fixture post, and circular overhead lighting. This Christopher Robin children's apparel unit, completed in 1969, is an early example of indoor use of HID illumination—the circular lighting drum contains a 400-W, warm deluxe mercury lamp.**

*Design:* Charles E. Broudy & Associates. *Photo:* Charles E. Broudy.

**Painted "To Market, To Market" murals lead the way to City Market on the lower level of the Century City Centre, Chicago.**

*Design:* Carl Wiemars.

143

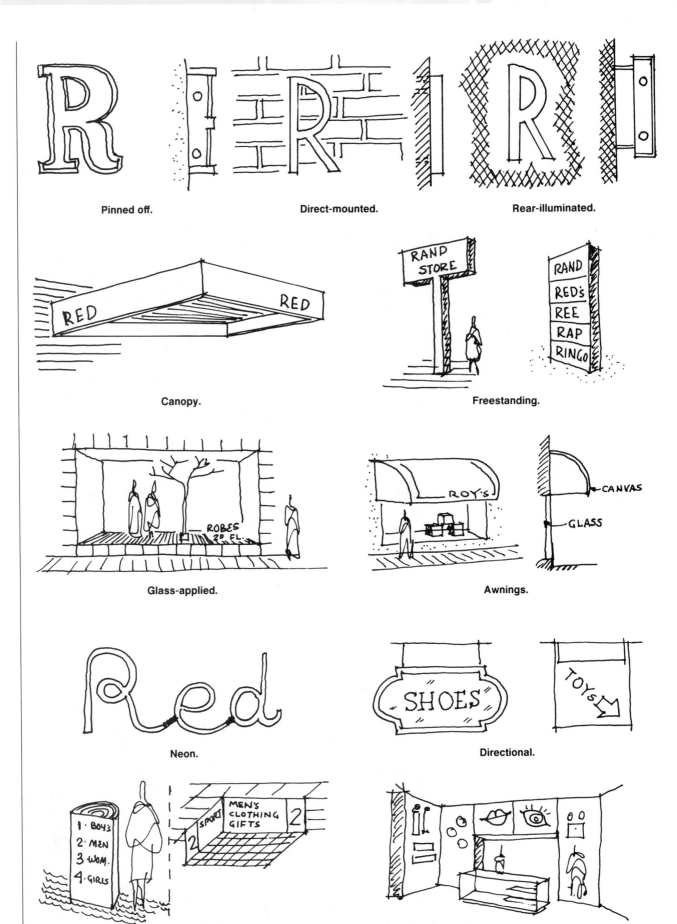

Pinned off.

Direct-mounted.

Rear-illuminated.

Canopy.

Freestanding.

Glass-applied.

Awnings.

Neon.

Directional.

Directories.

Photomurals.

**Retail Signage Sketchbook**

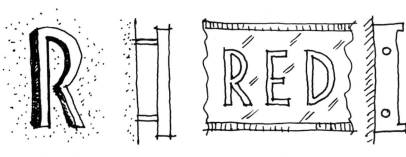

**Front-illuminated.**    **Box sign.**

**Hanging wood and metal signs.**

**Banners.**

**Brand or product category.**

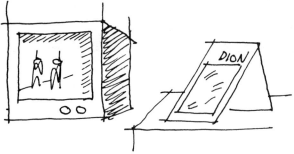

**Point-of-purchase.**

# Electronic signs

*Moving-light signage* has been available for many years to give information such as news, weather, time, and stock quotations. Some stores are now testing moving-light signage to augment media advertising. Typical messages carried include announcement of sales and special promotions, new merchandise arrivals, and the restaurant's daily specials. Small versions of a moving-light board can be used inside.

The biggest electronic selling device today is the *video tape player*. Customers under 40 have been brought up in the era of animated color images—television, movies, and now video. Eye-catching video-monitors, placed near entrances and showing apparel, sporting goods, cosmetics, home furnishings, and other items, have been effective in attracting people into the store. When placed within a department, they entertain and inform customers with fashion shows, cosmetic demonstrations, and bike touring. Tape players that tell a merchandise story have been installed in elevator cabs on a trial basis.

# Other considerations

- Check the building code for signage requirements for the handicapped. Braille on elevator floor location buttons, and on toilet room doors are two examples.

- Call in a graphics consultant when you need one. Some architects and space planners are also successful graphic designers; others are not. Within the graphic design discipline, there are firms that special-

Neon signage has evolved into an art form in the past decade. Though not well suited to very conservative stores, neon signs are effective focal points for other retail stores, when treated with taste and restraint. Neon tops an outdoor freestanding signboard at Baltimore's Harborplace. "The Museum Store" is translated in four different color ways at the Franklin Institute, Philadelphia. Neon "Sweet Stuff" across a top panel of windows is repeated in white glass-applied letters on panes of the center panel in Newmarket, Philadelphia.

HARBORPLACE   *Courtesy:* The Rouse Company.
FRANKLIN INSTITUTE MUSEUM SHOP   *Design:*
Charles E. Broudy & Associates. *Photo:* Vilma Barr.
SWEET STUFF   *Design:* Charles E. Broudy &
Associates. *Photo:* Vilmar Barr.

**Harborplace**

**Franklin Institute**

**Sweet Stuff**

ize in retail and shopping centers. Developers of major shopping centers will tell a merchant to hire a graphics consultant if it appears that the store's designer cannot meet the landlord's standards.

# Bibliography

Weiner, Steve: "Find It Yourself: Many Stores Abandon 'Service with a Smile,' Rely on Signs, Displays," *The Wall Street Journal*, Mar. 16, 1981, p. 1.

# 14

# Shopping Centers and Malls

This chapter will not deal with the many aspects and considerations of shopping center planning and design, an entire design subdiscipline in itself. The reader who is interested in information and guidelines regarding this type of building can refer to several fine books on the subject or contact the International Council of Shopping Centers in New York City.

For our purposes here, we will assume that the designer has been retained by the center or mall tenant.

Shopping centers and malls have taken many new forms in recent years: urban malls, vertical malls, factory outlet malls, discount malls, off-price malls and festival malls. "The shopping center industry is alive, well, and looking toward a bright future," said Martin J. Cleary, president of the Internal Council of Shopping Centers (ICSC), and president and chief operating officer of Jacobs, Visconsi & Jacobs Co., Cleveland, in an article in *Buildings.* "The gigantic spacious center courts are no longer common, and mall widths have been reduced. Energy mangement systems are being used extensively in shopping centers to improve energy use.

"Department stores now require less square footage. The average mall tenant store size has been reduced by about half of what it was, showing the individual tenant is merchandising more for his money."

Part of the tenant's program will be provided in the form of the landlord's criteria document. It tells what the owner provides and what he does not provide and what the tenant must provide to comply with the landlord's standards.

The owner or the owner's representatives are the final arbiters of taste. Any design deemed detrimental to the mall's established quality levels will be rejected. The landlord will provide designs at the tenant's expense if no other acceptable solution can be found. They are very serious and selective about the overall design message the center will communicate.

Milan's Galleria Vittorio Emanuele, built between 1865 and 1867, is a four-story arcade of shops and offices, covered by a glass barrel vault and a beautiful glass cupola, 160 feet high. Its monumental entrance dominates the north side of the city's center, the Piazza del Duomo. It is one of the best examples of a commercial space which is also grand, urban, and social.
*Photo:* John Stapleton. *Courtesy:* Prof. Mercia M. T. Garssi.

# HVAC

· In some cases, the landlord will provide full information on how the system works; the tenant then follows the basic rules established for the engineering design requirements. Other owners will provide tenant with air conditioning or just provide chilled and hot water. The tenant then has to pro-

The main entrance to Willow Grove Park near Philadelphia, a 350,000-square-foot project with 170 shops and restaurants and three department stores. "All aspects of Willow Grove Park, from the overall design concept to the details of the interior landscaping, have been designed to evoke the elegance, charm, spirit, and style of the old Willow Grove Amusement Park. The resultant character of the entire project will be one of a very special center with a unique sense of place." (From *Willow Grove Park: Store Design Criteria,* p. 2.)

*Design:* RTKL Associates, Inc. *Photo:* Robert Stahman. *Courtesy:* Willow Grove Associates.

**(Top right) A section of the feature court as shown in the guidelines publication, *Willow Grove Park Store Design Criteria* (p. 7).**

*Design:* RTKL Associates, Inc., Architects.

**(Bottom right) A typical page from *Willow Grove Park Store Design Criteria* has a format directed to future tenants and their designers. Tenants' criteria publications range from simple photocopied documents to handsomely designed and illustrated bound books such as this.**

*Design:* RTKL Associates, Inc., Architects.

vide air-handling equipment, duct work, and control wiring.

· The landlord can charge the tenant a sum based on a scale shown on the lease exhibit outline. If the landlord is making a profit on this charge, the tenant should understand this at the outset.

· The landlord does not want tenants "borrowing" any of the air conditioning in the public walkways and corridors. Tenants must have their air conditioning and air-handling equipment carefully calculated and documented.

· Penetration through the roof is controlled by the landlord. Openings required by ventilating and air-conditioning equipment may have to be performed by the landlord's roofing contractor because of liability insurance.

# Plumbing

In small communities, the landlord may provide a separate sewage treatment plant to handle the center or mall project.

Tenants' access to piping, valves, and sanitary facilities is most important. Depending on the size of the store, the tenants may be required to provide their own toilet facilities.

# Sprinkler systems

The cost of sprinklers is often offset by savings in fire insurance. Fire safety codes are very strict in some communities.

FEATURE COURT TYPICAL SECTION

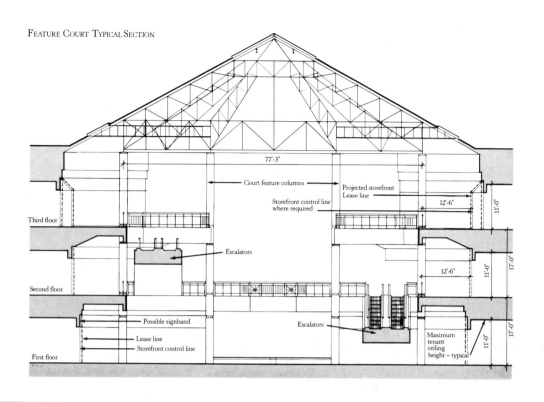

77'-3"

Court feature columns

Projected storefront
Lease line

Storefront control line
where required

12'-6"

Third floor

11'-0"

Escalators

12'-6"

Second floor

11'-0"

17'-0"

Possible signband

Escalators

Lease line

Maximum
tenant
ceiling
height – typical

Storefront control line

First floor

11'-0"

17'-0"

## PROJECTED STOREFRONTS

Projected storefronts have been specifically located along the Mall to provide variety in both physical appearance and merchandizing techniques, and to respond creatively to some unique building configurations. They are a design "bonus" to the Tenant in terms of identity and visibility and their use will be strictly controlled by the Landlord both now and in the future. The projected space is envisioned as a kind of show window for display purposes only. Racks of clothing, table displays, gondolas, or typical stocking shelves will not be allowed in the projected storefronts.

1. Construction of the projected storefronts shall be by the Tenant at his own expense.
2. The projected storefronts shall be predominately glass enclosed with sloping top and side panels as illustrated.
3. Materials shall be glass (clear, beveled, etched, or stained) with butt-joint or metal framing, including the sloping top and sides.
4. The Landlord will provide and install the Mall pavers up to the storefront control line of the projection. The Tenant is encour-

aged to utilize the entire area of the projection. However, if the Tenant chooses to recess any portion of his storefront from the projection line, i.e. at a recessed entrance, the Landlord will pro-

vide and install the Mall pavers to the closure line at the Tenant's expense.

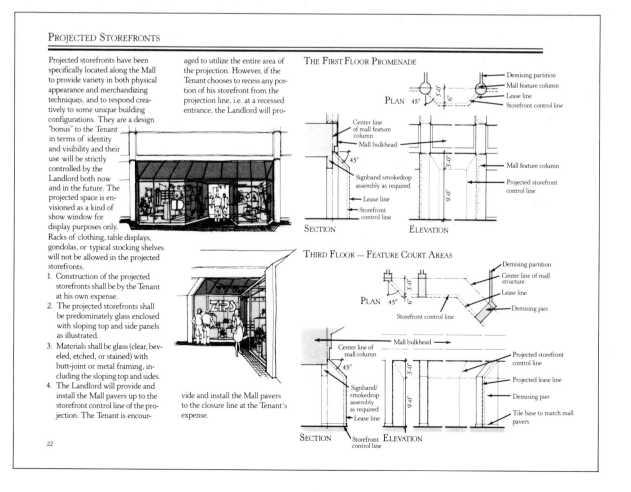

THE FIRST FLOOR PROMENADE

PLAN

45°

3'-0"

6"

Demising partition
Mall feature column
Lease line
Storefront control line

Center line
of mall feature
column

Mall bulkhead

45°

Signband smokedrop
assembly as required

Lease line

Storefront
control line

SECTION

ELEVATION

3'-0"

9'-0"

Mall feature column

Projected storefront
control line

THIRD FLOOR — FEATURE COURT AREAS

PLAN

45°

3'-0"

6"

Storefront control line

Demising partition
Center line of mall
structure
Lease line

Demising pier

Mall bulkhead

Center line of
mall column

45°

Signband/
smokedrop
assembly
as required

Lease line

Storefront
control line

3'-0"

9'-0"

Projected storefront
control line

Projected lease line

Demising pier

Tile base to match mall
pavers

SECTION

ELEVATION

22

Malls today require tenants to have their own sprinkler systems.

Flush, concealed heads have recently become available. These do not detract from the design of the store's ceiling.

# Electrical and lighting

· Usually, the electrical main is brought to the store's premises, and the merchant has the meter installed.

· A 220-volt (or higher) transformer or generator is provided by the landlord. The tenant provides a space in the back room wall for equipment such as meter sockets and panels required by local codes. Find out if service is being brought to the tenant's demised premises; it is costly later on to run lines and conduits hundreds of feet.

· A number of states have energy codes which limit the watts per square foot the store can use and the amount of energy used for equipment.

· Some developers are not allowing 2- by 4- foot exposed fluorescent fixtures. Look for this ruling in the lease exhibit.

· Check into lighting requirements, such as: adequate lighting and ventilation of showcases, shields on exposed lights (other than decorative); no glare from store area on the mall; and hours of operation for illuminated signs.

# Storefronts

· All designs have to be approved by the landlord, a process which can take weeks or months, depending on the landlord's organization.

· Landlords are starting to allow projecting or greenhouse fronts in an effort to relieve the flat, planar look that has characterized past mall design.

· Flooring in the public walkways may have to extend into the individual store's recesses or doorways.

· In high-rise buildings, the landlord may control 3 feet behind the front glass window of lobby shops.

· To protect the glass storefront, the landlord may require a 6- or 12-inch tile base so cleaning machines will not damage the surface. For a corner store, some will not want glass all around the perimeter.

**Exterior of the now-multiuse Philadelphia Bourse, a massive brick and stone landmark in the Independence Square area. Banners hung between the ground and first floors have right-angle exposure to street and vehicular traffic.**

*Design:* H2L2 Architects/Planners. *Photo:* Vilma Barr. *Courtesy:* Kaiserman Enterprises.

153

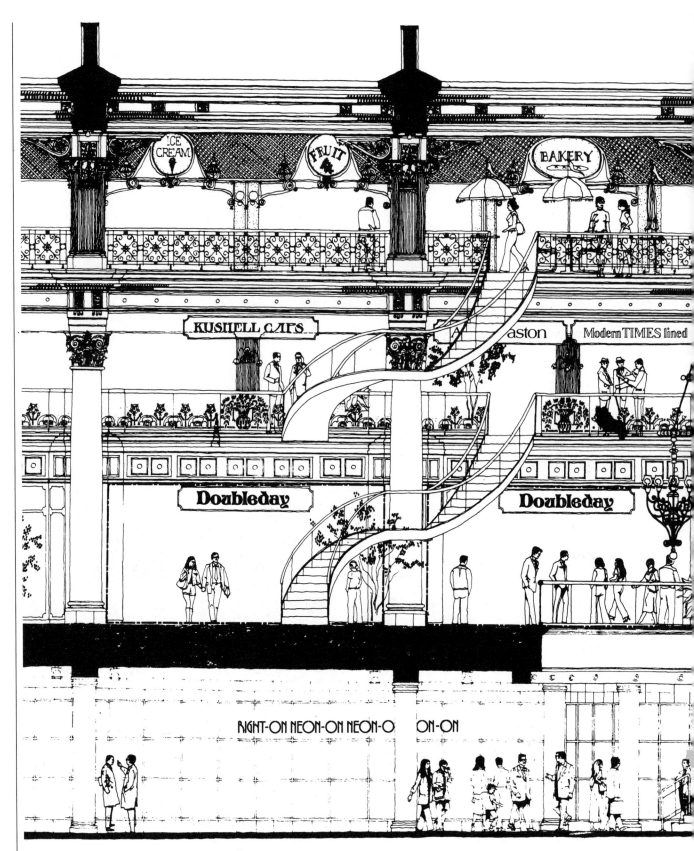

**This double-page spread from** *The Philadelphia Bourse Tenant Design criteria* **is a detailed line drawing of a section of the renovated building's center court with suggested signage typefaces.**

*Design:* H2L2 Architects/Planners. *Courtesy:* Kaiserman Enterprises.

The center court and stairway at the renovated Philadelphia Bourse. (A *bourse* is an exchange or money market.) A 1982 renovation created a vertical urban mall with offices above.

*Design:* H2L2 Architects/Planners. *Photo:* Vilma Barr. *Courtesy:* Kaiserman Enterprises.

A typical storefront and signage at the Philadelphia Bourse, following specifications by the owner and architect.

*Design:* H2L2 Architects/Planners. *Photo:* Vilma Barr. *Courtesy:* Kaiserman Enterprises.

## Sign Bands

Some sign bands usages are very strict; others are more liberal. Items like subheadings, logos, typefaces, lighting, painting on glass, size canopies and awnings have to be checked out before the sign design is presented.

Contract drawings and the interior finish sched-

ule are sent to the landlord for approval. It is a good idea to send the drawings and specifications out for bid at the same time so that work can begin on the store as soon as approval is received on the plans from the landlord.

In most communities, the individual tenant has to file for a separate building permit and certificate of occupancy. Approvals are required from the land-

The three-level atrium at Georgetown Park, Washington, D.C. The developer, Georgetown Park Associates, credits "professional planning, design, . . . local historians, review boards and governmental agencies" for assisting in the development of the final concept. "The collaborative work of these professionals addresses the historic origins and architecture of the Victorian and Italianate periods between 1875 and 1910." (From *Handbook on Storefront Design—Georgetown Park,* p. 3.)

*Photo:* Leonard Bogarod. *Courtesy:* Real Estate Research Corporation.

lord after inspecting the completed job, as well as the usual community inspectors.

# Bibliography

Gosling, David, and Barry Maitland: *Design and Planning of Retail Systems*, Whitney Library of Design, New York, 1976, pp. 109, 184.

Monroe, Linda K.: "Shopping Center Forecast 1984: A Mature Industry Looks to the Future," *Buildings*, January 1984, pp. 54–55.

# 15

# Specialty Retailing; Wholesale Showrooms

S**pecialty retailing**

Traditionally, "retail store" meant department, apparel, shoe, grocery, or drugstore. Today, this term has taken on expanded definition. Established merchants are offering broadened arrays of products and services within the standard stores. Also outlets concentrating on special products and services are opening all over the United States and overseas. Sometimes we export the concept; other times, successful European or Oriental merchandising will take hold and flourish here.

*Some newcomers to the specialty store field*

· *Optical centers.* In Hong Kong, the customer can have an eye examination and receive the results on a computer printout. The store has an on-site lab; the finished glasses are delivered in less than an hour.

· *Dental and medical centers.* Often found in shopping centers and free-standing strip centers, these "walk-in" units strive to demystify visits to the traditional doctor's or dentist's office. By promoting the idea that a visit to the dentist or doctor for a checkup or routine treatment need not take any more planning than the usual shopping excursion, the centers are targeted to both children and adults.

· *Food centers and food specialty stores.* Gourmet take-out establishments have sprung up to serve

**DDL Foodshow was a 12,000-square-foot gourmet food take-out extravaganza created by movie producer Dino De Laurentiis and located on New York City's upper West Side. A sweeping, all-glass barrel vault covered what was originally the Palm Court of the former Endicott Hotel. Incandescent theatrical lighting was used throughout the store. Stairs between levels were accented with concealed lighting. The floor material was a combination of deep blue and terra-cotta tiles. The estimated cost of the store, which also had a 5000-square foot kitchen, was $3.5 million.**

*Design:* Adam D. Tihany International, Ltd. *Photos:* Vilma Barr.

(Left) Part of the first floor in Strawbridge & Clothier's downtown Philadelphia flagship store has been transformed into an elegant and imaginative food hall. The entrance to the food hall off the main north-sourth aisle features a vintage delivery wagon. Strawbridge & Clothier was founded in 1868.

Design: Benjamin Thompson & Associates. Photo: Vilma Barr.

(Below) City Market opened early in 1984 in the lower level of the Century City Centre in Chicago's New Town section, offering up-scale take-out. An added feature (not shown) is an intimate adjacent restaurant. The Centre is a seven-level vertical mall, converted from a former movie palace, that draws on 140,000 persons (many of whom are middle-income and above) within walking distance.

Design: Planning and Design Group, Inc.

the residents of affluent sections in big cities. "Yuppies" (young urban professionals) with discretionary income are prime targets. Many of the recent U.S. food halls were inspired by Harrod's in London where world-class goodies have been dispensed for decades. In New York, Zabar's caters to the upper West Side cognoscente. In Chicago, Zambrano's and the City Market in Century City Centre aim for the same type of customer in the New Town area. Department stores with handsome new food halls and arcades include Strawbridge & Clothier, Philadelphia; Frederick & Nelson, Seattle; and Macy's New York.

- *Lawyer's offices, financial centers.* These service centers require less hardware and equipment than do medical offices. Outlets and provision for word processing stations and computer terminals are a consideration. Both storefront and shopping center locations are opening.

- *Catalog showrooms.* Catalog showrooms move lots of merchandise. Nearly every major market is served by a unit of Best Products, Consumers Distributing, Service Merchandise, or a strong local company. These are not mail-order businesses; catalog showroom customers carry their purchases out the door. Merchandise is boxed, and the larg-

Financial services are an important part of Sears, Roebuck & Co. At the end of 1983, there were financial service centers in 133 Sears stores, with that figure expected to more than double within a year. The centers offer the brokerage services of Dean Witter Reynolds, insurance services of the Allstate Insurance Group, and real estate brokerage services of Coldwell Banker real estate group.

*Courtesy:* Sears Merchandise Group.

This remodeled gift shop at Ingalls Memorial Hospital, Harvey, Illinois, features custom cabinetry and lighting. Personnel have a clear view of the activities around them from the cashier's island, a security factor. Rust-toned carpeting is identical to that in the adjacent main lobby, providing visual continuity with the rest of the hospital's first floor.

*Design:* Perkins & Will. *Photo:* Howard N. Kaplan.

est item handled will fit on top of the average automobile.

· *Museum and hospital shops.* Nonprofit museums, historical buildings, and health care institutions have found a source of considerable income from sales generated by their retail shops. Some of the major museums also do a brisk mail-order business from catalogs featuring their best sellers. These shops stock a wide range of items, ranging from 50-cent trinkets to original works of art and jewelry costing hundreds of dollars. New York's

Metropolitan Museum of Art has a midtown Herald Square branch located in Macy's.

· *Computer stores.* Computer manufacturers went into the retail business in the late 1970s to build a market for personal and small business-size computers. Now, dealers handle many different manufacturer's lines in stores located in both central business districts and outlying areas.

· *Runners' stores.* This type of store has emerged as interest in running, jogging, and physical fitness has risen. Runners' specialty stores can also be tied in with biking, swimming, and exercise. Health food products are frequently carried, along with books on sports.

· *Energy stores.* Rising fuel costs prompted the genre of stores handling ceiling fans, wood-burning stoves, insulation and weather stripping products, and solar heating systems.

### Checklist for specialty store design

1. Know the product lines: size, quantity, and quality. The Pottery Barn carries a large variety of products which vary in size and quantity. On the other hand, the Telephone Store has a product which has a limited number of styles and is basically the same size.

2. Know the targeted market: demographics, income, age, sex, buying patterns. Will shoppers tend to linger over the selection process, or do they look for the product they want as soon as they walk in the door? What are they willing to pay for in the way of attention from salespeople?

3. Analyze the products to be sold for their best features, and devise the most cost-effective and appealing means of display.

4. Develop a coordinated plan for graphics and signage. For example, stores selling computer hardware and software project their image with sleek, contemporary visual identification programs in both two and three dimensions.

5. Use appropriate colors and materials. Houston Hat & Boot, a leather goods specialty store with units in the East, Texas, and California, uses ceramic tile, natural wood, and textured painted walls.

6. Create a storefront and window design to communicate a statement of the store's uniqueness that will encourage shoppers to cross the threshold. Crate & Barrel stores in Boston and Chicago use large street-level windows to show bold, thematic displays.

7. Theft and security protection systems are a high priority for stores handling small items and for self-service outlets. Brookstone stores, which specialize in unusual hardware and gift items, display samples which are chained or fastened to counter anchors. The customer fills out an order form for the merchandise which is stocked out of sight; goods are brought forward to the wrap desk upon payment.

8. Areas hidden from visual surveillance by employees encourage shoplifters. Create an imaginative and manageable floor plan with careful placement of shelving, floor and hanging fixtures, etc.

9. Place cash-wrap counters so staff have a clear view of the entrance, displays, storage areas, and fitting room entries.

10. Make sure receiving and storage areas relate both to the requirements of the products (size and weight) and the speed of access (do customers want to take their purchases home?). For stores stocking furniture and other bulky items, warehouse aisles have to be wide enough so forklifts can easily maneuver. A shirt store, Chemiserie International, in the Short Hills Mall, New Jersey, has front-facing shirt displays so the customer can see the product as it will be worn; back-up shirts are stored in bins behind the samples.

11. Specify materials appropriate to the "wear level." Hardware and auto stores require heavy-duty finishes and fixtures. Steel shelving and vinyl floors are used in PEP Boys auto accessory stores.

Specialty stores have certain commonalities:

· *Potential for expanding:* Additions to existing product lines or new product line introductions require flexibility in the store layout. Avoid a preponderance of built-in fixtures. Benetton's, a women's apparel chain, has all store fixtures brought in just before a unit opens for business. These portable units can be moved around quickly and easily.

Safeway Stores, the largest food retailer in the world, opened a 61,000-square-foot prototype combo-style store in Arlington, Texas, in late 1982. In 1983 the chain earned $183.9 million on sales of $18.6 billion. Exposed structural framework, glass storefront, and inner skylight create an open, shopping-mall atmosphere. Red and white are the predominant colors. Departments, identified by photomurals, include cosmetics, delicatessen with salad bar and seating area, florist, pharmacy, and photo-gift shop. The plan of the store is a wide V-shape, with grocery items on one side and variety items on the other. The focal point for the store is where two sides meet in the "core," with new service areas.

*Courtesy:* Safeway Stores, Inc. 1984.

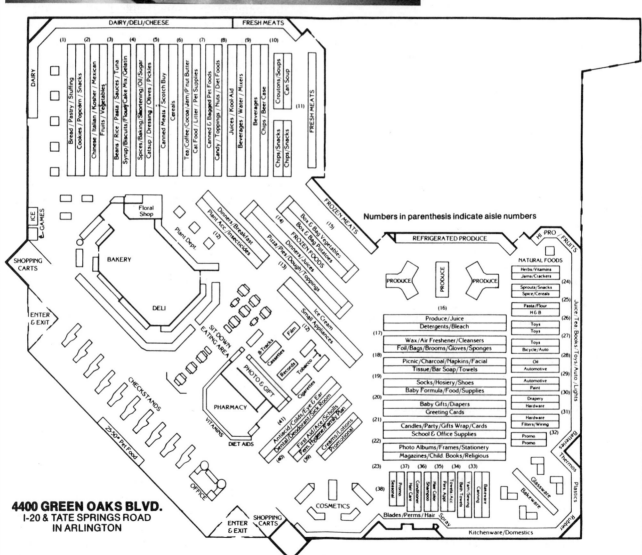

The ceiling and walls are illuminated by an overall system of fluorescent lights covered by a diffusing material.

- *Combination stores:* "Combo" stores were introduced in the early 1980s to make it easier for busy working people to take advantage of one-stop shopping. Some combinations are: food stores with banks; drugstores with book departments; book stores with coffee shops; cleaners with laundry service and shoe repair.

# Wholesale showrooms

Manufacturers and distributors establish permanent wholesale showrooms to display samples of their product lines for resale through retail outlets or other authorized agents. Architects and interior designers are familiar with trade showrooms for furniture, fabrics, floor and wall coverings, and decorative accessories located in major cities such as New York, Chicago, Los Angeles, Dallas, and Atlanta.

Showrooms for apparel, shoes, jewelry, housewares, tableware, and table and bed linens can occupy entire buildings (or districts, in New York). In recent years, new showroom buildings for both decorative and apparel goods have opened in Washington, D.C., Seattle, Philadelphia, San Francisco, and Miami. The store designer can transfer many of the concepts and recommendations outlined in earlier chapters to wholesale showroom design.

As in a retail store, the main function of the space is as a background to show off merchandise to its best advantage. Traffic, however, is more selective than in the typical retail facility; showroom sales personnel have one-on-one relationships with potential buyers who will be placing orders, in some cases, for many thousands of dollars worth of merchandise at one time. So another objective of a wholesale showroom design is to create a relaxed and comfortable atmosphere to make buyers feel that they will get all the attention needed to negotiate and place their order.

### Programming for showroom design

- *Merchandise display.*
Showrooms can be set up to display a great deal of merchandise (glassware, housewares, fabrics); as much merchandise as can reasonably fit (furniture, lighting); or very little merchandise (high-price apparel, furs, shoes). For the last category, a "salon" atmosphere is established. The salesperson puts together a customized selection from the maker's line and brings out items from concealed storage for individual consideration.

- *Conference areas.*
Buyers and salespeople will select samples on which the order will be based and then sit down in another area to discuss the store's open-to-buy, style modifications, colors, sizes, delivery schedule, etc. Catalogs describing goods not on display may also be examined.
Enclosures should be furnished with comfortable chairs, writing surfaces, and sound control. Shelving or racks to hold items under consideration may also be required.

- *Sales and executive offices.*
Some showroom locations also house corporate offices as well as work spaces for a team of showroom and territory sales representatives. Designers should determine during the data-gathering phase who will occupy office space full time, part time, or occasionally.
The office area may require computerized equipment for stock control and other management functions. Contact an office automation consultant to assist in the planning of complex installations. Large accounting and management consulting firms, office design specialists, and equipment manufacturers offer this service.

- *Special events.*
The showroom operator may want to hold receptions, luncheons, fashion shows, or seminars in the space. The designer should provide for changing

**The Garolini/Halston shoe showroom in New York City uses circular lighting fixtures and display islands, curved partitions, and built-in banquette seating. Individual conference areas are separated from the main display area.**

*Design:* Charles E. Broudy & Associates. *Photo:* Charles E. Broudy.

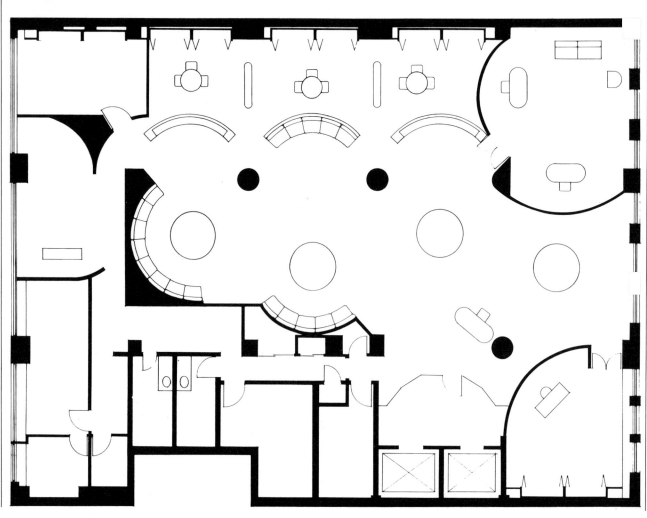

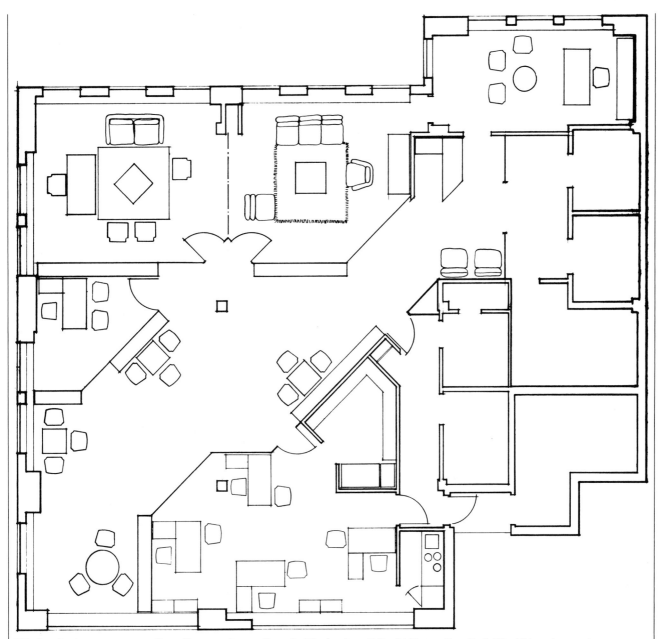

**Wholesale showroom, executive offices, and operations facility for Joan & David Shoes, New York City. This scheme places conference areas off the angled main display spine. Sound-absorbent materials help to keep conversations private.**

*Design:* Charles E. Broudy & Associates.

areas for models, extra seating with storage provided for guests, and a warming kitchen and wet bar. The floor plan should allow for efficient circulation of staff, guests, and service personnel for the various events.

# **B**ibliography

Pegler, Martin M.: "Food Glorious Food," *Visual Merchandising & Store Design*, June 1983, pp. 81–82.

# 16

# The Future of Retail Merchandising

## Introduction

Few industry observers would dispute the statement that retailing is a fast-moving business. Market trends and shifts in buying patterns need constant monitoring so that strategies may be developed, plans conceived, and monies allocated to keep retail stores busy and profitable.

Eight experts were asked to share their outlooks on "The Future of Retail Merchandising." Contributors based their comments on a list of questions that dealt with broad industry trends, short- and long-term planning, and examples of programs undertaken to improve competitive position.

Similar observations were mentioned in several of the essays. These include: targeting new departments or totally separate stores, to changing lifestyles and family work-leisure patterns; research and test marketing of new services, conveniences, and product lines; and making physical space more responsive to the needs of both the merchant and the customer. The contributors' statements provide valuable insight into the thinking of decision makers in the merchandising, development, and consulting fields.

### The store of the future

**by Edward A. Brennan**
President and Chief Operating Officer,
Sears, Roebuck and Co.,
Chicago

Sears, founded in 1886, now operates 390 full-line stores and 355 medium-size stores, most of which will ultimately be remodeled. In addition, Sears has 68 hard-lines stores. We have an incredible franchise with the American public, representing 36 million households who actively but selectively shop at Sears. That is 24 million with a current balance on their credit accounts, and another 12 million unduplicated, noncredit catalog customers.

With that kind of base, the challenge is not to get more people into the stores. We have the traffic. Rather, we want to sell those customers already there a broader assortment of goods and services. In some cases, we want to sell them the same goods and services but in much greater depth. Early in 1981, we began to discuss Sears strategy for the 1990s in terms of merchandise assortment and presentation.

First we studied what the competition was doing in department stores, discount stores, or specialty stores. Then we turned inward, asking our entire buying organization to analyze every product line and tell us where their particular industry is going and where they are taking us. The 6-month review climaxed in December 1981 with 2 months of meetings with senior management to discuss revising departments and discontinuing or adding lines of merchandise. The purpose was to develop a store more closely attuned to the Sears customer's shopping habits, wants, and needs.

# Sears strategy

Our strategy is simple and straightforward: to effectively combine Sears traditional leadership in hard lines with a new, more customer-responsive approach to such opportunity areas as men's and women's apparel, sporting goods, and home fashions. The goal is to maintain position for those product lines which already dominate their markets while identifying and strengthening those offering real potential for growth. As part of this process, we challenged each Sears buyer to literally lift up his or her line and examine it. If it needed fixing, fix it. If it couldn't be fixed, discontinue it.

That meant determining where the industry was for a particular product and more importantly where the industry was going. Then we asked the buyers to stand back and look at that line through the eyes of the target customer, asking themselves these questions: (1) If I were shopping for this merchandise, would I be motivated to buy? (2) Does what I see presented in the store or on the catalog page tell me that "this is the place" for this kind of merchandise?

In other words, does the line make a dominant statement? If the answer was "no," or even "maybe," we challenged them to make whatever adjustments were necessary in assortment, departmental adjacencies, or presentation so that all product lines could make a consistently stronger statement at point of sale.

# Implementation

As a result, we have literally torn apart the store on paper and then reassembled the more than 770 lines that comprise it into a new, more exciting environment. In many instances, we took a new concept for a department or group of departments and installed it in various existing Sears stores around the country. There we were able to accurately gauge customer response to a new departmental treatment by comparing the sales and profit results of the prototype with those of control stores in the same markets.

Some 200 merchandise lines were moved to new departments and were tested in existing stores. We have dropped 30 lines from the total assortment. Task forces from each area of the business took parts of the recommendations and tested concepts at different stores throughout the country. A prototype home improvement department was tested at Houston's Willowbrook Mall store, apparel at Vernon Hills near Chicago, automotive at West Dundee, also near Chicago, and home fashions in Burlington, Massachusetts.

We were so pleased with the test-market results of the experimental departments that we brought them all together and completely remodeled the 10-year-old Vernon Hills store from top to bottom with all the up-to-date improvements. Sears formally unveiled its first built-from-the-ground-up "store of the future" in King of Prussia, outside of Philadelphia. In November 1983, Sears announced a $1.7-billion, 5-year expansion and remodeling program that will bring the store-of-the-future concept to most Sears stores across the country.

Sears really is introducing dramatic changes to be made in the only true department store in the industry today, not in the sense of higher prices but in the context of offering a broad array of goods, soft lines and hard lines alike. This is particularly significant at a time when almost all the retailers who used to carry a wide assortment of merchandise have become increasingly specialized. Often, in selecting a niche, they have walked away from entire businesses such as appliances, paint, and automotive in order to focus more narrowly on others—apparel, home fashions, or housewares.

# The store of the future

Building on strengths and logical department adjacencies, the store of the future is truly a collection of powerful distinctive lines, *grouped in a manner that makes a dominant statement within the framework of the total store*. At a time when the word "innovative" is seldom used to describe the general merchandising industry, King of Prussia proves the exception:

- A retailing environment that is broad enough to accommodate the wide range in tastes and values we know our customers represent, yet is specialized enough to appeal to their ever-changing expectations and lifestyles
- A dynamic merchandising statement built around the right mix of Sears and important national brand goods, contributing to a stronger presentation in areas such as sporting goods, apparel, and home fashions
- A store that provides a perceptibly higher level of customer service at point of sale with an expense structure we can afford

We are running some of the largest increases in new departments created out of the fragments of others, boosting all categories in the process—a strong indicator that our new concept works. It also demonstrates what we have long suspected: Sears has the right merchandise. But often we made it too difficult, or confusing, for customers to find it. Three examples come to mind of how the store of the future has brought new organization and discipline to our goods:

· Our new housewares statement now includes a food preparation shop, table appliances, dinnerware, table linens, lighting, and clocks. To create this environment, we introduced lines previously scattered throughout four different departments and moved five others to departments where they more logically belong.
· An expanded lawn and garden area focuses on four key, related businesses: lawn mowers and riding equipment; growing goods; grills and outdoor furniture; and in season, Christmas trim.
· Sears' new electronics shop is undoubtedly the fastest-growing area in retailing today.

Overall, the theme is "soft tech." In addition to computers and software, major segments are video including the new dominant "wall-of-eyes" presentation; audio; photography; and communication. We want the customer to feel confident in the products offered and the people selling them. Both will become increasingly important as the trend to more in-home use of electronic gear gains momentum.

# Design elements

In the store of the future we have adopted a dual-aisle approach throughout apparel departments, which provides main-aisle exposure for all shops. Each of the following design elements contributes to the overall ambience at King of Prussia. The atmosphere has warmth and appeal often lacking in traditional Sears stores.

· Vaulted ceilings at the mall entrances, set off by indirect lighting
· Clearly defined ceiling heights with lower 10-foot ceilings in apparel and home fashions, rising to 12 feet in other areas of the store
· Individualized lighting throughout, giving a softer look to apparel and home fashions, with spots carefully positioned to heighten merchandise presentation
· Specially designed transition areas, set off by cased mannequins; decoratives; softer lighting, to gradually inform the customer that he or she is moving from one room in the store to another
· A glass-enclosed escalator that heightens the impact and drama of the total store

# Services: accelerated modernization

Financial services are an important part of the store of the future, offering the brokerage services of Dean Witter Reynolds, insurance services of the Allstate Insurance Group, and real estate brokerage services of the Coldwell Banker real estate group. At the end of 1984, 300 Sears stores across the nation had financial service centers. By that time, Sears also had 110 stores of the future. In 1985, we will open nine new stores and remodel 117 stores to bring the total number of stores of the future to 236 at the end of 1985.

Our 5-year program calls for remodeling of more than 600 stores and construction of 62 new stores. This decision is consistent with an overall facilities direction which emphasizes the accelerated modernization of existing retail stores over pure expansion.

## The retailer: on the outside looking in on the customer

Marion Katz

**by W. Scott Ditch**
Vice President and Director of
Corporate Public Affairs,
The Rouse Company,
Columbia, Maryland

Planning by hunch and imitation is out. In its place is analysis and investigation using increasingly sophisticated and scientific methodologies.

Major merchandising institutions and developers like The Rouse Company are studying lifestyles, trends, and buying patterns more closely than ever. This practice will spread down from the large companies to other segments of the industry.

Over the past 15 years, significant changes in the retail distribution field have hit the marketplace:

· There are fewer pristine cow pastures on which to construct regional megamalls. Interest has shifted to urban marketplaces, festival centers, and remodeling and remerchandising of existing shopping centers and malls.
· Sushi and quiche are now household words. How important is a gourmet take-out? What is a fad, what will become a trend, and what will turn into a standard item or service?
· Who heard of running stores 10 years ago? Or discount book stores? How thinly can the market be sliced? When and where will the shakeouts occur?

## Probing the market

I joined The Rouse Company as assistant director of research in 1963. There has been a steady rise in our marketing orientation as we have adopted more scientific methods of evaluating markets.

There are all sorts of ways to probe and test the market. A few years ago, the Stanford Research Institute developed a values and lifestyle approach. Our market research programs now involve working with focus groups and behavior groups, and studying lifestyles and price points.

We are redefining each marketplace where our shopping centers are located. Psychographic techniques help to determine the market profile. Is it younger, older? Do we want an upper-price women's specialty store or not? It is not enough today to just rent space; we must know precisely what we want to include as part of the tenant mix.

# Relate design to the consumer

The Rouse Company coordinates the design of its projects but does not design individual stores. We have developed or operate 61 properties and are currently working on a dozen more—St. Louis, New York City, San Francisco, Denver, Baltimore, and Atlanta, to name a few.

The most successful store design relates itself to what the consumer really is: natural, not flashy or garish. The materials used should be compatible with the surroundings.

We encourage retail store design innovations that will integrate the unit store to the larger whole in which it will function—center or mall, urban or suburban.

# The sleeping giants

A few years ago, critics were lamenting "The Malling of America," citing the proliferation of shopping centers ringing urban areas. Now, our firm's sights have shifted from finding underutilized farmland on which to build a commercial center to identifying and taking advantage of tremendous opportunities in existing centers. These are the sleeping retailing giants of the industry.

We are acquiring viable older centers and making changes as needed to reposition them in maturing markets. These centers range in size from 320,000 square feet to 700,000 square feet and include the Staten Island Mall, the Connecticut Post Center in Milford, the 28-year-old Mondawmin Center, Baltimore, and South DeKalb Center, near Atlanta.

We are actively involved with the return of retailing to center city in several metropolitan areas. We are concerned, however, that too much imitation and sameness will cause cities to lose their own character.

When chain stores replay their profit formula from city to city—duplicating store design, merchandise selection, and presentation—the chain operator can benefit handsomely. But, what will be the long-term effect on how downtowns will look in the next decade and beyond? Will the cookie-cutter school of merchandising lead to the elimination of differentiation in regions around the United States?

Cities should rediscover what they are. Retailing can help them do this.

How the development of retail clusters will be handled is crucial to the future economies of downtowns. Our company has done Grand Avenue in Milwaukee and Harborplace in Baltimore, among others. Our decisions were based on projected economics and benefits to the community from institutional and social changes.

In 1974, James Rouse addressed a design conference at the Harvard Graduate School of Design and told his audience of students and practioners that "design should no longer be a redefinition of visual delight but should support the ingredients of communities." His statement is just as true today for retailing and other elements of our built environment.

## The Gap broadens its appeal

John Blaustein

**by Donald Fisher**
Founder and Chief Executive Officer,
The Gap Stores,
San Bruno, California

The store of the future will appeal to a targeted market. We want The Gap stores to be known as "The Casual Clothing Store with All American Good Taste." Jeans-related casual clothing for men and women is what we have become known for. Each Gap unit is a no-nonsense store selling a very basic product. Our stores will be upgraded to have the most effective fixtures and displays.

The Gap has grown from a single store in 1969 to over 600 in 1985. The original stores in the now nationwide chain developed from the concept of a basic store selling 100 percent Levi, Strauss products. This then developed into a store selling private-label jeans, tops, sweatsuits, and athletic outfits.

Super Gap stores of approximately 10,000 to 20,000 square feet were opened starting in 1982. They have a high-tech look, with exposed roof joists, fluorescent lighting, vinyl floors, neon lighting, and an electronic message board.

The 10-year-old supergraphics theme will be replaced. Our aim is to attract more mature people to shop for themselves, as well as their children. A new storefront design will display quality merchandise so shoppers can see a sampling of the selections inside.

When customers enter the store, they will see Gap apparel against a tasteful, "soft look." In older Gap stores, side walls sometimes ran for more than 100 feet without a break. Now, there will be more intimate spaces which will tell individual fashion stories.

Typical round display racks are uninteresting and present a cluttered look. They will be replaced. We will exhibit merchandise in bins, tables, shelves, and display units of varying styles and colors. Our own family of fixtures will include such vehicles as ladders, dowels, and slat walls which will permit our salespeople to change displays themselves. Each store manager will receive a complete visual merchandise presentation kit with complete instructions on how to create effective displays. The manual will be the basis for design uniformity throughout the chain; it is a technique that a chain our size can and must do that a smaller chain cannot.

Other elements of our program are as follows:

· Energy-conscious lighting will augment the store's design and the merchandise. Fluorescent and incandescent spot lighting will be mixed.
· Colors and materials will have a timeless, nonintimidating appeal.
· Storage and receiving will be kept to a minimum. We want the merchandise on the sales floor.
· Fitting rooms will be upgraded. Security lights and locked doors (when the rooms are not in use) will be retained.
· Signage, packaging, and overall graphics will be improved. A coordinated identity program will encompass labels, tags, sizing, and even hangers.

A total of approximately 50 Gap stores a year will either be upgraded or will be new additions to the chain. Our units are in shopping centers and malls and in central business districts. Super Gap stores are freestanding and have adjacent parking.

The Gap stores' image is that of presenting a fair-value, moderate-cost, fundamental, quality-produced product. Our management will continue to be flexible in its response to the lifestyles and dress trends of its customers. We seek new opportunities to expand lines of merchandise into other areas and develop new types of retail to further the taste and style for mass America.

## Shifts in merchandising strategies spur store design responses

**by James B. Klutznick**
Senior Vice President,
Urban Investment and Development Co.,
Chicago

When designing a shopping center, we plan it by the mix of general merchandise categories (i.e., department stores, food and entertainment facilities, and smaller shops) in the center. The theory is similar to that used by individual stores where the design reflects the merchandising within the specialty, whether it is clothing, shoes, hardware, or whatever. Major trends in store design move with pricing policies and how they interact with one another. The logic I see in retail design stems from the pricing objectives the retailers set: what kind of margin they are trying to get, and where they are trying to get it from. Merchants who buy cheaply and sell on a thin margin with volume cannot afford as much embellishment in store design. As the margin grades up, it allows for more room to create an environment.

## Four types of pricing dictate retail design

The basic types of retail stores operating today according to pricing are:

· Factory outlet
· Discount
· Off-price
· Full retail

There have been very significant changes in the last couple of years, induced by economic conditions. The emphasis on value has spawned the "off-price" stores, which are proliferating today. From the standpoint of design, they are a different idiom from the old discount operation.

## Off-price's niche

The off-price concept fits the niche between what was traditionally discount and full retail. Some off-price stores have created nicely designed environments. At Cohos, in the metropolitan Hartford, Connecticut, area, the owner took what could have been a typical discount environment and very imaginatively put in the right motifs, just a touch of this and that. For example, there is a skylight in the middle. Now, you never saw that in a discount store. He created a new environment. He used nice-looking fixtures and decent carpeting. It is a mix between high tech and traditional.

With high tech, you can get a lot for the price. The engineering and design of a fixture actually can be stylish. Lighting fixtures can be hung without adding a dropped ceiling because girders themselves can be part of high-tech design. Thus, off-price retailers do not have to spend as much for finishing as full-retail specialty stores. Instead, they are using a good high-tech design.

# Design upgrade and service

There has been a general upgrading of retail store design. There is a significant difference in the quality of interior finishes as you go up the scale. The more merchants can make from their goods, the more they can afford to give the customer in the quality of the environment. Thus, full-retail merchants can and should provide the best design environments.

It is the same with service. I think some of the specialty and department stores missed the boat when they decided to cut service during economically hard times. People decided that, yes, it was nice to be in a pleasant environment, but if they could not get someone to wait on them, they might as well go to a place where they can get value, so they gave up the environment.

People have recognized where the variations are and how to adjust to them. They do not need service or environment if they can save 50 percent off the cost of a nationally, or internationally, known brand of merchandise. To counter this trend, many full-line retailers are going back to what they gave up years ago: private brand names. They are using their own label so customers can distinguish their merchandise from generally traded brands.

## Designing for a changing marketplace

Stuart-Rodgers

**by M. Leanne Lachman**
President,
Real Estate Research Corporation,
Chicago

A few years ago, we interviewed chain store owners to find out if they owned or leased their properties. Somewhat surprisingly, as many were switching from owning to leasing as were switching from leasing to owning. Each company's decision reflected its own cash and financial profile.

In our years of talking with retailers and observing the merchandising scene, it appears that the most successful merchants do the things that others in the business are not doing—and usually do not have the imagination or nerve to do. That is how they achieve a profitable edge in the huge and ever-changing market.

We have seen—not only in retailing but in housing and office development—a marked shift over the last 25 years away from a mass-market concept characterized by a relatively homogeneous demographic profile. There had been a standardized household profile that fit nearly every metropolitan area. Not everyone has realized that we have been steadily losing that mass market. The prototypical family of the 1950s (working father, nonworking mother, and 2.5 school-age children) today represents only 12 percent of the total U.S. households.

Some retailers are still thinking about the kinds of products that they want personally—and that their generally atypical families want—and not necessarily about what the larger and more diverse market wants. This is one of the reasons there has been slow revitalization of neighborhood strip areas. Older merchants in those centers are doing business the same way they have always done businesss, not recognizing that the surrounding population has changed dramatically, that a different kind of merchandising is appropriate for today's households. Now, there is child buying power, teenage buying power, wife buying power, husband buying power, young single adult buying power, middle-aged single adult buying power, and elderly buying power. And each of those categories has further socioeconomic divisions.

At the same time, there are innovative, dynamic younger retail companies that are burgeoning. Once they are successful in one area, they franchise across the country, and a whole new chain is born. These chains will be successful over time, though, only if they change their product presentation continuously.

## Changes in household composition

We have today a highly diverse population in highly diverse households. The biggest difference is between households with children and households without children. The latter have a much higher level of disposable income. They eat out more, they buy more luxury items, and they are the patrons of the gourmet food stores that are springing up around the country. They are the big discretionary spenders. Much of all high-end merchandise is sold to non-child-oriented households.

Families with children were caught as inflation rose in the late 1970s. They have more fixed expenditures: education, food and clothing, housing. Even though a high portion of adult female family members are now employed, there is just not the same quantity of discretionary income as in the nonchild families. Families with children are very important to discounters, however.

Discounters also take advantage of discretionary spenders' price sensitivity to basic goods. I have asked friends, "Where did you buy your can opener?" Eighty percent say, "At a discount store." Where they buy a fancy dress or a good-quality suit is not so price-sensitive a decision. But with a can opener, why should they pay more than they have to? They may go to the high-end outlet to purchase towels and sheets for a guest room. But for the children's rooms, they go to a discount store or wait for sales at the better stores.

The stores having trouble now are the traditional department stores. Those that have successfully adopted the boutique approach, like Macy's, are doing well. Flexibility is essential. Smaller retail businesses have less space to work with and a narrower image to change, but they have to be as adaptable as the larger stores.

## One-on-one retail design

The designer who wants to serve the merchant should read the trade papers. He or she should know the terms the merchant uses. In designing for a retail store, you are much closer to the client than when working with banks or office users. Merchants make the designer part of the family and want to work closely together—as they should because the retailer is the one with the real understanding of customer behavior.

To be good retailers, merchandisers have to be highly attuned to who their customers are and why they are purchasing. They like to see the same market sensitivity in their designers. They want that same "touchy, feely" quality. Designers are accustomed to the taste-arbiter role. Now, they are working for merchants who tell them what is going to work. That is a very difficult situation for most designers. If they are working with successful merchandisers, however, they should be listening and learning more than they are giving advice. Profitable retailers are constantly looking for ways to increase their share of the market. To have credibility with their clients, designers have to come across as equally motivated by higher profits as the merchants.

# Pace of retail construction

An average of 300 new shopping centers have been built each year since 1980. In the 1970s, the annual rate was 1000, or more than three times as high. We predict that the 300 figure will continue through the 1980s.

Half of shopping center construction expenditures are on expansion of existing centers rather than on new construction. Stores in renovated centers are smaller, which means there is higher productivity per square foot, based on denser selling. Merchants are stocking less and putting more out on the floor. Back-of-the-house areas have steadily shrunk. There is less storage on site because of the high rent. Merchants now use warehouses or require more frequent shipments from suppliers to the stores.

Chain retailers continually change prototypes and rehabilitate their stores. It is important for them to maintain a distinctive image in the marketplace as the population ages and changes. Merchants who attract a significant market will regularly budget expenditures for interior finishing and remodeling.

There is a basic rule in market research that you should never analyze your own neighborhood because of bias: You have your personal preferences, and you see your neighborhood your own way. Everyone who designs for retailing has to separate personal taste from what has marketing appeal—often two completely different things. Designers have to watch what people around them do when they shop and then tailor design for them.

# New categories of stores

Supermarket chains are now experimenting with combo stores. Food has the lowest profit margin in the business, and operators are trying to add products that have a higher profit margin, like electronics, books, liquor, and pharmaceuticals. These supermarkets and large drugstores are turning into convenience department stores. They are broadening selections so their customers, the majority of whom are busy working people, can make the most efficient use of their shopping time.

Specialty food stores are growing dramatically at the same time that giant one-stop shopping is expanding. High-end goods retailing is increasing concurrently with discounters. Similarly, fast-food sales are up, along with growth in upper-price restaurants.

There used to be a limited number of types of stores. No more. Now the variety is nearly endless—whatever somebody dreamed up last week is the latest category. This creates difficulties for the mass retailers but enormous opportunity for the smaller store that is carefully targeted. The target is constantly moving, however. What has evolved in retailing is a much richer and more diverse merchandising palette across the country.

## Store design and successful competitive differentiation

Frank Ziegler

**by Anthony W. Miles**
Vice President,
The Boston Consulting Group,
San Francisco

Competition has intensified as population growth has slowed and the endless expansion of suburbs, with new sites available at a steady rate, has ceased. The intensity of retail competition in cities like Houston and Phoenix—with out-of-towners rushing in and the threat of serious overstoring—is symptomatic of this phenomenon.

It is simply no longer adequate to assume that sites will always be available or that a few stores in a fast-growing area will do the job for a chain. The importance of maximizing the customer draw of a store and of maximizing the yield from a site—both closely related to a strongly differentiated and clearly evident presence in an SMSA—have never been greater. They will become more so.

To these pressures for a comprehensive and thoroughly thought-through retail strategy—covering everything from city selection through merchandising to store design—have been added economic fluctuations and a significant series of demographic shifts. There are more extremely well-managed chains to contend with, and there is more innovation in terms of new chain concepts. Retailers have come to need more professionalism, a fully coordinated approach, and a set of quick reflexes. These needs will only intensify.

Store design is one essential component of these new strategies. The external and internal appearance of the store, and its overall ambiance, are a critical part of making a competitively differentiated appeal to potential customers. Because retailers can no longer assume that people find shopping a pleasure, presence in the store must now deliberately be made into a pleasant experience, appealing in itself. Store atmospherics must then reinforce the investment of time in the store, reinforce the choice of merchandise, and reinforce the price-point choice—and they must subtly guide purchasing behavior. This is no small requirement.

Over the next decade it will be the chains who recognize these needs—and the fact that they will not be able to depend on a design's lasting 10 or more years—who will draw ahead of their competitors.

# Retail innovation

Retailing is a ferment of innovation. It is one area where experimentation is relatively cheap and easy. However, as with most businesses, it is not the biggest and currently most successful competitors who are usually the innovators—they are preoccupied with discipline and system consistency, and they feel they have the most to lose. Their organizational cultures rarely encourage much risk taking, and they do not know how to manage and reward individuals who want to try a daring experiment on the side.

The innovation takes place among the start-ups and spin-outs, by people with a fresh outlook, little to lose, and the prospect of building wealth for themselves. The ideas of the future are tried out in new store concepts that one has to search out on the streets themselves.

To this must be added a new component, the people from outside retailing whose business has been taking on a retailing flavor. For too long retailers have comforted themselves that theirs is a unique world and that only a lifetime in the business could prepare one for success. As retailing itself changes—for example, as a result of the increasingly pervasive impact of electronics—it is no longer so clear who has the comparative advantage. It will be a grave mistake to assume that all these "outsiders" who intrude into retailing will fail—they have none of the constraints on imagination that too much experience can sometimes bring, and they need to be watched with care and openmindedness.

Retailers need a carefully organized competitive intelligence-gathering program, one that is looking for ideas that will work. Nothing is more dangerous than an attitude of "dismiss it, lest it be evil." As store design has become more central to a strategy of successful competitive differentiation, this is one aspect of innovation that must be consciously monitored. This calls for a more outwardly aware, competitively focused approach to planning than most retailers currently practice.

# The impact of electronics

Many aspects of consumer behavior and the demographic balance of the population are bound to change over the next 15 years. These changes will affect retailing in ways that are still difficult to perceive. However, the key question facing retailers over that period is the likely impact of electronics.

A great deal has been made of the prospects for at-home shopping through telecommunications. There are many experiments underway.

The full impact is still unclear and will be for some time, but it is obvious that there will be some fundamental changes for the industry.

The key questions for store design will be:

· What is the role of the store? Does it become a showroom only, an order-taking point or a service counter? What will this mean for the atmospherics and size of the store or its location?
· What categories of merchandise will be affected, and in what ways? What will this mean for layouts and display techniques?
· How do you accommodate electronic retailing equipment in the store and still keep a consistent and appealing appearance and traffic flow? What takes precedence: convenient electronic equipment or merchandise?

Change will be slower than the wildest futurologists predict because too many behaviors have to change and a great deal of facilitating still needs to be done. But retailers are on the critical path in this process of change, and those who are planning now and preparing a steady and comprehensive program of innovation should emerge with a major advantage. Successful harnessing of electronics should provide a more substantial competitive barrier than has existed in retailing in the past, and consistent store design will be central to success in the overall electronic retailing strategy.

## Bendel's reduces space, expands sales

by **Geraldine Stutz,**
President,
Henri Bendel,
New York

In 1980, with a group of backers, I investigated the possibility of opening 12 Henri Bendel stores in major markets across the country—Chicago, Houston, Dallas, San Francisco, Beverly Hills, and others. We visited these cities and concluded that the United States was overstored in Bendel's markets. Stores like Lord & Taylor, Saks Fifth Avenue, and Marshall Field were already there and doing a good job.

We also concluded that these stores all looked very much alike. One after another—beige travertine marble, mobiles, chandeliers, and criss-crossing escalators floating in the middle of the store—they seemed to present the same message.

It was too costly to expand Bendel's New York store on 57th Street off Fifth Avenue, and too costly not to expand our business. Our decision was *not* to expand the store physically but to go into the catalog mail-order business. This seemed to be a solid, long-range approach to expansion. So "Bendel's By Mail" was established in the shadow of the Queensboro Bridge.

At the same time, we reduced the amount of space we occupy on 57th Street. This 10-story building is 100 feet deep and has a 72-foot frontage; we had occupied all of it, using six floors for selling and the remainder for receiving, marking, offices, and other back-of-the-house activities. Now, there are four and a half sales floors. Much of the back of the house is now in our Queens catalog location at a much lower rent.

Since we consolidated to four and a half floors, sales have increased 12 to 15 percent annually. Our current sales volume of $25 million is generated in 20,000 square feet.

## Visual presentation sets store's image

We cater to a very small audience and a very narrow segment of the population.

Twenty-five years ago, we remade our first floor into Bendel's Street of Shops—a concept that has become the single most important design trend in American specialty stores in the last half of the twentieth century. We believe it will continue to be a valid idea, and we will not change it. Bendel's pioneered fashions in living and supplemented our clothes areas with food, quality housewares, paper products, jewelry, linens, Near East decorative items, even hardware.

Our graphics and signage are characterized by a dark brown and white stripe, and it is used in many ways: advertising, direct mail, and point of purchase.

# Importance of lighting

Lighting is the most important decorative tool in the store. It is as important an element in a store as it is in the theater. The quality of the lighting can make or break merchandise. If the lighting is great, it does not make any difference if the merchandise is on mannequins or pinned up on display boards or done as still life.

# Lofts for the future

To maintain our position as a front-runner in fashion merchandising, we will continue to try for exclusivity, originality, and innovation.

My ideal store for the future is an expanse of space—open, not enclosed, divided only by lighting and portable screens. We are presently remodeling a floor that will have open spaces. It is an abstraction of the "Street of Shops"—the same concept, really, but more illusionary.

**Specialty store retailers will build loyalty by helping customers express individuality**

Moffett Studio

**by Robert J. Witt**
Chairman and Chief Executive Officer,
Boyd's,
St. Louis, Missouri

One way for a specialty store to keep its customers and gain new ones is to give more service, more advice, and more of a shopping experience. This may fly in the face of current theories. Actually, specialty store merchants who want to communicate their store's mission will focus policies and operations so that the message gets to the target customer.

For years, men and women customers have been asking, if not pleading, "Put it together for me." Creative retailers of tomorrow will come closer to fulfilling this request, and become more profitable.

Specialty stores must demonstrate how they can satisfy each customer's wardrobe needs, not only for the highly competitive business environment but for weekend, leisure, and sports activities. Specific wardrobe presentations will offer "options of dressing," showing how various outfits can suit individual personalities. In-store display groupings will suggest ways in which men and women customers can enhance their own personality as well as confidence level through clothing selection, while shopping itself is made easier and quicker. Limited shopping time is a very real constraint. Busy people do not have much time to shop—they want to get in and get out.

## Professional fashion advisors

Boyd's, founded in 1876, has always been characterized by a high service level and has continually searched out new ways to help its customers. For example, back in 1880, Boyd's laundry service was established for the benefit of discriminating customers who deemed no other laundry compatible with the standards of care necessary for their fine shirtings.

Today's commitment to servicing its customers is evidenced by a major emphasis on sales training and the development of professional fashion advisors.

The 63-year old, six-story downtown building will soon undergo a renovation which will reduce the selling area to two and a half levels totaling 25,000 square feet of selling space. Women's wear presentations will be increased to approximately 40 percent of the selling area. The upper floors will be converted to office space by the developer.

Emphasis is on sales per square foot and productivity. We are planning to reduce square footage and increase volume; our goal is to have *more* sales help per square foot. As the volume grows, we can increase sales service. Better-trained people will produce more: The more they produce, the higher their incomes will be.

These "professional fashion advisors" will receive ongoing training and current fashion information so that they can effectively counsel their customers.

Merchandise assortments viewed on video-display terminals will never replace the appeal of well-displayed merchandise that can be seen in three dimensions and touched. The specialty store customer does not want to be served by robots but by pleasant, better-informed store personnel.

## The specialty store environment

The design of a retail specialty store should be distinctive enough to let the customer know that no other store has the same personality. The setting must project the mood and the appeal that turns customers on. At the same time, it must not detract from the merchandise. Colors and materials should blend together *to highlight merchandise*. If the customer leaves a store and does not remember what the store looked like but recalls seeing some very exciting merchandise, then the store design can be considered successful. If the customer can envision the store setting *and* the merchandise, so much the better. If only the setting and not the merchandise stands out in the customer's memory, the design has not done what it was supposed to do.

We are constantly looking at our energy usage and the ways we use our lighting, both fluorescent and incandescent sources. Many stores today are overlit. Lighting can create a mood and an atmosphere in a store. As in many areas of design, less can be more.

Energy use discipline needs to be implanted in the minds of both managers and visual merchandisers. Do not be stingy with lighting, but handle it to its best advantage without overuse. Operating expenses and taxes per square foot keep escalating. Savings from controlled energy costs can be a very significant factor in controlling expenses.

# Merchandise mix and presentation

Specialty store sizes will range from the very small with finely focused merchandise offerings making full use of cubic space to large spaces presenting big assortments showing dominance in each merchandise classification.

Boyd's is reviewing sites of varying sizes in the St. Louis area. Our primary target audience is men and women in the 25- to 45-year-old age group. A new location should have the kind of customer traffic we want—by income, age, and education levels.

The Rouse Company is developing the St. Louis Station, a national historic landmark, into a dramatic new retail marketplace and a luxury hotel. The excitement of a festival mall near the downtown area is good for the city and good for business; I believe that most major cities can support at least one center of this type. People like to combine fun, dining, and serious shopping.

Boyd's is considering a "showcase" store which would have a very high space utilization. The men's section would cater to evening and weekend traffic coming from the mall and from the hotel. The women's department would concentrate on the professional woman looking for business and leisure apparel. A tightly defined merchandise presentation should produce high sales per square foot.

Finely edited assortments of merchandise carefully focused at its target customer and presented in a helpful and coordinated manner will give specialty stores a positive, updated image.

# Developing a Retail Store Design Practice

The market for retail store design services is a broad one. According to the Small Business Administration, there are over 1.2 million retail stores in the United States. This figure includes branch units of chains but does not include wholesale showrooms or catalog stores. (The same planning and design concepts discussed in this book for traditional retail stores also apply to the design of wholesale showrooms of both hard and soft goods.)

If you would like to get into the retail store design field or do more of this type of work, you should mount a marketing and promotional effort to win commissions. Most designers would prefer that new jobs came in over the transom. But that era has vanished, and in its place is a highly competitive environment. In many cases, architects, interior designers, contractors, and fixture manufacturers are all vying for the same jobs.

The hard economic fact is: To get the job, you have to go after it, often aggressively. The job-getting process is just that—a process. It takes planning, organizing, time, effort, and money. You have to be persistent, positive, and realistic about your "hit rate." With a systematic approach, you should start to see results in the form of new work in a reasonable period of time.

"But," you say, "I have never done [or have limited experience in] retail store design. How can I compete?"

Be generic. If you cannot point to a binder full of photos of completed jobs, *create* solutions to hypothetical case studies. Identify three to six stores in your area that could stand physical improvement (new or vintage) and sketch a couple of solutions for each. In a brief written description, tell what prompted your design decisions.

To lend more credence to the exercise, you can put some of your "designs" out to bid. Contractors with whom you work on other types of jobs or those who have a track record in retail store design should cooperate with you and submit valid figures. With these, you have material for a presentation folder or brochure.

This appendix presents an overview to planning and implementing a program to attract new business in the retail store design field. There are several fine books that deal with the marketing of professional services, and they are listed at the end of this section. Books dealing with store design are also noted.

## Analyze

A. The Market

1. Where do you want to do the work? In your neighborhood, city, state, region, or nationally?

2. What kind of work do you want to go after? Apparel, drugstores, food stores, specialty stores? To find out more about where growth has been in your market area, contact your local or state business development office, federal agencies such as the Department of Commerce or the Small Business Administration, or any of the trade groups in the fields in which you are interested. Your local business librarian can be of considerable help in this research.

B. The Competition

1. Who in your area has a strong retail design practice? Visit retail stores and find out who did the design—an outside consultant or the in-house design staff.

2. Make notes on what you like and do not like about the finished product. You might talk with some of the employees and find out what *they* think works and does not work.

3. A word of caution about photographing the inside of stores: Get approval from the owner before you take a whole series of shots. If you are doing a visual survey and prefer not to bother with photo permissions at this stage, do quick sketches or layouts.

C. Your Firm

1. What are your firm's strengths?

   a. Creativity

   b. Full-service planning, architecture, and engineering

   c. Quick response to client's needs

   d. Effective project management

   e. Computer-aided design

2. Find your niche, and promote it.

## Develop the tools

### References

Unless you have never been in business before, you have a list of satis-

## Brochures and Direct Mail Pieces That Sell

Brochures and direct mail pieces are sales-supportive tools. They must have a dynamic quality. The can be elegant and understated, and still be dynamic.

To make a sales piece come alive, it needs a clearly defined personality. Getting some photos together, making a statement of philosophy, listing some past clients and writing some brief descriptions does not make a sales piece. It is better than nothing, certainly. But does it have a market or markets? What is its objective? What goals will it help you reach? Will it strengthen your position in the marketplace?

A brochure is not going to get where you want to go by itself, overnight. Remember that a brochure is the vehicle that communicates your product, your staff, experience and quality of work. Potential customers and clients have needs. You have solutions. They get the benefits. Tell them that, clearly and emphatically, in your brochure and in person.

### Analysis and Planning

List all the design decision makers you want to read your brochure. On one side list the broad category; on the other, be specific.

| GENERAL CATEGORY | SPECIFIC GROUP |
|---|---|
| What are they interested in? | High return on investment? |
| | Wise spending of funds? |
| | Own advancement? |
| What kind(s) of training do they have? | Business? Engineering? |
| What is the general condition of their company? | Design? High growth? Flat? Operating funds reduced? |
| What would they find unique about your firm? | Cost saving examples? In-house computer? |
| Who have they used previously for your type of service? | Did themselves? Large national firm? Small local firm? |

Once you have profiled your firm's markets, profile your firm. (Or do it the other way around, if you'd prefer.) What you are really doing is developing key sales themes.

Set down what you believe you are to the outside world and then back up your statements. *Be realistic.*

| APPEAL | JUSTIFICATION |
|---|---|
| Reliable. | Tested in-house procedures. Thorough follow up to correct problems. |
| Experienced project management. | Specialists and technicians assigned to coordinate job details. |
| Full service. | Firm has own architect and engineer(or architect has interior designer and engineer, etc.) |
| Unique capability. | Offers lower fees. Computer aided design. |
| Size. | Principals give personal attention to each project. Have office in Milan to handle overseas work. |
| Excel in planning. | Have planned 10 million square feet of office space. |
| Renovation experts. | Use laser technology. |

### Give Your Brochure Readers What They Want

What do prospective clients want your sales piece to tell them? The brochure should be:
1. honest
2. as short as possible
3. written in the language of the reader
4. interesting and stimulating
5. give usable information about the projects or products shown
6. attractive

Briefly, this is the information core for a brochure or sales piece. Select what is applicable.
   Who you are and what you do
   Your location
   Your size
   Your clients/customers
   Projects, completed or underway, and location
   Services offered
   How you are organized
   Key staff members

Some firms want a brochure that is an expanded calling card. Others want a compendium of their career's work. Flexibility allowing customizing of brochures to fit specific users or groups suits some firms quite nicely. Others want a bound brochure they can just pick off the shelf at any time.

**This checklist contains the elements of an effective print piece for a design firm.**

A compact four, six, or eight page brochure that can be carried by the dozen in a briefcase is favored by some to give out like a business card and follow up with a complete brochure sent in the mail. Still others like a combination of a "quicky" handout brochure followed up by another form of collateral, either a more in-depth brochure or a series of project or information sheets, bound in a folder.

### What To Say and How To Say It

Not only should the copy be brief, it should sound natural and effortless. So many brochures are written in "designese." People do not talk in stiff and stilted designese or "technese," but many are written that way. The best brochure copy when read aloud sounds as if someone were talking or making an oral presentation. It could be well-rehearsed, but it sounds natural. *It contains punchy statements and dramatic words that evoke clear and exciting mental images to the reader.*

### Tips on Layout and Printing

■ **Visual Comprehension.** To test the quality of a graphic design, ask the question, "Is there an obstacle between the message and the reader?" Is the copy prosaic, the type face too small, the copy block too solid? Do the illustrations convey the message, focus attention?

■ **Copy and Type.** Use subheads, bullets, dingbats and other graphic techniques to break up copy and make it more readable. (A dingbat is a typographical ornament or symbol.)

Graphic designers believe that both serif and sans serif type faces can be used to give either a traditional or contemporary look. (A serif is: "any of the short lines stemming from and at an angle to the upper and lower ends of the strokes of a letter." "Sans serif" or without serifs lacks these extensions.)

■ **Illustrations and Photos.** The larger the image, the stronger statement you are making with it.

### COSTS

There are no hard and fast rules relating to how much you should pay for a brochure. If you are a six-person firm and can afford a 16-page, all-color piece that will cost $10 to $12 per copy because it makes good marketing sense in your analysis, that is what you should consider. If a 200-person firm wants a one-color four-page brochure that cannot cost more than $1.50 per copy, this constraint should be plugged in early.

The bigger the run, the lower the cost per piece. Small runs are expensive for the product received because the printer's set up charges have to be absorbed by fewer pieces.

Depending on the market, the brochure can last from 12-48 months. To take advantage of printing economies, order sufficient initial quantity so you will not run out in six months. Do not be careless about distribution, but do not be stingy either.

If you want to do a speculative mailing, do not send out a $5 brochure to 2,000 names from a rented mail list. Instead, get a simple companion direct mail piece and respond to qualified leads with the $5 brochure.

Should you print full four or five-color, one-color or two-colors? It really depends on the subject matter. If there is sufficient dimension in the product so that the lack of color does not significantly diminish the desired impact, b&w can be effectively used. No doubt about it, four-color commands attention.

Costs for printing vary regionally. Printers bid each job separately, depending on the number of photos and illustrations to be stripped in, and other technical factors. Most printers will not guarantee a price for more than 30 days from the date of the bid.

Make sure you get good advice on paper stock. It contributes to the overall look and mood of the piece as much as the type style and layout. The best way to narrow your choices is to do research on printed pieces you admire, and then ask your artist or printer if the stock that appeals to you will work with what you want your brochure to achieve.

fied clients. Ask them for letters of recommendation. Most will be glad to comply. Tell them that you are putting together a portfolio or brochure and that you plan to submit proposals for retail store design work. Call or write three or four current or recent clients, and request a brief note about your firm's performance. Suggest that they mention whatever qualities you want to emphasize to the retail market: style, flexibility, management capabilities, etc.

### Print pieces

The ingredients of an effective print piece are described in "Brochures and Direct Mail Pieces That Sell" (pages 190–191).

# Contacting prospects

### By mail

If your firm does not already have one, put together a mail list. Even a one-person firm can have 200 or more names as a base. The categories below will help you begin to compile your mail list.

*Mail list categories*

1. *Current clients:* Names from project files.

2. *Past clients:* Firms that have not been active with you in the past 12 months.

3. *Prospective clients:* firms you have not worked for but would like to.

4. *Vendors:* Suppliers of products or services used by your firm or specified by your firm for project work.

5. *Professional consultants:* Firms which maintain professional business relationships with your company, such as engineers, labs, accountants, bankers, and lawyers.

6. *Contractors:* General or subcontractors.

7. *Community leaders:* Elected or appointed public officials or heads of community or volunteer organizations.

8. *Press:* Local metropolitan or community newspapers; radio and TV stations; and trade and business publications reaching your identified markets.

9. *Other:* Friends; relatives; alumni association members.

With the wide availability of word processors and small computers, designers can store their firm's mail list on their own equipment. Names can be added or deleted, and updating and changes can be made easily. A simple code can recall groups of names by geography or by type of business or professional affiliation. If you do not own information storage equipment, contact a local mail house to set up and store your mail list and keep it current.

To obtain names for a mailing, you can also get in touch with a list broker. Brokers usually rent lists on a one-time basis, so you will not own the list for reuse.

What should you send? You can produce a basic brochure about your firm's work, either a special retail design brochure or a general capabilities brochure with your retail work included. If you have limited retail experience, a simple "idea" or generic brochure will get prospects thinking about your firm as store designers.

You could also send out a simple announcement that your firm is set-

ting up a new "Retail Store Design Division" to give some identity to this activity and tell what services you will be offering. Once you have completed a job, print up a case study about it (get your client's permission first) and send this out.

A periodic newsletter about your firm's work is an effective business stimulator for all areas of your practice. If you do not have a writer or graphic designer in-house, consider outside professional help in these areas. It is a wise investment. See "Where to Get Promotional Help" at the end of this section.

### By phone

Follow up your mailings with phone calls. Keep a record of this activity on 5- by 8-inch cards. (A suggested form is shown here.) Go through them regularly. Set aside a time for phoning new prospects. Early morning is usually best for many people. When you are asked to call back at a certain time, put this down on your calendar, and, as your day allows, try to call again.

Write future project information on the back of the cards, using additional cards as necessary. Keep complete prospect files, including news clippings when they apply. Add new prospects to your mail list.

# The proposal

A formal written proposal can be presented to the prospect at a meeting or by correspondence. Whether weeks of work have gone into the preparation of the offer or whether it is a simple confirmation of a conversation, the proposal still has to convey all the things which might be said by the design firm representa-

## TELEPHONE CONTACT RECORD

### LEAD

Date: (first contact)

Firm name:

Address:

Phone:

Type of business:

Lead source:

Contact(s): Prime
Secondary
Other

### PROJECT DESCRIPTION:

Where:

When:

Existing conditions:

No. of square feet:          No. of levels:

Other

Projected

No. of square feet:          No. of levels:

Other

Activities performed:

Estimated scope of project:

### ACTION

Date:

Write:

Phone:

**Calls to prospects should be recorded on a form such as this Telephone Contact Record.**

193

tive were he or she present when the proposal was under consideration.

The proposal package must communicate to those who review it the image which the design firm wishes to project. The proposal will be the most tangible product the buyer will have until the final results are available, and it becomes a measure or symbol of whether value is being obtained.

The designer's proposal to obtain a commission to create a retail store should contain the following elements:

- Background (why the proposal has been prepared)
- Approach to be used
- Scope of the product (Checklists or conceptual sketches may be included here if the designer feels this information will gain a competitive edge without giving away too many ideas that can be copied.)
- Methodology to be adopted
- Time
- Cost
- Staffing
- Conditions of contract

It would be unusual if the prospect accepted a proposal without further discussion. The offer as it is presented becomes a chopping block. The client may require more details in one section, or a facet of the services described may be eliminated or divided between the sponsor's own staff and that of the design firm. Whatever changes are introduced must be agreeable to both parties; otherwise, the likelihood of clashes at the end of the contract, if not before, is very high.

# The interview

Interviews are exercises in human chemistry. All professionals can tell when they meet a client with whom they would like to work. The client reads the professional in the same way. The purpose of the interview is to convince the client that working with you will be an interesting and rewarding experience.

The starting point of the preparation for each interview is to learn as much as possible about the conditions under which it will be held:

- *The interviewers:* How many people will be present? What are their names?
- *The physical setting:* Can slides be shown? Will there be a screen, or should your firm bring its own? Are there easels for charts?
- *The timetable:* Is yours the first or last interview of the day, or in between? How long should it last?
- *The agenda:* Are there particular subjects the interviewers would like to see or hear about?

The best source of this information is a phone call to the person scheduling the interview. Find out if the interview will be formal or informal.

Sometimes the interviewing client will be a single individual with complete authority to define the criteria, establish the terms of the working relationship, and make the selection. Developers, corporate entrepreneurs, and small-business people frequently operate in this manner. This format usually calls for an informal interview aimed at establishing rapport with the single decision maker.

Or the interviewers could be a

committee to whom has been delegated the responsibility for selection. Committees to select retail store designers are often composed of executives in merchandising, finance, engineering, visual merchandising, and administration. For this type of formal interview, five basic questions should be answered in order to plan an effective presentation:

1. What do we have to say to fulfill the formal selection criteria?
2. Who on our team will best relate to the personalities of the clients?
3. How should our people project themselves in the presentation?
4. What type of presentation media (slides, flipcharts, overhead transparencies, photo enlargements) will make it easiest to project our style?
5. What is the most important point we want the prospect to remember 10 minutes after we have left the room?

# Fee guidelines

### Negotiated fee

Negotiating a fee is an art unto itself. Experience is the best teacher: unfortunately, there are no all-purpose guidelines that clearly delineate responses to the various negotiating scenarios the designer might encounter. One basis for fee setting is knowledge of what the competition is charging for comparable work.

In the past there were standard fees endorsed by design associations, but this practice has been banned by the federal government.

### Percent of construction costs, furnishings, and fixtures

This conventional system is a holdover from the architectural profession's former standard method of compensation.

### Fee based on square footage

This form of compensation is calculated by dollars times square footage. It is often used in the office space planning field. Charles E. Broudy & Associates has used it only once, when it was requested by a large retail organization.

### Cost plus (cost-based compensation)

Compensation is computed by multiplying hourly rates by a factor of 2.5 or 3 to allow for overhead and profit. Clients often accept this arrangement with a cap, not-to-exceed, or an educated guesstimate, all of which allow the client to include the fees in the overall budget.

### Fixed fee

When all design elements are known before the actual design work begins, a fixed fee can offer fair compensation. The designer has to analyze past production time and judge the profit outcome from similar jobs. If the project runs past the projected completion date, there should be periodic fee increases; inflation affects employees' hourly rates as well as the cost of materials.

## Where to get promotional help

Personnel at headquarters of local offices of professional writing and graphics organizations can suggest consultants for you to contact for help in preparing a print piece or publicity effort. If you interview an advertising or public relations agency, find out if they really know how to sell a professional service. Many agencies are too product-oriented to make the shift into services marketing. The following list is a good starting point in locating a helpful agency.

- *Society for Marketing Professional Services:* Headquarters, Alexandria, Virginia; chapters nationwide.

- *International Association of Business Communicators:* Headquarters, San Francisco, California; chapters nationwide.

- *Public Relations Society of America:* Headquarters, New York City; offices and chapters nationwide.

- *Society for Technical Communication:* Headquarters, Washington, D.C.: chapters nationwide.

- *Graphic design organizations:* Names change from city to city. In Chicago, the Society for Typographic Art maintains an office. Many cities also have a creative directory of designers and writers which can be used as a reference.

- *Others:* Start a file of direct-mail pieces and ads that you like and then track down who prepared them. Most cities of medium size and larger have a pool of talented free-lance writers and graphics design firms who can do a good job by combining your input and a reasonable budget. Major area printers also offer design and layout services and can often recommend editorial help if they do not have writers on staff.

## Recommended references

Coxe, Weld: *Marketing Architectural and Engineering Services*, 2d ed., Van Nostrand Reinhold, New York, 1983.

Jones, Gerre: *How to Market Professional Design Services*, McGraw-Hill, New York, 1973.

Redstone, Louis G., FAIA: *New Dimensions in Shopping Centers and Stores*, McGraw-Hill, New York, 1976.

*Stores of the Year: A Pictorial Report on Store Interiors, Vol. II*, compiled and published by the Retail Reporting Bureau, New York, 1983.

White, Ken: *Bookstore Planning and Design*, McGraw-Hill, New York, 1982.

Wilson, Aubrey: *The Marketing of Professional Services*, McGraw-Hill Book Company (UK) Ltd., Maidenhead, Berkshire, England, 1972. A classic, and still the best book written on the subject.

## Bibliography

Barr, Vilma: "Sell with Your Firm's Brochure," *Interior Design*, May 1982, pp. 282–291.

Coxe, Weld: *Marketing Architectural and Engineering Services*, 2d ed., Van Nostrand Reinhold, New York, 1983, pp. 122–127.

Wilson, Aubrey: *The Marketing of Professional Services*, McGraw-Hill Book Company (UK) Ltd., Maidenhead, Berkshire, England. 1972, pp. 47–48.

# Glossary

**Accessibility.** The ease or difficulty which the customer has in reaching a given store by different forms of transportation. The three forms of transportation usually considered are automobile, public transportation, and walking.

**Additional markons.** Upward revisions of original selling prices.

**Anchor store.** A major store, typically a department store in a downtown or regional shopping center, that is able to draw customers to a shopping area.

**Associated office.** Also known as a "cooperative office," it is owned by a voluntary association of independent stores or groups of stores. The operation of the resident office is one function of the association. Other functions may include research and exchange of operating figures.

**Attraction.** The pulling force exerted by a shopping center or business district due to the presence of one or more of the factors of merchandise availability, price advantage, physical comforts, and convenience.

**Back of the house.** Stockrooms; nonselling area.

**Ballast.** A device that modifies incoming voltage and current to provide the circuit conditions necessary to start and operate electric discharge lamps.

**Book inventory.** The retail value of the inventory. It is presumed to be correct until physical inventory is taken.

**Breadth of selection.** The offering of a variety of different merchandise lines in one store or in one shopping center.

**Cash-wrap.** A counter that houses cash register and wrapping facilities.

**Central business district (CBD).** The downtown commercial area of a city. The CBD is an area of historically high land valuation; high concentration of retail businesses, offices, service businesses, and sometimes hotels and theaters; and heavy traffic flow.

**Circulation plan.** A plan showing expected customer movement throughout the sales areas. It is the basis for the location of fixtures, displays, sales counters, cash-wrap desks, and other facilities to assure maximum merchandise exposure to the maximum number of shoppers.

**Community shopping center.** A shopping area which has as principal tenant a limited-line department store unit, or one full-line department store plus a complement of other shoppers' goods facilities, as well as convenience goods units. A community shopping center usually contains an average gross leasable area of between 150,000 and 300,000 square feet on 20 to 30 acres of land.

**Comparison shoppers' goods stores.** Included in this category of stores are (1) general merchandise stores, (2) apparel and accessory stores, (3) furniture, home furnishings, and equipment stores, and (4) miscellaneous shoppers' goods stores. GAF stands for the first letters of the first three categories; the "M" and "O" in GAFM and GAFO stand for "miscellaneous" shoppers' goods and "other" shoppers' goods, respectively. Customers will typically travel farther to purchase comparison shoppers' goods than to purchase convenience goods, and they often are inclined to compare the offerings of more than one store before making a purchase.

**Compatibility.** The benefits which can be derived by placing two or more types of stores beside one another.

**Contrast.** The relationship between the brightness of an object and its immediate background.

**Convenience goods.** Merchandise that is consumed daily and purchased frequently, such as food and drugs.

**Convenience goods shopping center.** A shopping area that usually contains between 30,000 and 75,000 square feet of gross area and occupies between 4 and 8 acres of land. The principal tenants in a neighborhood convenience goods center are a supermarket and a drugstore.

**Convenience goods stores.** Food stores, eating and drinking places, and drug and proprietary stores. Customers typically will not travel as far for convenience goods as for comparison shoppers' goods, and they are not as apt to compare the offerings of more than one store before making a purchase. As a result, convenience goods stores generally have much smaller trade areas than comparison shoppers' goods stores do.

**Convenience services.** A category which includes personal service facilities, such as barber shops, beauty shops, shoe repair shops, and dry cleaning shops. Like convenience goods, these services are used very frequently.

**Cumulative attraction.** The sales advantage that results when two or more compatible retail facilities are clustered together at one location rather than being widely separated.

**Curtain wall.** A wall that "hangs" on a structural frame. In the store interior, it may be installed above the wall cases to give them a "built-in" effect.

**Demand.** The highest amount of kilowatt consumption recorded in a 15- to 30-minute period. This charge for one period of time can affect an electric bill for one year.

**Depth of selection.** A variety of different styles, sizes, and prices in any one given merchandise line.

**Diffuser.** A device commonly put on the bottom or sides of a luminaire to redirect or spread the light from a source. It is used to control the brightness of the source and in many cases the direction of light emitted by the luminaire.

**Discretionary income.** That portion of a consumer's income that remains after the necessary expenditures have been made for food, clothing, and shelter.

**Dollar sales per square foot of sales area.** The result of dividing annual sales of an area, department, or store by the number of square feet occupied by the specific area. This is an accepted method of determining the sales potential or performance for each merchandise category in each sales area, for each department, or for the entire store.

**Double hang.** Two hang rods, one over the other.

**Economizer.** A system of controls and duct work that permits "free" cooling of a building with outside air when the outside temperature and humidity are suitable.

**Energy management system.** An integrated group of products that regulate energy usage in a building. It may be a load control, an environmental control system, or a combination of the two.

**Environmental control system.** An integrated group of products that control the heating-cooling-ventilation equipment in a building.

**Exposure (or visibility).** The ability of potential customers of a store to see and recognize the store.

**Face-out.** A sloping hang-rod with balls to permit a waterfall effect in display of apparel, handbags, etc. Can be flexible.

**Fixed expenses.** Expenses that are not expected to fluctuate significantly dispite considerable changes in sales, service, or manufacturing activity. These expenses may be fixed for a year or more. Such expenses normally include rent, taxes, salaries, depreciation, etc.

**Fixture density.** The ratio of the area occupied by the sales fixtures to the total area of the sales space. The fixture density should not exceed 50 percent of the total sales area.

**Fixtures, sales.** The cases and displays used for merchandise presentations and storage.

**Fixtures, stock.** Units that are mass-produced by certain manufacturers as opposed to custom designs for specific needs of retailers.

**Footcandle.** The basic measure used to indicate level of illumination. One footcandle is equal to one unit of light flux (one lumen) distributed evenly over a 1-square-foot surface area.

**Full-line department or discount store.** A unit which offers a complete selection of soft goods, housewares, domestics, drugs, shoes, hardware, paints, auto supplies, sporting goods, toys, furniture, and appliances.

**General merchandise stores.** Retail stores that sell a number of merchandise lines, such as dry goods, apparel and accessories, furniture and home furnishings, housewares, hardware, and food. This category includes department stores,

discount department stores, variety stores ("five-and-ten-cent stores"), and miscellaneous general merchandise stores (smaller stores selling a line of merchandise similar to department stores, general stores, and catalog showrooms).

**Gondolas.** A free-standing shelving unit, usually many shelves high.

**Gross leasable area.** The total area designated for tenant occupancy and exclusive use, including basements, mezzanines, and upper floors; or the total area on which a tenant pays rent.

**Gross margin.** The amount of revenue that remains to cover fixed costs and yield a profit after all variable costs have been deducted. It is determined by finding the difference between the net cost of the goods (after cash discount) and the net sales (after all price changes, workroom costs, and inventory shortages have been subtracted).

**Gross margin percentage.** A figure calculated by dividing the dollars of gross margin by net sales for the period.

**Hardware.** Shelving and hang rod metal fixturing components.

**HID.** High-intensity discharge lighting, including mercury-vapor, metal-halide, and high-pressure sodium light sources. Although low-pressure sodium lamps are not HID sources, they often are included in the HID category.

**Household composition.** The number, sex, and age of the people in a household.

**HVAC.** Industry terminology for heating, ventilating, and air conditioning.

**Inboard.** The territory lying between the subject area and the central business district or other dominant trading centers. "Outboard" is in the opposite direction of "inboard" and includes the territory from which a proposed new facility theoretically can expect to intercept a substantial number of consumers.

**Independent office.** An enterprise whose management offers its services to such stores as wish to subscribe.

**Initial markon.** The spread between invoice cost (plus transportation, before discounts) and initial retail selling price.

**Kilowatt.** A measure of electric current and voltage equal to 1000 W.

**Lamp.** A light source, commonly called a "bulb" or "tube."

**Lens.** A glass or plastic shield that covers the bottom, and sometimes sides, of a luminaire to control the direction and brightness of the light.

**Level of performance.** A measure of operation determined through a quantitative evaluation of individual retail stores. In most retail complexes, one or two individual stores exert far more attraction than the other stores.

**Light trespass.** Distribution of light from an outdoor source onto areas where the illumination is not wanted; caused by lack of adequate beam control.

**Limited-line department or discount store.** A unit which concentrates on a complete selection of soft goods, housewares, drugs, and shoes.

**Louver.** A series of baffles arranged in a geometric pattern and used to shield a lamp from view at certain angles to avoid glare.

**Luminaire.** A complete lighting fixture including one or more lamps and a means for connection to a power source. Many luminaires also include one or more ballasts and

elements to position and protect lamps and distribute their light.

**Magnet.** The store in a shopping center or district which exerts the prime attractive force in drawing customers to the center or district. In a convenience center the magnet could be a supermarket. In a regional shopping center the large department stores would be the magnets.

**Major retail center (MRC).** A concentration of at least 25 retail stores, including at least one general merchandise store with a minimum of 100,000 square feet of floor space.

**Major shopping district.** A shopping area that contains one or more major magnets, or major department store units.

**Mall shops.** Stores in a regional shopping center other than the major department stores, typically located between two anchor stores.

**Markdowns.** Downward revisions of selling prices.

**Market penetration.** The amount of personal consumption expenditures which a specific retail operation, or a retail complex captures in a specific market area. Also called "share of the market."

**Merchandise mix.** The types of merchandise offered for sale in a specific retail facility.

**Merchandise planning.** An analysis of merchandising records and possible achievements, leading to attainment of higher merchandising goals. Studies of department areas and locations, turnover, and similar factors are helpful in determining requirements for lineal footage including space for forward and reverse stock. This type of planning, used as a guide in deciding the size and layout of a new store, is also

one of the best ways to determine whether a modernization program is indicated.

**Mezzanine (or balcony).** An area that equals less than 50 percent of the first floor and is above but open to that floor. Before completing plans, local and state building codes relating to exits, ceiling height, and other conditions should be checked.

**Minor shopping district.** A shopping district which contains a minor magnet, such as a junior department store, a large apparel store, or a number of specialty shoppers' goods facilities along with convenience goods facilities.

**Multiple packing.** Many items are bought in twos and threes if they are packed that way—with or without a reduction in price. Sheets and pillowcases packed in pairs are a good example.

**Neighborhood center.** A shopping area that provides for the sale of convenience goods (foods, drugs, and sundries) and personal services (laundry and dry cleaning, barbering, shoe repairing, etc.) for the day-to-day living needs of the immediate neighborhood. It is built around a supermarket, which is the principal tenant. In theory, the neighborhood center has a typical gross leasable area of 50,000 square feet. In practice, it may range in size from 30,000 to 100,000 square feet. The neighborhood center is the smallest type of shopping center.

**Net income.** Income before income taxes; determined by deducting from net sales or net revenue all the expenses for the year or the accounting period under study.

**Net selling area.** The area devoted wholly to retail sales, not including storage, mechanical, and office space.

**Open-to-buy.** The open-to-buy tells a merchant how much merchandise, at retail, can be added to inventory at a given time without exceeding planned figures.

**Operating profit.** The amount remaining after expenses are subtracted from gross margin.

**Overcounter selling.** The showing of merchandise to a shopper by a salesperson stationed behind a showcase or counter.

**Owned office.** An office under the same corporate ownership as the stores it serves. Its facilities are not usually available to outsiders.

**Pedestrian circulation.** The pattern of pedestrian movements between shopping facilities. Circulation patterns are determined largely by the desire of consumers to accomplish their shopping with maximum efficiency.

**Personal consumption expenditures.** The amount of total gross income which consumers spend for goods and services. The amount which consumers spend for various types of goods varies greatly depending upon income level, stage of family development, and many other factors.

**Primary shoppers' goods.** Goods whose expense, rate of depletion, and frequency of purchase make them intermediate between convenience goods and secondary shoppers' goods. Apparel, shoes, and books, are examples. These goods are typically more expensive, less rapidly used up, and less frequently purchased than convenience goods. However, they are typically less expensive, more rapidly consumed, and more frequently purchased than secondary shoppers' goods.

**Primary trade area.** The area in which a shopping area or establishment will have its greatest influence (highest capture rates). The primary trade area is typically defined so that residents of the area will account for 60 to 70 percent of the sales of the area or establishment, although this figure varies considerably.

**Private brands.** A private-labeled brand of merchandise carried in a department or specialty store.

**Productivity.** Annual sales per square foot of gross leasable area.

**R-factor.** Resistance of an insulating material to heat flow. The higher the R-factor, or R-value, the better the insulator.

**Reflector.** A device used to redirect the light from a lamp or luminaire by the process of reflection.

**Regional shopping center.** A major center that has two or more major department store units as its principal tenants. Such centers also contain a full complement of other shoppers' goods units and normally a full complement of convenience goods facilities. The gross leasable area of a regional shopping center may range from 400,000 square feet to more than 1 million square feet. The land requirements are normally approximately 50 acres, in some instances they are 100 acres or more.

**Rounders.** Circular hanging racks.

**Secondary shoppers' goods.** Expensive shoppers' goods, including such items as furniture, major appliances, and automobiles. Because of their expense and their relatively long useful life, these goods are purchased less frequently than primary shoppers' goods. Consumers typically will travel much greater distances to shop for secondary goods than for most other goods, and brand names assume much greater importance.

**Self-selection.** Merchandise displayed on fixtures to encourage the shopper to touch, examine, and select items without pressure by sales personnel. Salespeople are present to give service when asked to do so.

**Self-service.** Merchandise is on open display so that the shopper selects items from the gondolas or wall units without sales help. Very often, shoppers enter the area through a gate and exit via a checkout counter. Signage is essential since shoppers are on their own.

**Set appeal.** The attractiveness of articles sold in sets, such as dinnerware.

**Shopping center.** A group of commercial establishments planned, developed, owned, and managed as a unit related in location, size, and type of shops to the trade area the unit serves. It provides on-site parking in relationship to the types and sizes of stores.

**Shopping district.** A shopping area of varied composition; may range from a neighborhood convenience goods facility to an extremely large complex including full-line department store units and a full complement of shoppers' goods and convenience goods facilities. In most instances, business districts are referred to as "unplanned centers," and new shopping centers which are controlled by one ownership are normally referred to as "planned developments" (cf. Strip development, Minor shopping district, and Major shopping district).

**Standard metropolitan statistical area (SMSA).** Metropolitan areas defined by the federal government for purposes of data reporting and allocations of certain federal grants. In general, an SMSA includes an urbanized area with at least 50,000 inhabitants and the county or counties in which it is located.

**Standards and brackets.** Metal hardware that supports shelving or hang rods. An adjustable system.

**Stock overage.** A condition in which the physical inventory of a store or department is higher than the book inventory.

**Stock shortage.** A condition in which the actual physical inventory of a store or department yields a lower retail figure than the book value.

**Stock turn.** A measure of the velocity with which a store's inventory turns over. Within reason, the more times each year that a stock is sold, replaced, and sold again, the more profitable the merchandising operation is likely to be.

**Strip development (or ribbon).** A planned or unplanned shopping area that usually stands apart from other major commercial centers and is often limited to a few stores along one side of a traffic artery. Strip developments do not usually contain major shoppers' goods facilities, such as a department store, but there are exceptions to this rule.

**Superregional center.** A shopping area that provides extensive variety of comparison shoppers' goods (general merchandise, apparel, furniture, and home furnishings), as well as a variety of services and recreational facilities. It is built around at least three major department stores of generally not less than 100,000 square feet each. In theory, the typical size of a superregional center is about 750,000 square feet of gross leasable area. In practice, the size ranges to more than 1 million square feet.

**Time-of-day.** A calendar-clock preprogrammed to turn designated equipment on and off at specific times that may vary according to day of week or for holidays.

**Trade area.** The geographic region from which most of the continuing patronage of a shopping area or store is obtained. Some analysts designate primary and secondary trade areas; others also define a tertiary or fringe trade area.

**Trading up.** Shifting a portion of the merchandising emphasis from the lower-price lines toward those nearer the top of the scale or even to new higher prices not previously stocked.

**Turnover.** The number of stock turns achieved in a year.

**Valance.** A horizontal band shielding lights which shine on merchandise; or a sign band above products.

**Variable expenses.** Expenses, or costs, which vary in total in direct proportion to production or sales volume. Raw materials, cost of merchandise, piecework labor, and sales commissions are examples.

# **B**ibliography

"Energy Management Terms," *Buildings*, November 1983, p. 115.

*Guide to Lighting Cost Savings for Stores*, National Lighting Bureau, Washington, 1981.

Helfant, Seymour, and Beatrice Judelle: *Management Manual for the Independent Store*, Independent Stores Division, National Retail Merchants Association, New York, 1969.

*Lessons for States and Cities: A Handbook for Analyses of the Impacts of New Developments of Older Commercial Areas:* Prepared for the Office of Community Planning and Development, U.S. Department of Housing and Urban Development, by Real Estate Research Corporation, Chicago, 1982.

*Retail Location Analysis Manual:* Prepared for the Ford Foundation by Real Estate Research Corporation, Chicago, 1967.

Telchin, Charles S., and Seymour Helfant: *Plan Your Store for Maximum Sales and Profit*, National Retail Merchants Association, New York, 1969.

# Index

# About the Authors

**Vilma Barr,** manager of the Public Relations Center of Chicago's Harza Engineering Company; received a B.S. degree in business administration from Drexel University and did graduate work in management at Massachusetts Institute of Technology. She has held merchandising and planning positions at Strawbridge & Clothier and worked as Philadelphia correspondent for Fairchild Publications. A former contributing editor to *Contract* and other professional journals, Barr co-authored *Promoting Professional Services* with Dr. Stuart Rose. She is a member of the Society for Technical Communication and an affiliate of the American Society of Civil Engineers. With her co-author, Charles E. Broudy, she participated in "Design for Profit," a seminar series on retail store design.

**Charles E. Broudy,** AIA, heads Charles E. Broudy & Associates, P.C., in Philadelphia, an architectural and planning firm which specializes in merchandising facilities. His firm has received several awards for the creation of over 1000 specialty shops, department stores, chain units, shopping centers, art galleries, and showrooms nationwide. The client list includes the Ann Taylor stores, Hart Schaffner & Marx Stores, Liberty of London, Lytton's, the Boston Museum of Art, the Chicago Museum of Science and Industry, Johnston & Murphy, and the National Trust for Historic Preservation in Washington. A graduate of Drexel University's Department of Architecture with over twenty years of experience, Broudy was a featured speaker in *Architectural Record*'s retail and commercial building planning workshop. He is a member and former president of the Philadelphia chapter of the American Institute of Architects.

# THE MER-CHILD

## ALSO BY ROBIN MORGAN

### Poetry

*Monster*
*Lady of the Beasts*
*Death Benefits*
*Depth Perception*
*Upstairs in the Garden: Selected and New Poems*

### Fiction

*Dry Your Smile*

### Nonfiction

*The Demon Lover*
*The Anatomy of Freedom*
*Going Too Far*
*Sisterhood Is Global* (ed.)
*Sisterhood Is Powerful* (ed.)
*The New Woman* (ed.)

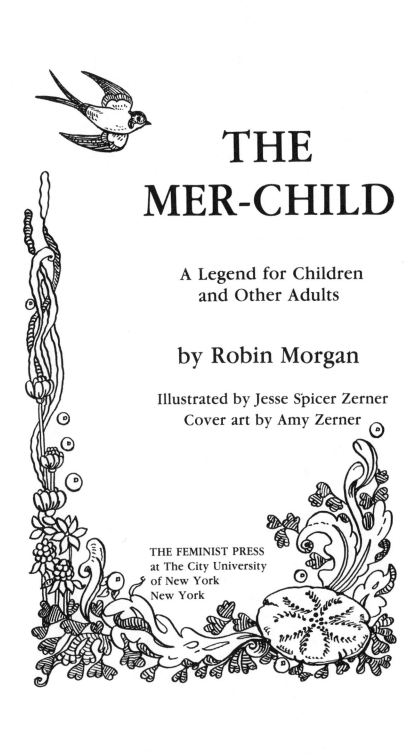

# THE
# MER-CHILD

A Legend for Children
and Other Adults

## by Robin Morgan

Illustrated by Jesse Spicer Zerner
Cover art by Amy Zerner

THE FEMINIST PRESS
at The City University
of New York
New York

Published 1991 and 2005 by The Feminist Press at The City
University of New York, 365 Fifth Avenue, Suite 5406,
New York, N.Y. 10016

10  09  08  07  06     6 5 4 3 2

*Library of Congress Cataloging-in-Publication Data*

Morgan, Robin.
   The Mer-Child : a legend for children and other adults / by
Robin Morgan ; illustrated by Jesse Spicer Zerner ; cover art by
Amy Zerner.
       p.  cm.
   Summary: Relates the friendship between a little girl whose
legs are paralyzed and a young boy whose mother is a mermaid
and whose father is human.
   ISBN 1-55861-053-7 (alk paper)
1-55861-054-5 (pbk. : alk. paper)
   [1. Friendship—Fiction. 2. Mermen—Fiction. 3. Physically
handicapped—Fiction.] 4. Prejudices—Fiction.] I. Spicer
Zerner, Jesse, ill. II. Title. PZ7.M8263Me   1991
[Fic]—dc20

                                        91-3246
                                          CIP
                                          AC

Cover art: Mixed media collage © 1991 by Amy Zerner
Cover and text design by Paula Martinac

Printed in the United States of America on acid-free paper by
McNaughton & Gunn, Inc.

This publication is made possible, in part, by public funds from
the New York State Council on the Arts. The Feminist Press is
also grateful to Alida Brill, Helene D. Goldfarb, Joanne Markell,
Nancy Porter, and Gen VAughan for their generosity.

*For Blake, a mer-child*

nce upon a time that
may or may not come again, there lived a Mer-
Child.

He had pale green skin translucent as sea-
foam, and his body sloped to a tail that glit-
tered like a prism in the sun, each scale reflect-
ing a different shimmer of the rainbow
—crimson and cobalt, lilac and gold. His hair
was surf white, ringleted as the froth that
crests a wave. But his eyes were the strangest
of all: they were speckled and whorled like
the spirals of the sundial shell.

He was very beautiful.

His mother was a mermaid, his father a
human. Long, long ago, they had fallen in
love. For her sake his father, a mariner, forsook his own kind and entered the depths of
the sea. His comrades thought him lost. The
sea folk, in turn, forsook the mermaid, pro-
nouncing her lost, for mermaids were not supposed to love mortals. The sea folk would not

even own the mermaid's child, because it was half human. Only the dolphins pitied the lovers, and remained their friends.

Still, the mermaid and her mariner had one another. They loved their child dearly, of course. But their suffering had made them forever grown-up, and they were now a special kind, complete unto themselves. The Mer-Child had no one of his own.

He was very lonely.

Sometimes he played with the young porpoises, leaping along the surface of the sea, stitching together air and water with one long graceful thread of motion. Sometimes he sang with the great whales. Sometimes he joined in the favorite game of the whiskered walruses —in which you deliberately entangled yourself in seaweed chains and then tumbled through the depths, bouncing lightly against the coral reefs and bonking into one another.

But the Mer-Child was, after all, not a young porpoise. Or a great whale. Or a whiskered walrus. He never quite belonged.

And he was very lonely.

 e had tried to play with human children. The first time he ever saw one paddling about in the water, he swam right up and, not knowing what else to do, bonked playfully into it as he would into a friendly walrus. The child screamed and darted back to shore, where it babbled about sea monsters and was cooed over by laughing adult humans.

Another time, there was a tiny girl. She was not afraid, but she tried to catch the Mer-Child and drag him up onto the beach. He barely escaped.

Once, he saved a child from drowning, bearing him to the shallows and peeping from behind a rock while he staggered safely onto land. But when the child blurted out what had happened, his parents didn't believe him, and they forbade him the water again all that day for telling such a "tall story."

Still another time, he came across a group

of girls and boys all giggling and splashing —but they quickly covered their astonishment at seeing a Mer-Child by throwing stones at him and yelling, "There's something fishy about you!" and then screeching with laughter.

One summer, the Mer-Child actually did make friends—he thought—with a boy about his own age, a boy who seemed fearless, and almost as at home in the water as the Mer-Child himself. But a day came when the boy insisted on racing him. Even though the Mer-Child refused again and again, and even though when he finally gave in, he then paddled as slowly as he knew how, still he reached the finish point long before his human companion. The boy turned on him, eyes aglow with hate, and sputtered,

"Who cares, anyway? Who could be jealous of *you?* If your mother was a mermaid, then she lured your father to death, that's what. Mermaids do that to humans, everybody knows they do. Your mother was a murderess and your father was a dummy. Or maybe your father tried to catch your mother and fry her for dinner, huh? Either way, it makes me want to throw up, it's so disgusting.

4

And you, you're not a person *or* a fish. Freak! You don't fit in anywhere!''

"That's not true!'' cried the Mer-Child. "My mother and father loved each other! How could you ever, *ever* understand them? He never tried to capture her and she never tried to drown him. You're lying! All your stories about the sea folk are lies!''

"Oh yeah?'' sneered the boy. He clambered up on some rocks and stood with his legs planted wide apart and his arms folded. He wiggled his toes. He bent his knees in a deep squat and then straightened up. He kicked out first one leg and then the other. He balanced on his left foot and waggled the right foot in the air defiantly, as if it were a flag.

"Lemme see you do *this,* Scaly-Tail. Race me on *land* and see who wins. You're not a *real* boy. I bet no self-respecting fish plays with you, either, else why're you hanging around people so much, huh? Where's all your fishy friends? Or are you mister special hot stuff, the only Mer-Child in the world?''

"What if I am? I mean—'' the Mer-Child stammered, "there are lots of other sea folk! Ondines and naiads and tritons. There are water nymphs and river sprites and mer-ones.

And—and—they all love me! They play with me whenever I want and do whatever I ask them to!" He fell silent, drenched with the shame of his lie.

The boy was not impressed. Still jeering, he danced off further inland. But his taunts floated back to the Mer-Child in a singsong snarl on the wind.

*"Fish-boy! Fish-boy! You and your squid-kid pals! You're not even real, I made you up, you never existed at all!"*

The Mer-Child watched him go through shell-whorl eyes.

After that, he didn't try to make friends with human children, although he often gazed at them from a distance, longingly. He learned that he could show himself from the waist up, and never too close. Then the children might wave, thinking him human like themselves, or sometimes they might even yell admiringly at him, "Hey! You're some swimmer!"

In the late afternoon, when their parents would call them in from the water to help gather up towels and picnic baskets from the beach, the children would point at him, out beyond the breakers, and whine enviously.

"Look, *that* boy's still swimming! Why do *we* have to go?"

"If that kid wants to stay in all night and get blue lips, that's his concern," a father would snap.

"Where are his parents, anyway?" a mother would murmur, shading her eyes with one hand and squinting at the lone figure in the distance. "How can they let a child go swimming all alone at a cove like this where there's no lifeguard? You! Boy!" she would sometimes call, "You'd better come in now, it's getting late!"

But the Mer-Child knew he must swim no nearer. He merely gazed at the creatures bending and kneeling and straightening and wobbling along the sand. At last they would move off, a mother perhaps muttering, "I've never seen such a swimmer! I suppose he must know what he's doing. Maybe he's in training for the Olympics or something." Or a father might scold at his laggard offspring, "Will you hurry up? Stop staring backward and look where you're going. If some crazy kid wants to stay in the water this long and his parents don't care, it's none of our business." Yanking

and shoving at one another, they would disappear up the path from the cove.

The Mer-Child would watch them go through shell-whorl eyes. He would watch until the beach was utterly deserted, and then turn his gaze toward the vast unbroken surface of the sea.

Sometimes a sea swallow might fly overhead and drop him a graygreen feather, like a promise of pity.

But he himself was not a sea swallow. Or a fish. Or a person. The sea folk would not own him. The human folk would not own him.

The Mer-Child was very lonely.

ummer ebbed slowly from the cove and, as he had done in other years, the Mer-Child found himself missing even the few encounters, however distant or hurtful, with other children. For as the air grew cold, fewer and fewer humans came to the beach. Sometimes in autumn a single figure might be seen walking along the shoreline. But it was always an adult, and as the air grew sharper, even adult visitors were rare. The Mer-Child bobbed aimlessly on the choppier waves, bored.

One day, as he was wondering whether to follow the dolphins to the southern seas, or go ride the Gulf Stream, or visit the Great Barrier Reef, he heard the overhead calls of startled sea swallows, and he looked up to see the glossy black-helmeted birds dip and swoop their pearlish graygreen bodies out to sea, as if they'd been surprised during their stroll along the shore.

But there, on the beach itself, moving slowly across the sand toward the outcropping of rock, was what seemed at first a bulk with a double head—but which soon became a man carrying a human bundle: what looked like a child wrapped warmly in sweaters and blankets. The man set the child down on a rock and settled himself alongside. For a while they gazed out at the sea, seeming to talk now and then, until the man drew a pad from his pocket and began to sketch. Then, after a while, he lifted the child again, and carried his bundle up the path from the cove.

The Mer-Child was curious.

The next day, the strange pair was back. And the next. Within the week, the man had begun to leave the child tucked safely into a blanketed nest along the rock outcropping, which gave her a fine view of the sea. He would then go for short walks, returning with shells he had gathered, or a drawing he had made of the seascape around the bend of beach. The child meanwhile sat peacefully on the rock perch, sometimes reading a book, but mostly just looking out to sea, often singing a wordless little song unashamedly loud against the crash of surf.

The Mer-Child watched all this through shell-whorl eyes. The human child seemed lonely.

One day, he dared swim nearer. He hid behind a jut in the natural seawall of rocks, in order to see the small human more closely. From his hiding place, he could spy on the odd person who was, he thought, a little girl, although he couldn't be certain. She seemed to him like no other child he had ever seen.

For one thing, she appeared to move only from the waist up whenever she reached for her book, or leaned to adjust the blankets tucked about her legs. Legs which never seemed to move. She didn't scramble over rocks, or run along the sand. Or even walk. And she never swam.

But her voice went places her body didn't. It bounced off the rock surfaces and echoed over the waves. The Mer-Child thought he had never heard anything so beautiful as her queer mournful melodies, although they did remind him a little of the courting songs of the humpback whale. Her singing seemed to draw him closer. He edged in, still hiding.

She was indeed like no other child.

11

Her skin was not pink like that of many early-summer children who came to the cove, nor was it the rich glazed black of the island children on the other shore, the far side of the sea. Instead, she seemed to glow as if from some inside brightness that flickered through the silvery sealbrown of all her surfaces—the face and hands giving off light like a sunspotted flounder, the eyes almost greenblack as the ocean floor and shot with the same tawny flecks. Her hair was short, and exclaimed itself in a rush of wiry tight black curls all over the proud head. When the wind touched her hair, that head looked like a sea anemone riffling itself underwater. Or so the Mer-Child thought.

Sometimes, to his amazement, she bent her graceful neck and buried that head in her arms. Then peculiar sounds came from her, more like the grunts of a sea robin than the whalesong melodies he loved so. When she lifted her head again, her eyes seemed to have rained tiny rivers down her cheeks. The Mer-Child puzzled all this from his hiding place, and did not understand.

Yet she was lonely. That he recognized.

The day came when her father had made

certain she was comfortable in her perch and had gone a bit away to set up his easel and paints, and she turned to find her book—but saw, wedged cunningly in the crack beside her usual place, a circle of seaweed, as if woven into a crown.

She smiled, then placed it promptly on her stiff black curls and sat looking out to sea—a small monarch surveying her immense realm. The circlet had dried brittle by the afternoon's end, but she kept it, pressing it in her book.

The next day, she found a piece of driftwood in the crevice, a curve of creamy bark scoured by water and salt into a shape like interlocking wings arched above a double bird-body.

The next day, she deliberately waited until her father was far off down the beach, savoring the expectation. Then she looked. There, in the treasure-crevice, was wedged a shard of mottled blue glass, its edges worn smooth by tidal scrubbings. She peered through it at the sun and saw a horizon bluegreen as if she looked up through seawater into air.

The next day, her father offered to sit

with her awhile, but she impatiently urged him to get on with his painting, and only when quite alone did she dare search beside her, down between the stones. Fragile but perfect, a sanddollar lay there, nestled on a cushion of sea moss.

The next day, the shell, strung by its natural hole on a velvet ribbon the color of willow leaves, hung round her slender throat.

Her father would comment in surprise on his return each afternoon.

"The sea must like you, to wash up gifts like these," he smiled as he lifted her into his arms. But privately he thought how well she had learned to see treasures right around her, unlike other children who were freer to ignore their immediate surroundings, given a luxury of movement that let them explore wherever they wished.

She herself said little. But she always took her treasures with her, and once, when a light rain caused her father to sweep her up in a hasty departure, she made him turn back to retrieve the black-and-yellow streaked pebble she had "found" that day.

All this the Mer-Child watched through shell-whorl eyes.

14

Day after day, he watched her from his hiding place just the other side of the rock outcropping. Hour after hour, the two of them watched in silence on either side of the seawall, gazing out to sea.

It was she who spoke first.

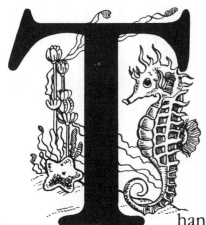
hank you," she said simply, in the clear voice he knew so well from her singing. "Thank you for my treasures."

The Mer-Child was so shocked at being addressed directly that he flipped from his ledge by reflex and splashed loudly into the water. He had darted two miles out to sea with excitement before he could slow down and tell himself calmly that she doubtless had been talking to the waves and not to him at all. Ashamed of himself, but unable to keep away, he alternately glided and inched back to his observation place.

The Little Girl still sat on her rock. But she seemed to be smiling to herself, and she hummed softly as she tickled her chin with the sea-swallow feather that had been that day's gift.

They spent the rest of the afternoon in

silence—although the waves did seem excessively loud.

The next day, as they took up their positions on the seawall, she spoke the moment her father was out of earshot.

"I'd bring you gifts in return, you know, but I don't get about much. I couldn't gather land flowers or bird feathers or pinecones very easily, you see."

The Mer-Child clung to his ledge for dear life and strained to hear her over the thudding of his heart, which whammed in repeated tidal waves against his ribs. He told himself again, *Don't be a fool. She's talking to the sea. She doesn't even know you exist.* But then she seemed to twist her upper body toward him and call directly across the rock that separated them.

"I thought of bringing you a book, you know. But I couldn't think whether a child like you would care for reading. Besides, almost all my books are about sea life, which is hardly something *you* need to learn about."

The Mer-Child's tidal-wave heart seemed to stop, and he found himself seriously wondering whether it would ever start again.

17

But start it did, although from the delightful melting sensation that came over him he all at once realized how a jellyfish must feel. He wriggled a few inches closer. He edged himself up toward the top of the seawall. Holding his breath, he peeked over the barrier rock.

The Little Girl was looking directly into his eyes.

"Anemone," was all he could manage.

"Ann who?" she asked.

"An—sea anemone," he whispered. "Anemone," he repeated foolishly. "Like your head." Then, overcome with embarrassment, he slid down from his rock and vanished in the next wave.

The Little Girl serenely went back to her singing.

Still, that was the beginning.

The space that separated the two grew smaller day by day, the Mer-Child lying at last in full view of the Little Girl, although still hidden from sight of anyone on the beach. The afternoons grew shorter, as autumn sifted toward darkness. But the conversations grew longer, so much so that the Little Girl's father

ol hand with its exquisitely webbed
sped her strong brown one and
t.

she burst into laughter through her
aid,

urse! I never thought of it that way
f I were a sort of mermaid. It makes
kind, then. How lovely! Oh, love-
lovely!" She squeezed his hand,
ed it to clap hers in celebration.
er-Child, too, broke out in smiles
ng her, beat his hands one on the
elcome.

wondered if his daughter had taken to talking
to herself in her loneliness. He could see her
up on her beloved throne, as she called it,
from his walk along the beach or his position
with his paints. She seemed to be in animated
conversation with the sea, gesturing with
those strong little arms that tried to compen-
sate for the motionless legs. Yet he trusted his
daughter's wisdom. He had learned she knew
as well as anyone (sometimes better) what she
needed for her own survival. She did in fact
seem happier than he had ever seen her.

As for the Mer-Child, he could no more
be kept from his daily appointment than the
tide could be kept from coming in. He was
delirious. He would chase his own tail with
joy.

"Your eyes," she announced one day,
"are nice. Weird and shivery. Dizzy-making.
But nice. Did you know that?"

The Mer-Child allowed as how he hadn't
known that. He got suddenly shy, but his
tailtip twitched with pleasure in the shallows.

"Well," she went on, matter-of-factly,
"they are. They sort of . . . spiral. They seem
to look in and out at the same time. And they

shine so! Do you cry often?'' she asked abruptly.

"Cry? Like the gulls, you mean?''

"Well, no. You know, cry tears. I mean, weep.''

"I don't know what 'weep' is,'' replied the Mer-Child, feeling shamed by his ignorance.

"I cry a lot sometimes,'' the Little Girl confessed in a low voice, as if she hadn't heard his admission.

Slowly it came to him that she meant when her eyes rained rivers.

"Oh,'' he blurted out, "I know when you cry. You 'weep,' and your eyes . . . waterfall. I've never done that. I don't even know if I can. Is it to be sad or happy?''

"I think it can mean either one, or both,'' she answered, "but I've only ever wept from being sad.''

"Ah,'' the Mer-Child replied. And they said no more that day.

But on other days they talked of many things. She asked his name, and he replied that he had none. And he felt ashamed again until she laughed and said that was wonderfully

because he had no
was the only Mer-C
one of a kind.

He never tho
then—since she, to
one of her kind in
ply the Little Girl.

He did ask he
never moved, or w
her very tenderly, a
her, even if he cou

"Oh,'' she said
My legs are paralyz
move or hold me u
someday there mi
eration, or cure
know. But until th
—my body's like
the waist up.'' He
springs, welled u
Fascinated, the M
realized that she w

"Please,'' he c
He reached out to
"I know what you
also like other chil

ly.'' His c
fingers gr
held it tig

Then
tears, and

"Of c
before! As
us *two* of
ly, lovely,
then drop

The M
and, imita
other, in v

heirs was a special world, all unto themselves, its only reality the few hours each afternoon when the Little Girl's father left her and watched from a distance, until the dreaded moment when he came to gather her up and carry her home again.

Between those moments and their return the next day lay unreal endless hours for each child, hours of going through the motions of living as if in a dream. Only when they were together did the Mer-Child and the Little Girl feel fully awake.

There was no confidence they couldn't share. She told him how her legs had been useless since her babyhood, probably damaged in the same accident that had taken the life of her never-known mother. She showed him a photograph of that mother—a halibut-skinned woman with the same anemone hair and a smile that warmed your own until you found you were grinning back at the square piece of picture paper. She told him how her father somehow thought the doctors hadn't done all they could have, how her father thought that was because he and her mother weren't welcome in that hospital since they loved each other but had different color skins.

No matter how often she explained this, the Mer-Child couldn't understand it. Her parents had both been human, hadn't they? And the doctors, too? Patiently, the Little Girl tried to tell him some of the ways in which humans often saw themselves as being of different kinds.

They returned to this conversation again and again.

"It isn't only the shade of skin or hair or eyes, you see. Look, I knew a girl once, at school," she cleared her throat as if telling a story, "and this girl liked to play a game with a ball and wooden stick that mostly boys play. I wasn't much interested in it myself because you had to run a lot and of course I . . . well, anyway, the boys wouldn't let her play this

game, just because she was a girl.''

"Well, human children aren't always —kind,'' the Mer-Child argued diplomatically, remembering his own experiences.

"But don't you see? The children only copy what the grown-ups do. My doctor—the nice one I have now—she says some men tried to stop her from becoming a doctor, because she was a woman.''

"But aren't they all *human?*'' he would persist.

To change the subject, the Little Girl would ask about the sea, and the Mer-Child would enchant her with stories of the ocean floor, its valleys and volcanoes, meadows and mountain chains. He described the irresistible pull of undersea eddies. He let her ride the great *tsunami,* the giant Pacific wave, through his words. He made the magic of the male sea horse giving birth come alive for her.

But always they returned to sameness and difference.

"Aren't all humans more alike than different?'' he asked.

"Yes, but . . . they don't always see it that way,'' she sighed. "Older ones sometimes

don't trust young ones, and younger ones can be cruel to old ones. It's so *mean*. My father's family didn't want him to marry my mother, nor hers to marry him. Then, after she died, he was so angry at all of them he said he didn't need their help, he would raise me all by himself, even though he's an artist and not rich.''

The Mer-Child knew by now what ''artist'' meant, from the easel and paints and sketches. But ''rich'' was a new category.

''What's 'rich'?'' he almost winced to ask.

The Little Girl sighed again. Sometimes each explanation required another, she had discovered.

'''Rich' is when you have more stuff than others do. Who are then called 'poor.' Rich people don't like poor ones, and poor ones don't like rich ones right back.''

''But aren't they all—''

''—human? Yes,'' she anticipated, ''and you promised to tell me how the female dolphins help the mother dolphin give birth to her baby.''

So he told her about the dolphin midwives. And he told her how the sun didn't set

26

for months on end over the summertime Greenland sea, and which deep-sea fish were luminous, and how fairy shrimp swam upside down. He told her that sponges were animals, not plants, and he described for her the swift underwater grace of the huge leathery turtle, so unlike its lumbering gait on land. (Her father wondered how, even with all the books she'd read, she could know so much about the sea. He wondered how rare shells from the South Pacific could wash up unbroken on a North Atlantic shore, how strange names like whelk and stomia and manatee could come so readily to his daughter's lips. But he was a wise father, and said nothing, rejoicing in his daughter's happiness.)

Still, at every chance, the Mer-Child's curiosity about humanity drew him back to that subject as surely as the moon draws up the tides.

"Why," he thought out loud to her as if she were part of himself, "don't the rich just give some of their being rich to the poor ones? The poor ones could give back some of their being poor. Then each *one* could be different, but *together* they'd all be the same. You know

what I mean? It's like . . . each carp and snapper is different from every other, but they're all *fish*. And fish are different from crabs or coral, but they're all sea creatures. And each of the sea folk is special, but we're all part of one—"

"—family?" she cut in gently. And they both fell silent, thinking of what he had told her about his own family, how his human father and mermaid mother each had been cast out from their own folk for the sake of their love, the love that had given him birth.

He looked down at the trumpet triton shell she was cradling, a gift he had brought her from a dashing overnight swim all the way to Trinidad, the island where her mother had been born. Then he murmured,

"My mother once said that beings crowd together and move against other beings because each one feels separate and scared, alone in the universe."

"My father said something like that once," the Little Girl whispered back. "He was painting a portrait of my mother from memory, and he started to cry—you know, his eyes began to rain rivers—and he came

and rocked me in his arms and said over and over, like a song almost, 'So alone, each of us, forever. That's what your mother and I broke through, for a while.'"

The Mer-Child and the Little Girl sat together, holding hands. Only the sound of the youngest waves could be heard, plashing mildly against the rock base.

t was the middle of October. One day, the Little Girl was unusually quiet. It was only as the afternoon lengthened toward dusk that she burst out,

"Tomorrow we must leave."

The Mer-Child felt as if a sudden undertow had gripped his mind and was tugging it away from his body.

"Leave? Where? How? You can't leave!" he stammered wildly. "I'll follow you. I'll come wherever . . . You can't go . . . " In his despair he thrashed himself against the seawall, leaving scales of mangled iridescence on the rocks.

His friend strained to catch the webbed fists pounding the stones in panic. Finally she caught and clasped them tightly in her hands.

"You can't follow me, dearest Mer-Child," she cried, "not where we're going. It's far inland, where we live. We only came to the cove because my doctor said sea air would be good for me—and we came in after-summer season because we couldn't afford what they call the real vacation months. And now we have to go, but maybe . . . maybe we can come again next—"

Then the sea robin sobs rose from her throat and blurred in the wind with the unearthly moans the Mer-Child keened. All that gray October afternoon they sang this way, for their loss of one another, on the wet rocks by the autumn sea.

Only when her father approached did they release one another. Only then did she whisper, more like a prayer to no one than a promise to anyone, "Perhaps next year . . . "

But the Mer-Child, retreating to his huddle behind the seawall, watched in mute grief how she was plucked like a sea anemone from her rocky home and borne away, to land.

He watched all this through shell-whorl eyes. And did not cry.

> This is a song the sailors sing,
> though none knows how it came to be;
> some say a voice from the waves would ring

out in the night, bitterly free,
sighing *What is so cursed as an autumn sea,*
*now you are lost, lost to me?*

All through the ice and wind and snow
—none could find how it came to be—
that voice would mock the sailor's show
of fear where he knelt on stiffened knee,
chanting *What is so damned as a winter sea,*
*once you are lost, lost to me?*

In April drenched, in May becalmed.
None dared gain where the voice might be,
but that song would echo like a psalm
above the sailor's scurvy plea,
mourning  *What is so doomed as a*
   *springtime sea,*
*and you still lost, lost to me?*

In August oven or monsoon
none might win. Yet could it be
this voice seemed at last a clue, a rune,
to a sailor's blistered soul the key
unlocking even to such as we
*What love can be found on a summer sea,*
*gained, won, or saved, with you lost to me?*

ll that winter and spring and summer the Mer-Child roamed the waters of the world, finding summer and autumn and winter on the other side of the planet. But none of the seasons or wonders of ocean or river, brook, bay, inlet, stream, or open sea could tempt his interest or penetrate his sorrow. The clownish dolphins could not coax an answering smile from him, and the whiskered walruses, after many tries, gave up attempting to involve him in their old shared pastime.

His only comfort seemed to be in wandering alone along the ocean floor and exploring its caves until he spied great undulating clumps of sea anemones. To these flowerlike creatures he would drift and crawl like a wounded thing, and rest his head amidst their beckoning tentacle-petals.

Late northern-hemisphere summer came,

and with it, terror and hope so mingling in his thoughts that the Mer-Child barely let himself know what he was doing as he returned to the familiar cove. There, from far out beyond the sandbar and the breakers, he watched the final summer stragglers litter and then desert the beach, group by group, family by family, one by one.

Then they were gone. The air grew sharper, the water grew colder, the waves grew choppier.

No one else came.

Finally, late one afternoon, the Mer-Child turned his back toward land and his face toward the wide sea, admitting to himself that she would not return.

And he began to swim into that emptiness.

Except that the sharp quick calls of startled sea swallows froze him in mid-stroke. He paused, heart bursting with dread and longing, and slowly turned again—to see, moving slowly across the sand toward the outcropping of rock, a man carrying what looked like a child wrapped warmly in sweaters and blankets.

The Mer-Child leapt from the water as the dolphins had taught him, high high into the air for pure praise, and then sped like the sea-arrow, toward land, toward her.

She was settled in place by the time he arrived, cosily tucked in, breathing rapidly with her own excitement, having imperiously (and a bit rudely) dismissed her amused father. A somewhat withered ear of corn—the most inlandish object she could think of—lay tied with a red bow in the crevice where the Mer-Child had always placed his gifts for her. She sat, head high, hands folded neatly in her lap, the sanddollar magically still unbroken and secure on its willowgreen ribbon around her neck.

Each fin and scale and pore quivering with delight, the Mer-Child flung his whole prismatic length alongside on the rock, panting, laughing, exhausted, exhilirated, beside her. Then she reached out and laid a small brown hand on all that heaving rainbow.

"I came back," she said.

o that was the second summer, even better than the first.

That was the summer she told him about her room at home, about her little aquarium and pet angelfish, about school, about how as they grew older the children teased her less but ignored her more as they ran off to their games and their lives. That was the summer he sang her the song he had made up when he feared her lost to him forever. That was the summer they sang together—low enough so that her father down the beach couldn't hear, but also low enough so that the sea sound-waves bore their melody out to the great whales, who wauled in answering refrain.

That was the summer she declared she knew what she wanted to be when she grew up—a notion that disconcerted the Mer-Child more than he showed.

"An oceanographer," she pronounced

proudly. "That's what I'll be. A scientist who studies all about the sea and sea life—marine biology, they call that—and helps preserve the world's oceans and sea folk from pollution and destruction and things."

There were so many new words in her announcement that it took her an entire afternoon to explain them all to the Mer-Child. But he liked each explanation more and more, nodding his surf-white ringlets vigorously as she outlined her plan. Clearly, this meant that she would always be near the sea. Just as clearly, it seemed to him a superb idea.

That was the summer he brought her the rare black pearl. That was the summer she told him that her father said the black pearl she had found could buy her the best education an oceanographer ever had. That was the summer she read to him the Hans Christian Andersen story *The Little Mermaid.* He found it marvelously sad, and he was astonished to discover that his mother was so famous as to be in a humans' book—even if the storyteller did get some of the facts wrong.

And that was the summer he said, "I bet you could swim."

At first, she was shocked and frightened. But he explained how every creature was lighter in water, even fish and mer-ones. "Remember the leathery turtle?" he asked. And he told her how he himself never kicked when he swam—how could he, without legs?—but instead sort of arched his back the way she herself did when she stretched, and mostly stroked and spun and wove the water about with his arms. Then there was pure floating, of course, and the simple trick of riding the waves and letting the water do all the work, and . . .

They spent hours talking about it: how he would teach her to bob and skim and coast the wave roll, and how together they could roam the world's waters and he could show her their secrets. What an oceanographer she'd be then!

That was the summer they dreamed together.

But it was a dream.

The wind of late autumn breathed its chill along the sheltered cove, and the time of their parting drew near.

Again, wild loneliness was borne in upon the Mer-Child. Again, the Little Girl wept for both their sakes.

Then she was gone.

Repeating to himself the memorized words of Andersen's story, and absurdly clutching a withered ear of corn, the Mer-Child swam slowly seaward, and did not cry.

**L**ike a wheel the year turned. The sea breathed its tidal rhythms more slowly, or so it seemed to the Mer-Child, than ever before. Perfect snowflakes fell unseen by any eye onto the blank face of the open sea, each crystal as brief and unique as an hour the Mer-Child and the Little Girl had shared. Spring came, and the wild geese flew northward, their calls like alarms to waken the coastline before them. Then summer warmed the surface of the northern seas and the great sperm whales moved massively through the depths toward their mating grounds.

The Mer-Child had visited the giant glaciers of the South Pole, and had permitted electric eels (who were more show-offs than helpers) to light his way through seablack caverns no mer-one had ever traveled. He had rescued six baby dolphins from tuna nets and courteously disengaged two deep-sea divers from a disagreement with an irritated squid. (Their story of the odd hero who saved them was never believed; the crew aboard their boat said they had experienced "depth mirage," and in time they too came to believe the Mer-Child had been a hallucination.)

But none of these adventures could, for the Mer-Child, be as precious as a single quiet conversation with his friend. This year, though, he had faith she would return, and as summer waned he turned with a quickening pulse toward the direction of the familiar coast.

He had not expected obstacles.

There were undersea earthquakes that season, caused, it was thought, from off-shore explosions by humans testing strange new weapons. Whole landscapes shifted under-water; sunken galleons, moored on the sea-floor for a thousand years, now rose and drifted through the churning fathoms like ghost ships. The Mer-Child was pinned for two days beneath an ancient Phoenician galley that had been dislodged and then had sunk again—on him. When he finally squirmed free, he had to force his way through schools

41

of maddened fish darting in terror from debris and from equally terrified predators. The mystical balance of the sea had been disturbed, and until it righted itself all would be chaos beneath the surface.

The Mer-Child helped where he could, but he kept fighting his way back to the cove, back to the Little Girl who would be—where? Safe from this disaster? He knew he must get to her, though to save her or save himself he could not have told. He knew only what was driving him: an energy strong as that propelling the salmon upstream to spawn each year, risking death as if it were a mere inconvenience that might slow one down, like the waterfall to be leapt up, like the sargasso swamp to drag oneself across, like the weariness and hunger, the flesh scarred, the scales broken—but the passion intact. The water grew colder, and he knew, as he broke the choppy surface waves, that the air had grown sharper.

He was late. Very late.

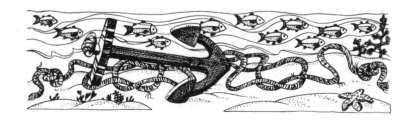

efore him, in the near distance, there lay the cove, tranquil as ever on a sunbrilliant afternoon, the coastline eroded by fractions only his skilled glance could detect. Was it possible, then, for humans to cause such a catastrophe undersea and remain completely unaffected themselves, on land? He realized how little human beings really knew about the ocean, and how little most appeared to care.

But all of this, and his own painful cuts and gashes and aches of exhaustion, seemed to slide away from his consciousness as he approached the cove, and the anticipated meeting with his friend fountained new strength through him. He was prepared that she might, this time, have reached their meeting place before him—indeed, he was secretly terrified that she might already have left.

But he was not prepared for what he saw.

Two separate figures were moving slowly down the path toward the beach. One was a familiar tall shape, complete with easel and sketch pad and paint box. But the other?

It was the Little Girl—but standing. Or almost standing. Almost walking, if it could be called that. Shiny spines, like scales glittering in the sun, gleamed along both her legs, and she leaned on two strange wooden masts. With the aid of these, and a hand from her father, she lurched and stumbled toward the seawall.

The Mer-Child was frantic for her to be settled, her father dispatched, and some explanation made of this extraordinary change. Were these then scales, in fact? Had she become some kind of walking mermaid? (He thought her capable of marvels.) He flailed like a beached minnow in his haste for news.

But in good time she did arrive, and as soon as her father had turned back to the beach, she called out a greeting to the Mer-Child. But her face clouded over with concern when she saw his condition, and she refused to give her explanation until he gave his. Only after she could be reassured by first-hand in-

spection that his wounds were relatively minor would she answer his flurry of questions, explaining in a glad voice what her shining "tails," as he called them, were.

"Braces," she said, and showed him how they held her up the same way its exoskeleton held a lobster together. The wooden masts had nothing to do with a ship and weren't masts at all. She called them "crutches"; she could lean her upper body's weight on them for further support. In time, she said, she might even be able to do without one or the other—braces or crutches—but that depended on how she could build up what her doctor called "muscle tone."

"And *that,*" she bubbled, her dark eyes flashing their gold flecks in merriment, "is where you come in, my dear friend."

The Mer-Child was confused.

"I'm all at sea," he frowned, using an expression he had learned struck her as particularly funny.

The Little Girl brought out her news as if it were the greatest treasure she might offer.

"I'm to learn to swim!"

There was a great *thwack* somewhere

45

below the Mer-Child's pale green chest but above his rainbowscaled tail. He suspected it was his stomach, completely flopping over inside him.

"Yes," she almost sang, "I'm to learn to swim. None of this would've happened if it hadn't been for your idea that I might move in water better than on land. I asked my father if such an idea could possibly work (I didn't tell on *you*, of course), and then he asked my doctor and then she said maybe I was after all ready for what they call water therapy and so all last winter and spring they kept dipping me into shallow pools at the clinic and I did special exercises and learned to float and develop my arms and then I got these braces and now here I am and I'm allowed into the water out to that buoy my father says but with a lifeline and probably water wings, oh my own dear Mer-Child how can I thank you for what you've done?"

All in a rush it came, like hurricane winds, but bringing gusts of hope.

That was the summer they talked less, because her father hovered nearer. The Mer-

Child watched daily while her father carried, then floated, his daughter along a lifeline to the buoy. It was at least a week before she could convince her father to leave her alone, swearing to remain knotted to the buoy on her line and wearing the ridiculous orange water wings the Mer-Child a bit too honestly had announced made her look like a sunburned blowfish.

But finally it happened. And there, out beyond the breakers, secure within the sheltering cove but equally secure from well-meaning fatherly interruption, the Mer-Child joined her. They were alone, and swimming together—she as light and free as the Mer-Child, who circled her with the greatest watchfulness, scolding her more than her father did when she let go of the lifeline for a second, but laughing with glee at her courage and at the way she made herself at home in his element.

Never had there been such an afternoon.

hat was the summer the Little Girl grew taller and stronger and more certain of herself. That was the summer the Mer-Child for the first time found himself afraid of what the sea's power could do. That was the summer the Little Girl's father pretended to believe her story of the tame porpoise who sometimes bobbed alongside her out there when she swam unattended.

That was the summer the Mer-Child and the Little Girl sat together in the warm shallows while her father napped on a blanket up the beach. The Mer-Child showed her how thousands of tiny coquina shells buried themselves in the soaked sand and made air bubbles after each wave receded. They scooped up handfuls of sand and sifted out shell after shell of peach and periwinkle and azure, magenta striping lavender, gray swirling around chartreuse—each creature designed like no other, perfect and alone, each buried in sand but releasing its solitary bubble upward like a signal.

"Nobody fits anywhere—except in not fitting," he mused softly.

"But all life once fitted in the sea," she answered. "At least it all came from there."

"You fit," he murmured, "in water now."

"Almost," she whispered, "just like you almost fit on land. 'Course, one element we haven't tried is air." She squinted up at the sunsplashed blue above them. "I wonder if we'd fit there."

"At any rate," he smiled, "we fit with each other. Here, finally, we belong."

"Yes. We belong."

Then the Mer-Child felt inside him a tearing as when whole sections of the sea-floor had been ripped apart in the earthquake. His throat seemed as if it would rupture with unspoken words. Waveshine, shellstripe, silverbrown skin and anemone hair above eyes black with pain and love all shimmered

together in the sea sun. The light stung his eyes.

"Oh look," she cried. "Just as you knew that I could swim—as if that would make me a sea being, so I knew that you could weep—as if that would make you a human." She touched her fingertip to his wet face and brought away a tear. Amazed, he did the same. He tasted this river his own eyes had rained.

"It tastes of salt!" he exclaimed. "It tastes like the sea!"

"Mine too!" she laughed through her own tears, and he touched and tasted hers as well. "It's as if humans kept a sign of the mother sea in ourselves, a secret token of grief or gladness."

"But I'm not sad," the Mer-Child said. "I've never been so happy."

"Nor I," wept the Little Girl.

That was the summer they discovered the tears of joy, under a canopy of gulls and sea swallows wheeling in the sun.

ven today, there is a legend told along the rocky coasts of North America. It's difficult to know where the legend begins and where the true story leaves off—although many people will admit to having actually met the famous oceanographer who returned, year after year, decade after decade, in late summer to one special cove.

For years, they say, during her youth and middle age, she had come regularly to swim in this spot, her powerful arms and upper body making her a fine swimmer despite the withered legs that trailed through water after her, almost like a tail. They say she had a way with all sea creatures, with gulls gone lame or baby octopi washed ashore, or the occasional curious seal exploring the rocky promontory. They say the year of the oil-spill from the wrecked tanker she was a wild woman, furious as a sea-squall while she directed the clean-up operation. They say she toured beaches all over the globe, not merely to collect specimens as easily as she collected prizes and honors in the cities and universities of the world, but to go swimming. And they say she was as graceful in water as she was awkward on land.

They tell how she never married, but loved children. They tell, too, how she became stooped with age and limped more heavily than ever; how she would inch along the beach toward the cove in chilly autumn and firmly refuse the company of others; how she would sit for hours far out along the seawall, talking to herself the way old people do, sometimes laughing out loud or singing at the sea.

She had a friend, some say, who sat with her—or seemed to. Stories differ about this. But it appeared from a distance to be an old man—someone with white hair, that was certain. Nobody ever met this companion. He was never seen to accompany the famous old oceanographer into town, or during her walks along the beach.

The legend they tell still along the rock

coasts of the North Atlantic has it that on the night of the Great Storm, the old woman was seen willfully lumbering her way down to the cove. A child had tried to stop her but, as the child reported later, the old woman had patted her on the head and told her to run home quick and get safe from the coming storm. The woman had said she'd be fine, that the child wasn't to worry. And before turning to the sea, she had pressed a perfect sanddollar into the child's small palm.

That night the wind and the sea met in the wildest howling dance ever witnessed by that coast. The seawall crumbled into pebbles and was washed away, and as it fell with a great crash, dolphins far out in the open ocean clicked in concert and smiled their wise secrets at one another.

In the indifferent dawn, the coastline was forever altered, the water's surface and sky's bowl scrubbed clean of any sign of life.

As for the famous old oceanographer, she was never again seen along the coast. Or anywhere.

The human folk, of course, say that she was drowned.

The sea folk doubtless believe that he, in turn, was lured by her onto land—which would explain his disappearance from their depths on that same night.

But two such souls as these, long long past "fitting" anywhere but in the transformations each made possible for the other, might have given this story a different ending—an ending suspected by that same child when she stood the next morning on the storm-swept beach, still clasping the sanddollar in her hand. She was watching how, from far out at the horizon where water met sky, two sea swallows came gliding toward her, air-swimmers of ease and skill. They dipped and then ascended, nearer and nearer, until they were wheeling above her head, and she could see them clearly.

Pearlish graygreen their bodies were, their heads sleek with dark silverbrown helmets, identical. Except that one had a marking of bright willowgreen ringing the throat—or was that a trick of the light?

Then, interweaving their wakes of flight with one another, they rose again and, beating their four wings as with one pulse, flew out into the sunrise, and disappeared.

## *About the Author*

Robin Morgan is a prize-winning author who has published 13 books of poetry, fiction, and nonfiction, including the now-classic anthologies *Sisterhood Is Powerful* and *Sisterhood Is Global*. Her work has been translated into eight languages. She is Editor in Chief of *Ms.* Magazine.

*Monte Farber*

## *About the Illustrators*

In a career spanning more than 40 years, Jesse Spicer Zerner has written and illustrated hundreds of children's books for Grosset and Dunlap, Waldman Publishing, Playmore, Inc., Moby Books, and other publishers.

Amy Zerner has received major awards including a 1986 Visual Artist's Fellowship in painting from the National Endowment for the Arts. She is illustrator and co-creator with her husband, Monte Farber, of *The Enchanted Tarot* (1990) and *The Alchemist* (Fall 1991), published by St. Martin's Press.

Jesse Spicer Zerner and Amy Zerner are mother and daughter. This is their first artistic collaboration.